JEWISH SURVIVAL

JEWISH SURVIVAL

THE IDENTITY PROBLEM
AT THE CLOSE
OF THE TWENTIETH CENTURY

Ernest Krausz
Gitta Tulea

EDITORS

TRANSACTION PUBLISHERS

New Brunswick (U.S.A.) and London (U.K.)

Library of Congress Catalog Number: 98–27167
ISBN: 1–56000–395–2
Printed in the United States of America

Library of Congress Cataloging-in-Publication Dat

Jewish survival : the identity problem at the close of the twentieth
    century / edited by Ernest Krausz and Gitta Tulea.
        p.   cm.
    "This volume is the outcome of the international workshop . . . at
Bar-Ilan University on the 18th and 19th of March, 1997"—P. ix
    Includes bibliographical references and index.
    ISBN 1-56000-395-2
    1. Jews—Politics and government—1948-   —Congresses. 2. Jews—
Identity—Congresses. 3. Israel and the diaspora—Congresses.
4. Judaism—20th century—Congresses. I. Krausz, Ernest.
DS143.J4595   1998
305.892'4—dc21   98–27167
                                                                                    CIP

This publication is sponsored by
Isidore and Nathalie Friedman
New York –Jerusalem

Contents

Acknowledgments

This volume is the outcome of the international workshop, which was organized by the Sociological Institute for Community Studies at Bar-Ilan University on the 18th and 19th of March, 1997. The workshop, which marked the twenty-five years anniversary of the Institute, dealt with the topic of "Jewish Survival—The Identification Problem at the End of the Twentieth Century."

There were participants from six countries, drawn from different areas of the social sciences, who presented papers and contributed to the discussion on the various aspects of Jewish survival in postmodern society, in Israel and in the Diaspora. The workshop was sponsored by the International Center for Jewish Identity at Bar-Ilan University and by our Institute, and was supported by the Schnitzer Foundation for Research on the Israeli Economy and Society, Bar-Ilan University, the World Zionist Organization to mark the centennial anniversary of Zionism, and by the Leon Tamman Foundation for Research into Jewish Communities. The workshop was also supported by the president of Bar-Ilan University, Professor Moshe Kaveh, by the rector, Professor Yehuda Friedlander, the director-general, Dr. Shabtai Lobel, and the dean of the Faculty of Social Sciences, Professor Benzion Zilberfarb. To all of them we are most grateful.

We wish to express our gratitude to the following: the Organizing Committee—Professor Leo Davids, Professor Paul Ritterband, and Dr. Avraham Leslau; the chairman of the board of the Institute, Professor Nissan Rubin, and the other members of the board; and Professor Charles Liebman, who gave the main address at the public session.

We also wish to thank Susie Grossman, the administrative head of the Institute, and Sara Nussbaum, member of the academic staff of the Institute, for the most efficient way in which they organized the workshop.

In the process of editing this volume, we were greatly helped by the expertise and thorough work carried out by Sarah Geiger Leslau.

This collection of presentations appears as Special Volume VI of our journal, *Sociological Papers*. The papers express the personal views of the authors.

The Editors

Foreword

The International Center for Jewish Identity at Bar-Ilan University was established last year to provide a framework for academic research into, and educational outreach regarding, the continuing quest for the preservation of the Jewish people and its age-old religion and culture. The Center ties technology and tradition together in a new, dynamic tapestry, and marries Internet and other state-of-the-art means with the creative skills and broad knowledge of Bar-Ilan University educators. Another Center aim is to support dialogue between Jewish youth of all origins and persuasions.

I am pleased, therefore, to support and encourage the activities of Bar-Ilan University's Sociological Institute for Community Studies. The international workshop it organized on the topic of Jewish Survival in 1997, as well as the publication of this volume summarizing the workshop proceedings, make a meaningful contribution to the academic literature on this important topic. We were particularly fortunate to have been joined at the workshop by eminent social scientists from other universities in Israel and abroad.

I salute the director of the Sociological Institute, Professor Ernest Krausz, for his leadership, as well as his ongoing advice and counsel.

Professor Moshe Kaveh
President
Bar-Ilan University

Introduction

Julius Gould

This volume from the Sociological Institute for Community Studies workshop on Jewish survival speaks for itself, and in that sense needs no introduction. But I am happy to introduce it to a wider audience and, in so doing, testify to the enthusiasm and scholarly zeal which marked the proceedings—qualities with which Professor Krausz and his colleagues at the Institute are richly endowed.

1. The chapters are written by experts in many disciplines, and deal with carefully chosen but diverse aspects of the subject. They illuminate most of the key questions about Jewish survival. Those questions are not matters of ghetto-angst or existential pain. They relate to the continued evolution of an ancient people, and a long-lived body of thought, as well as to the fate of a modern polity. The chapters are marked—as they should be—by a high degree of sophistication. For no historian or social scientist should need reminding of the great dangers in simplistic contrasts—not least in the sociology of religion. As is almost always the case, the observer of religious life uses a language that has its origins in the language of those who are observed: and such a language is seldom clinical or value-free. There is a constant risk of confusing theology with real or supposed social trends and of allowing beliefs or opinions to color the interpretation of evidence. There is also the omnipresent question of what constitutes evidence where the empirical or contingent levels overlap so steadily with metaphysics and spirituality.

The volatile issues of contemporary Jewish life, in Israel and within the diverse countries of the Diaspora, do not lend themselves to summary classification. Firstly, "ideal" and "material" interests (to use Max Weber's still serviceable contrast) intersect interminably. Secondly, the peculiarity of Jewish history has long been seen to be the way peoplehood has been supported by religious faith—often in the most unpropitious settings. That the Jews maintained for so long a sense of identity while they lived within the boundaries of other peoples has long seemed a unique historical conjunction. In 1943, in his masterly survey of anti-Semitism, Morris Ginsberg did not seek to "explain" it, but observed that

> It is difficult to account for this save by the strength of the faith in the Jewish religion as distinct and different from every other religion, a faith strengthened by persecution, upheld by a powerful religio-legal discipline, and producing or strengthening a bond of union which survives *even among those over whom religion has lost its hold.* (Ginsberg 1947: 201 [emphasis added])

This is the historical fact that makes the study of today's Jewish acculturation and secularization so complex: and, as is by now so glaringly obvious, these complexities are found within Israeli society and have continuing implications for relations with the Diaspora. Morris Ginsberg was writing at an anguished turning-point in Jewish and world history. Of course, times have changed. As Irving Louis Horowitz said in his opening address to the workshop, "the Jewish people are no longer the people they were between the Anschluss and Auschwitz." Yet the change is not quite total. Ginsberg's reference, so many years ago, to "a bond of union which survives even among those over whom religion has lost its hold" may still be relevant as applied to contemporary Israel. Did not Horowitz call the workshop's attention to "the most pronounced tendency in present-day Israeli society itself, the manifestly weak levels of religiosity and religious participation"?

Given this history, the ostensibly simplest of topics bristle with difficulties, stemming from theological currents, vested interests, and struggles for power. Controversy swirls about basic definitions. I do not, for example, expect early agreement on what an innocent observer might have thought quite simple—the question of "who is a Jew?"

The ways in which the workshop faced these matters reinforced for me the conclusions I set out in 1984 in a survey study of London Jews (Gould 1984). I sought to ventilate the issues in deliberately clinical terms—asking about "the attributes which Jews share with each other but not with those who are not Jews"—and made a vital distinction between *internal* and *external* dimensions. I argued that

> [I]n an open contemporary society there is an intricate linkage between (a) what Jews do or believe that is peculiar to them and marks them off from others; (b) how (quite diverse) "others" perceive such differences; and (c) how Jews receive what others perceive. This process can acquire its own dynamic. For the Jewish perception of the perception of others may come in turn to modify such perceptions. So there can be no routine or final outcome to such a process. (Ibid.:5)

I went on to note that while the Jewish sense of difference hinges, of course, on outside benevolence or hostility, the *internal* dimension is governed by the fact that Jews are legatees of a tradition that is religious, ethnic and moral. Changes in their circumstances make them shift the balance between the various elements in their inheritance. (Ibid.: 5–6)

I urged too that the existing variety of structures and underlying factors made it impossible

to insist upon a "religious" definition—one which would distinguish those who practice the Jewish religion (believing in certain abstract ideas and values and performing stated sets of religious/ritual observances) from all those who do not. (Ibid.:4)

This remains abundantly true today. One wishes it were not the case. Yet it could hardly be otherwise in a consumer age when theologians vie with commentators in speaking of "religious preferences" and religions are described (by their leaders) as "faith communities."

2. It would be invidious to single out specific offerings among the workshop papers—though I found the contributions of Professors Horowitz and Poll to be especially resonant. Reading the papers, I am struck, first, by their quality, and, secondly, by their *diversity*. This is bound to be the case in such a collection. For the striking diversity of the Jews in Israel and the countries of the Diaspora (notably though not exclusively the United States) is inescapable. The content of *identity* is also bound to be heterogeneous—reflecting not only the internal dimension that I have described, but also the political and cultural histories of the societies (Israel included) in which Jews are found. Even the patterns of alienation by "born" Jews from their Jewish milieus have historically been marked (some would say marred) by motifs and passions that are authentically "Jewish." Where Jewish self-hate actually exists, it abounds in such passions—with tragi-comical effects.

The size of the different Jewish populations is equally crucial—hence, of course, the countless contrasts to be found in the workshop papers, between the United States and Israel, as the two largest Jewish populations. It could also be argued that vigor is proportionate to size, even when much of the vigor is expressed via disputes between the groups and layers that can proliferate and flourish in such large populations. And perhaps underplayed in most of the papers, with the exception of that by Naftali Rothenberg, is the powerful role of *language*. Rothenberg notes (and it is of the foremost importance) that Jewish identity in Israel is grounded as much in the Hebrew language as in the other cultural themes and symbols of common citizenship. Furthermore, the place of religion in the Jewish state, open as it is to controversy—often of the bitterest and most uncompromising kind—is inevitably different from what is found in Diaspora countries. There, the mode and thrusts of secularization among Jews mirrors the variety of secularization that have emerged in the general societies (British, French, Russian, and so on) in which Jews reside. And when it comes to the attitudes and attachments of Jews in such countries towards the Jewish State, it is clear that many in the younger generation do not consistently show (nor could they be expected to show) the same level or kinds of commitment to, or even interest in, Israeli problems or concerns as their parents' generation did. For example, however crucial the notion of a "peace process" conducted by a normal established but imperilled state may be, it does not have the same aura or glamour that many Diaspora Jews once found in the earlier rhetoric and symbols of the nascent Zionist experiment.

3. Much of the debate about Jewish survival turns upon the real or supposed impact of two processes: assimilation and secularization. It is important to recognize that these are complex processes. Assimilation shades into acculturation within the wider societies (and this does not entail the elimination of all or even most dissimilarities). Secularization may appear to some as a concept that applies to Jewish structures in ways other than its application to Churches. But it *is* applicable—and illuminating. No Jewish writer has written more eloquently on the contrast between secularization and modernity than Chief Rabbi Jonathan Sacks (of Britain)—or in fuller benefit of insights drawn from the sociology of religion.

> By this is generally meant the transfer of territory, property and more generally, society's institutions and culture from ecclesiastic to lay power. Modernity is marked by the fact that religion ceases to dominate the way society organizes itself, or the way individuals explain their decisions. (Sacks 1990: 4)

Drawing upon seminal and influential analyses by Peter Berger, Rabbi Sacks contrasts traditional forms of religion with their modern counterparts. These are ideal types and, to be sure, such polarities mask the differences within each polar opposite.

> [P]rivatised religion is a matter of the "choice" or "preference" of the individual or the nuclear family, ipso facto lacking in common, binding quality. Such private religiosity, however "real" it may be to the individuals who adopt it, cannot any longer fulfil the classic task of religion, that of constructing a common world within which all of social life receives ultimate meaning binding on everyone. (Ibid.)

No one, myself included, feels it an easy task to conjoin the religious issues of secularization with the social stories of acculturation. Possibly none of the workshop papers tackled this systematically. But Solomon Poll put his finger on an important point. First he contrasts the two meanings of—and paths towards—assimilation: on the one hand, in a Diaspora country (the United States), and on the other hand, in Israel. We should note that he highlights the gulf between contemporary possibilities and what he calls with justice, "the traditional meaning of being Jewish" as linked with the observance of Jewish rituals.

The concern of assimilation in the United States is that Jews gradually become non-Jews. In Israel, the concern for assimilation assumes a different dimension. Jews living in a Jewish state, serving in the armed forces, paying taxes, participating in the Jewish community, and associating with other Jews, are instinctively Jewish. They do not need to practice any traditional religious ritual in order to be considered Jewish. By definition, in Israel a Jew cannot become a non-Jew, but one may become an Israeli without the traditional meaning of Jewishness. (Poll, this volume.)

And, significantly too, Professor Poll recognizes that, in the unique Israeli reality, the religious and secular populations may, as the cant cliché puts it, constitute two rival camps. To call them "camps" is itself an oversimplification. For in tense reality they rather resemble a warring array of tents in which factional disputes, demands on public funds, attachments to (and repulsion from) zealotry all take on an extraordinary variety of forms.

Professor Horowitz also invokes the diversity of Jewish peoplehood when he urges that "the inner reality of Jewish life is tripolar, it is not simply manifested in choices dictated by statist considerations." The case of the Jewish State is, by definition, unique. Putting matters in a theologically very controversial order, Professor Horowitz, in a rather striking phrase, talks of Judaism's "special religious Trinitarianism: Israel, the Torah, and God" with three secular correlates: the *State of Israel*; *peoplehood* (in which the Torah belongs to the Jewish people as a whole, a legal entity without a physical nation, but a national people; and thirdly "there is *the Hebrew God*, in which a collection of moral sentiments, legal precepts, and cosmological concepts are joined and fused to make Judaism a religion" (Horowitz, this volume).

He sees our age as a period of intellectual ferment and cross-fertilization bringing with it the need to scrutinize "the foundations of Zionism." That remains a task for Israeli and Diaspora scholars for years to come. Such scrutiny can clarify, without solving, issues of key importance. It would be wise to acknowledge that such issues are never solved for all time—but that temporary, often wounding solutions, are imposed by *events*. It is a waiting game, calling for endless patience—an existential game at which Jews have had long practice.

References

Ginsberg, Morris. 1947. *Reason and Unreason in Society*. London: Longmans.
Gould, Julius. 1984. *Jewish Commitment*. London: Institute of Jewish Affairs.
Sacks, Jonathan. 1990. *Tradition in an Untraditional Age*. London: Vallentine, Mitchell.

1

Keynote Address
Minimalism or Maximalism:
Jewish Survival at the Millennium

Irving Louis Horowitz

By common consensus, the two most extraordinary events of twentieth-century Jewish history were the destruction of European Jewry in the Holocaust, and the construction of the State of Israel. They bracket the 1940s, and they define Jewish parameters in the 1990s. Whatever the interpretations of these events, they clearly conjure up powerful and contradictory emotions: defeat and victory, peripheries and centers, helplessness and heroism, and of spirit and matter itself. The purpose of this article is to identify Jewish survival prospects in a post-Holocaust world, and in a world in which Israel is soon to celebrate the first half-century of its existence as a modern nation-state.

How the Jewish religion, national integration, and cultural identity are forged in light of these two immense events is at the core of this analysis. It is evident from any close examination of the subject of Jewish survival that contradiction is far more characteristic of Jewish life than consensus. This was the case in the past and remains so in the present. Struggles between orthodoxy and reformism, nationalism and cosmopolitanism (for want of a better word), Israeli national interests and Jewish universalistic claims, and capitalist individualism and socialist collectivism, have all hardened into postures rather than been resolved over the course of the century. Add to this mix such volatile private concerns as intermarriage, conversion, ethnic heritage, secular-

1

ization, and the task of analysis appears daunting, while that of synthesis seems well nigh impossible.

Policy makers repeatedly claim that even were Israel not to exist, conflict among Arab and Moslem interests would continue to fester. Dare one add in reverse that even were Arab hostilities toward Israel and Moslem animosities toward Jews magically to dissolve, conflict among Jewish interests—political and religious—would continue in force? Urgent questions have been raised about generational concerns: the evolution of Israel as a national entity with "normal" state proclivities to monopolize force, and the prospect that Judaism may become a minority religion even within Israel, much less within the context of most open societies. It behooves the social science community to answer whether Judaism is any different than other world class religions, and what constitutes Judaism as a frame of reference in national and cultural terms with nominal regard to issues of religious observance or theological discourse.

There is also the thorny, if largely unspoken, issue of how strategies of becoming Jewish enhance or impede principles of scientific research. Concerns for Jewish survival strongly imply that such survival is a positive value. But whether a moral center of gravity, much less a teleological purpose, can be deduced from the history of religions as a sociological concern merits examination. Within these heavy domains of relevance I should like to consider minimal and maximal approaches to Jewish survival. To be sure, the topic of Jewish survival in the period ahead is so broad and pervasive that the potential for saying something new, much less presenting a startling set of findings or conclusions is more presumptuous than ambitious. Yet, it is in the nature of human nature to persist in lurching forward, no matter how slightly, and to seek closure no matter how tentative.

I take as my text a highly personal point-counterpoint: the collection of my essays published a quarter century ago under the rubric: *Israeli Ecstasies and Jewish Agonies*, and the work I have pursued in the intervening years called *Taking Lives*. Risking a digression before addressing the wider issue of Jewish survival directly, I ask the reader's indulgence on how I view my own work in tandem, as book-ends separated by a quarter century.

The purpose of *Israeli Ecstasies and Jewish Agonies* was to explain how a dialectical set of relationships emerged as a result of a new centrality for Jewish life, Israel; and the evolution of a new periphery as well, in North America. For what seemed to be at stake in the late 1960s and early 1970s was the serious weakening of Jewish life as an entity of value apart from the existence of Israeli society. Now, the situation is curiously reversed. There is a widespread recognition of the work of Jewish life and a growing skepticism of the centrality of the Israeli center! My intentions in *Taking Lives* were somewhat less global: to develop a social scientific framework for understanding the Holocaust in terms of state legitimacy, or more specifically, variables of class, status and power familiar to those who work in the Weberian tradition. Curiously, we have a huge literature based on personal testimonials and biographies, and only a slightly smaller amount of writings exploring theological and religious considerations that emerged from the Holocaust. Yet the social analysis of this monumental tragedy is only now receiving its proper due.

What makes the study of Jewish identity complex is that we are not dealing with a unilinear phenomenon, but one more akin to a multiplexed phenomenon moving in a variety of historical as well as structural directions. To discuss the Jewish condition is to examine religiosity, nationality, and culture all at once as well as one at a time. Indeed, to separate these elements of Judaism, results in distortions and reductions that can, and sadly enough often does, lead to little light and much heat.

To be sure, the arguments between those who emphasize issues of class stratification on one side, and cultural identity on the other, indicate that exaggerated claims for any one sort of social scientific method are likely to result in frustration and futile argumentation. I turned from a study of Israeli-Jewish relations to an examination of the deeper roots of the Jewish condition as such, because the explosion of literature on the Holocaust led to serious distortions in the intellectual landscape; and no less important, the social scientific accounts, while attempting to repair distortions resulting from a variety of reductionists in the popular literature, introduced a few new sins of their own.

We have an astonishing amount of personal narratives (some serious, others self-serving) providing eyewitness reports of horrors and human degradation, but failing to place the Final Solution in any larger context. So what we are left with is a series of uplifting or depressing stories of living with the past, or getting beyond horror and degradation. On the other extreme are what might be called the theological exegeses, in which issues of an ultimate sort are examined: from questions like, "Can we believe in God's goodness after the Holocaust?" to a variety of messages, intentional or otherwise, that serve as Providential warning signals for those who fall from grace. Again, the quality of such human examinations of Providential intentions shift from profound to trivial—and worse.

Because they constituted a collective unit, the Jewish people, were uniquely singled out for total and complete annihilation; Christian and Hebrew scholars alike have tried to interpret the Nazi war on the Jewish people in Biblical, revelatory terms; frequently laced with reflections on the historical status of Jews living in a Christian world, and extending into the particular economic drives, political motives, and cultural longings of each world religion in relation to the other.

In the midst of these larger trends—what we may call the biographical and the theological, respectively—a third trend has emerged: the empirical study of how the Holocaust took place, what happened when, where it did, and why it surfaced in relation to the Jews of Europe. The major and admittedly bowdlerized answers given are: first, Germans have a unique propensity for racial purity and animus toward strangers in their midst who do not share in the national value system; and second, it is not the nation but the system, the Nazi-Fascist system that created the foundation for implementing the final solution.

I do not want to enter a polemic with other viewpoints, or argue issues examined at length in the text of *Taking Lives*. Rather, I want to note emphatically, that my own view is that however multiple the sources of anti-Semitism, and however broad the base of emotive support for the Final Solution, the actual implementation and execution of the Holocaust was a function of state power, of the legal and military monopoly of power that resided in the hands of the National Socialist state, which allowed for the Holocaust to move ahead in its grinding, vicious wholeness. The emergence of Israel as a state implicitly recognized as much. It made Jew and non-Jew alike aware of the modern as well as ancient sources of power and authority. The monopoly of power rather than the beneficence of rulers became the touchstone of Jewish life after the Holocaust. It provided the grounds of legitimacy for the Jewish State of Israel.

However "banal" the perpetrators of the Holocaust may have been as private persons, they acted in concert as part of a killing machine, comprised of a hugely expanded and swollen bureaucracy dedicated to surveillance, a military establishment that dwarfed anything hitherto known in the annals of European armed force, and a disciplined political party apparatus that had as its exclusionary membership mission the extirpation and destruction of Jewish life wherever Nazism held sway, including occupied zones and lands not known in earlier eras for anti-Semitism as national preoccupation. In this sense, *Taking Lives* is an effort to concretize the work of political sociology, of the interaction between state and society. It is also a way to lay claim to the fact that the very act of taking lives and counting bodies is the sociological equivalent to locating the essential variable by which a society and a state are to be judged.

The analysis of Jewish survival in post-Holocaust terms is immediately made complex by its triadic nature. We must simultaneously deal with the state of Israel, its model of democratic rule rooted in Westminster; a divinely inspired Torah passed on to Jews over centuries and millennia as a guide to ethical and legal behavior; a Jewish culture filtered through many nations and conventions and languages that are encapsulated in an adherence to some form of community living; and certain personality characteristics. Add to this mixture the relationship between persons who claim a common adherence to Judaism in philosophic terms, and any ensuing analysis of the Jewish condition becomes numbingly complex. But we have set ourselves the task of clarifying these relationships; we are seeking to establish an analytical model rather than a clerical muddle. Essentially, I do this by taking a minimalist, rather than maximalist view of the Jewish-Israel relationship. Along with Abba Eban, I assume that being a Jew implies commitment to the fate and fortune of Israel, and to a community of like-minded souls. Whether being an Israeli implies, in reverse, a commitment to the fate and fortune of world Jewry, is a question perhaps best left in abeyance for the present. Let me immediately note that this minimalist approach carries risks. Marginalization within Jewish religious life can, and often does, readily translate into complete secularization, or as is sometimes the case, into varieties of alternative civil religious persuasions.

Before we examine current struggles, it might be useful to remind ourselves how military matters stood only a quarter century ago. It might help explain why I entitled my work *Israeli Ecstasies and Jewish Agonies.* In the period that followed the euphoria of the Six-Day

War in 1967, it is understandable that a dominant wing of Israeli leaders could argue, as David Ben-Gurion had earlier, that commitment to Zionism could have no validity without Jewish immigration to Israel. Without such a pioneer vision, Jewish life in the Diaspora was bankrupt.

> I don't know how long it will take, whether ten years or fifty years, but in time, America will be a unitary nation, just like any other nation. It is entirely different with Jews in Israel. The roads in this country are Jewish roads, they were built by Jews. The houses that you see here were built by Jews. The trees are Jewish trees; they were planted by Jews. The railway is a Jewish railway; it is conducted by Jewish workers, by Jewish engineers. The papers are Jewish. We do not live a group life. Here we are living a national life. There is another difference between Israeli Jewry and Diaspora Jewry. We are also an independent factor in international life. We appear like any other free people at the United Nations. We meet with representatives of large and small states on an equal footing. We do not need *shtadlanim* (intercessors) any more.

Those amazingly proud words uttered in the glowing aftermath of military victory now appear quaint, inspiring more response than regard. As a consequence of military struggle, one which resulted in a political stalemate, redefinitions of Israeli realities topped the agenda. Claims of sovereignty and autonomy have been tempered by a renewed realization of the special relationship between Israelis and Jews, without much outward concern for who is preeminent in this interaction network. Thus, in a new book by Geoffrey Wheatcroft on *The Controversy of Zion* we have a summary of arguments against Zionism that have become as strident as they are commonplace.

> It is the very absence of the kind of ethnic nationalism and cultural homogeneity exemplified by Israel which has made possible their own triumphant story. What Jews outside of Israel have come to recognize very clearly is not only that Israel is not their home, but that the Israelis, however much they admire them, are no longer their people. . . . The final paradox might be that Zionism has succeeded in everything but its ostensible purpose; to resolve the Jewish Question by normalizing the Jewish people and to end their chosenness. . . . And yet the Jews remain in some manner chosen. . . . Today there is a Jewish state which is a source of healing pride for millions of Jews, but also a source of anxiety. Should they defend the religious zealots and right wing settlers who play an ever larger part in Israeli life? Or is Israel increasingly irrelevant to the fabulous success story of the Jews of America?

More contradictory general propositions on Israeli-Diaspora relations are hard to envision. But we need to determine whether such varied sentiments represent something deeper than the changing fortunes of warfare and statecraft. Do these two ideological frameworks define, not only the limits of Israeli existence, but the survival capacities of the Jewish people as a whole? In exploring this question, we must confront a reality in which a center (Israel) remains relatively weak while a periphery (American Jewry) is relatively powerful.

Israel's geographical rationalization, in the current period, and the Arab countries' own continuing struggles between tradition and modernity, have led to a renewed search for religious, ethnic, and cultural elements within Judaism. Do the political and social structures that divide Jews along national lines permit unity or fusion in religious and cultural terms? I suspect that even posing the issue in this way makes a positive answer possible. Definitive political and theological responses cannot be concluded with respect to Israeli-Jewish relationships. Dialectical people have a habit of maintaining long-standing differences, broken in moments of crisis by tactical synthesis. This certainly characterizes the present condition of Jews and Israelis. The state of Israel is an irreducible fact, one that Jews must live with—even those who might not celebrate such a fact. In this sense, Zionism and anti-Zionism are less policies than postures in present-day Israel. National realities now seem indifferent to internationalist ambitions.

In a broad series of stages, the Arab effort to convert Jews into a pariah people, and Israel into a pariah state, have failed. This is no small accomplishment in its own right. Beyond these, a series of issues within Judaism were also resolved in the past quarter century. Arabic adversaries, by ceaselessly questioning the legitimacy of Israel as a "settler state," provided the foundations for wide-ranging reexamination of the contemporary state of Jewish affairs, culminating in relatively successful efforts by Israel to come to terms with its position in the Middle East. Again, no small achievement for a land that felt far more tied to Europe than the Middle East only a quarter century ago. Such self-exploration might be a constant in Jewish affairs without external pressures, but with them, the sense of immediacy takes on dramatic proportions.

The repudiation of the Zionist-as-racism canard, not without the firm support of Western democracies, was coupled with a series of negotiated arrangements starting with Egypt and Jordan, and now expanded to include Palestinians and Syrians. A variety of diplomatic as well as military arrangements have modified the sense of Israeli estrangement. The question however remains whether weakening the threat to Israel as a pariah State translates into a weakening sense of identification of Jews with the fate and fortune of Israel. More bluntly, do Jews now view Israel as a place to visit archaeological sites and go scuba-diving rather than a place to restore political commitments or make an issue out of vigilant support?

Debate about whether Israel is central or peripheral to the Jewish experience in the United States or elsewhere in the Diaspora is only one half the essential paradigm. The other half is whether Judaism is central to Israeli political integration. It might well be that underlying these questions is whether Judaism is central to Jews wherever they are. Posing the issue in these admittedly harsh terms is not an exercise in dialectics, but an effort to examine the empirical state of affairs that makes the issue of Israeli sovereignty profoundly meaningful. For example, if migration from Israel to America far exceeds Jewish-American immigration to Israel, does this weaken or strengthen world Jewry? If one believes in the organic incompleteness of Jewish life outside Israel, the answer is self-evident. But for those who believe that the Jewish nation resides wherever a Jewish congregation exists, temporal problems of the state of Israel are of only limited significance to what Herzl called "the Jewish company." The extent to which orthodox positions on Israeli centrality have broken down is best illustrated by the current demographic situation. At least 10 percent of Israelis, or approximately 450,000 of Israel's citizens, are currently living in the United States on a relatively permanent basis. Beyond that, new migrants to Israel from Russia are often interested in moving to the United States, Canada, New Zealand, or Australia, what might be referred to as the Anglo-democracies, rather than staying in Israel. Whatever the explanations offered—hardships of settlement in Israel, limited knowledge about or interest in Jewish religious life, fears of new military hostilities, oppression of tax burdens, or limits to upward mobility and career opportunities—Jewish dedication to Israel remains highly questionable under present-day circumstances.

Whenever the existence of Israel has been threatened by hostile, military dominated states, and the survival of the Jews of Israel is clearly imperiled, Jewish solidarity has been evident and made near total by the "facts on the ground." Witness the outpouring of international Jewish support for Israel in the 1967 and 1973 Arab-Israeli conflicts or, most recently, the solidarity of Jews against Iraq, Libya and Iran—the so-called terrorist states. Ultimate questions about survival always obviate niceties of discussion and disputation. The choice between social life and death, like individual life and death, makes intellectual hairsplitting seem fatuous. To the extent that the Jewish state has, from its inception, been engaged in a survival-crisis-response syndrome, one can speak with confidence of the centrality of Israel to the Jewish experience.

However, when minimum conditions of Israeli security are met and, in consequence, the needs of a large portion of Jewish peoplehood are met, the question of the centrality of Israel to Jewish life becomes thorny. When Israeli survival is not in jeopardy, but to the contrary, relatively normalized, conventional distinctions between socialism, nationalism, and religiosity, slip back into the rhetoric ordinarily employed by Jews inside and outside of Israel. The state of normality thus unleashes national rather than overseas concerns. The relative lack of such normal, peaceful, conditions in the Middle East since the founding of Israel has obscured real differences between Jews in the Diaspora and in Israel with respect to a variety of issues affecting the international Jewish community. The data indicate some clear guidelines in this respect.

First, Reform Jews, adults and youth, who are presumably representative of American Jewry as a whole, rate the relationship of American Jews to Israel as very important; but only a quartile agree with the statement that Israel is the center of contemporary American Jewish life. As orthodoxy continues to hold sway in Israel, and Reform and Conservative religious movements inside Israel are confronted with problems of legitimacy, even that figure may be inflated. Second, regional studies of American Jews reveal noticeable differences in the strength of Zionism between fathers and sons. Fathers scored significantly higher on indicators of Zionist persuasion. For the most part, all available data support the argument that the Zionism of American Jews, is less an intent to migrate than a general belief in Israeli claims. Pro-Israel sentiment is directly linked to perceived threats to the survival of the Israeli state. Third, American Jewish attitudes vary significantly depending on whether Middle East wars are perceived to have negative consequences for the United States. Thus, the reaction of American Jews to the Six-Day War of 1967 was more favorable than their attitudes toward the Yom Kippur War of 1973 or the Lebanese adventure of 1982 precisely because the synergy and consistency of American and Israeli interests in the earlier war did not hold true for the later conflicts.

Israel has registered genuine achievements in various spheres of life-science and medical research, cyberspace technology, humanistic education in kibbutzim, folk music and dance, basic agricultural self-sufficiency, army efficiency and *esprit*, and so forth. Beyond these areas, the caliber of Israeli society is not notably higher than say, Western Europe. In politics, academic life, industry, labor leadership, religion, *belles lettres*, the media, the dramatic and fine arts, Israel, while surely not lagging too far behind other developed countries, is far from producing standards of excellence sufficient to inspire its own citizens or the Jewish Diaspora. As long as the relationship of the Diaspora to Israel is strictly financial, with no genuine joint responsibility in planning for Israel's development, or real accountability to contributors abroad for the funds collected, one cannot (outside the religious clusters) expect thoughtful Jews around the world to express a sustained sense of personal involvement in Israel at the intimate, or subjective level.

It may be argued that an adequate reexamination of Israeli-Diaspora relations should begin by understanding Israel as both a Third World entity and a European democracy operating in an unique context. Perceived in this way, tendencies toward growing separation of Jewish life in the Diaspora from identification with Israeli society might be seen as part of a long-term secular trend distinguishing nationhood from religiosity and ethnicity. Diminishing Jewish involvement with Israel may have long-term benefits as well as costs for center and periphery alike. For Israel, such secularization could lessen overseas pressure in the formation of national and international policies, and hence permit Israel greater flexibility in its decision-making processes. For Diaspora Jews, such a distinction might compel greater attention to Judaism as such, to the role of religion, culture, and ethnicity in the contemporary West, apart from concerns about military annihilation currently shrouding Middle Eastern affairs. Evolution of the debate over Israeli centrality and Diaspora marginality has moved a considerable distance beyond inherited Zionist and anti-Zionist shibboleths.

The question of Israel's centrality to Jewish life cannot be resolved by the wave of a magic wand. The inner reality of Jewish life is tripolar, it is not simply manifested in choices dictated by State considerations. Judaism has had its own special religious Trinitarianism: Israel, the Torah, and God. Corresponding to that, in secular terms is first, Israel as a state (in the Hobbesian sense of retaining a monopoly of power). Second, peoplehood, in which the sacred documents are invested in the Jewish people as a whole, a legal entity without a physical nation, but a national people. Finally, there is the Hebrew God, in which a collection of moral sentiments, legal precepts, and cosmological concepts are joined and fused to make Judaism a religion.

The centrality or marginality of American Jews to the Israeli experience can similarly be broken down into a kind of tripartite arrangement. Survey data have repeatedly shown that American Jewry's response to Israel depends on whether Israel is being talked about as a nation-state, as part of a worldwide communion of Jewish people, or as a theological-religious phenomenon having transcendental as well as immanent goals. When Israel is physically threatened by military activity, there is a high degree of international Jewish mobilization. But it is hard to imagine any responsible American Jewish leader calling on the Jewish people of the world to respond exclusively to Israeli needs as a state power in the Middle East, or for that matter even to urge support of the specifics of everyday life in Israel.

The historian, Melvin Urofsky who has done significant research on American Zionism, put the matter of Jewish response to Israeli appeals forcefully. Being Jewish is not the central concern of most American Jews: being American is. With the exception of one or two "gut" issues, such as anti-Semitism or Israel, American Jews are divided, indeed fragmented on every other question. They want to consider matters relating to religion as private; secular issues, even those which might affect Judaism, are to be treated in a secular, an American manner. Another way to express this same opinion is to observe that Jewish communities are themselves seriously affected by the centrality of American society and economy as a whole to the continued existence of Israel. In this sense, to the extent Israel as a society remains peripheral to American centrality, Israel compromises its claims for cultural or religious centrality with respect to Jews, especially those who live in the United States.

The notion of centrality, or the direct impact of Israel on a peripheral Jewish population, has three distinct frames of reference: the state of Israel, the Jewish people, and the Hebrew religion. This is a critical differentiation inherent in the history of Judaism. Its tripartite character underscores a great deal of ambiguity in Jewish life. But it also gives Jewish life considerable strategic resilience. What falsifies a great deal of data and statistics on who is or is not a Jew, or *when* a

Jew becomes a non-Jew, and so on, arises precisely within the American context, where this kind of tripartite structure becomes intolerably manifest. National Jews, ethnic Jews, and theological Jews all confront each other as total ideological solutions (i.e., assimilationist or survivalist) to fragmented political frameworks. As a result, contemporary Judaism exemplifies a feeling of pluralistic peoplehood that involves many diverse elements. Judaism cannot easily be destroyed or eliminated: but neither can it be easily synthesized into a single supreme frame of reference. The universalism, or if one prefers, the very porosity of Judaism, even if it causes moments of grief to Israel's particular concerns, provides residual strength to Jewish survivalist impulses. One indicator of this strength is the multiple problems encountered in conversion efforts. The source of so many failures in evangelical efforts to "convert" Jews is the narrow fundamentalist definition of what constitutes Jewishness. Christian fundamentalism tends to limit its interests in Judaism to one of theology. To the extent that Islamic theology also sees Judaism as exclusively a religious faith, it has the same interpretive problems as the Christian West. Consequently, their efforts to eliminate Judaism via theological conversion have had limited success. Jewish strength resides in its plurality, clerical and secular alike. The gigantic historical ambiguity involving God, ethnicity, and nation is a positive and healthy factor in Judaism's survival. But it also makes it exceedingly difficult to reach a definitive answer to the question of how central Israel is to Jewish life.

In the past, Israeli centrality has implied Jewish marginality. The ideological bridge between Israel and Jews is much more heavily traversed in one direction: from the Diaspora to Zion. Yet in demographic terms, the bridge carries more traffic from Zion to the Diaspora. Increasingly, an older pattern, in which Jewish leaders are frequently asked to define the role of Israel in the life of the individual American Jew, is being replaced by a newer pattern, in which Israeli figures must begin to explain the role of Diaspora Jews in the life of individual Israelis.

As this pattern of intellectual cross-fertilization ripens, the foundations of Zionism themselves undergo scrutiny. The totality of the destruction of the European Jewish communities that thrived between 1789 and 1939 served to vindicate classical Zionist persuasions. But the continued vitality of Jewish life in Anglo-American democracies has, with equal force, compelled reconsideration of Zionist ideological tenets. Earlier maximalist demands that Diaspora Jews resettle in Israel have reduced themselves to a minimalist approach. Now the durability, permanence, indeed, the absolute necessity of a viable Diaspora has replaced older, more religious-oriented visions of a return to Zion. What this does to Israel's centrality in the lives of world Jewish communities becomes a question of some urgency.

Do Conservative and Reform varieties of the Jewish religion have anything to contribute to Israeli society or theological attitudes in Israel? To ask this question is to ignore the most pronounced tendency in present-day Israeli society itself, the manifestly weak levels of religiosity and religious participation in Israeli society. Israel's secularization approximates secularization in other modernizing societies. Regular synagogue attendance is probably lower than Sunday morning churchgoing in American society. Indicators such as worship in a synagogue may prove little, by themselves, but at least they help make quite plain the differences between support for Israel and active participation in Jewish community or religious experience.

We need to confront uncomfortable questions within both Jewish life and Israeli society. To what degree can one have American Jewish identification with Israel that corresponds to a highly secular Israeli society? This is a more difficult question than whether one identifies with Israel in a strictly crisis scenario. Here the touchy issue becomes under what global conditions might support for Israel not be forthcoming by American Jewry? For example, what kinds of military action or capabilities would make it permissible or even theologically mandated to withhold support of Israel by Jewish communities? We witnessed the beginnings of this sort of distinction in the Israeli-Lebanese struggles during the early 1980s. Israeli military victories in the field were greeted with far more unease than were the threats that confronted Israeli society in earlier periods.

Such extremely sensitive questions are being raised with increasing frequency. If Israel enters a period of protracted political stalemate, in which it is part of pluralistic goals, and dynamic development in the Middle East as a whole, the capacity for quick mobilization of world Jewish support will diminish. As the war-peace syndrome recedes, stagnation-growth issues emerge. In such a scenario, matters taken for granted between Jews in the Diaspora and Israelis in Zion, are far fewer and less compelling than in the grand dialogue of the formative period of Israeli existence.

Whether the Jewish question rather than the Israeli question has once more become central is the thorny problem of the present decade. Throughout the twentieth century, every decade has thrown up a master problem which has occasioned realignment, reshuffling, and rethinking. Old alliances tend to dwindle with a decade's end. Those who found themselves united around opposition or support for the Vietnamese conflict in the 1960s, found old alliances sharply curtailed during the 1970s under the impact of the Middle East crisis. This is not to say that new forms of association between Jews as an "interest group" and other social movements cannot be forced, only that the foundation of such associations tend to be more domestic than global concerns.

The American experience has become more intertwined with Jewish experience than at any time in the past. Quite apart from military support to Israel, whether posed in terms of integration of Russian Jews, Jewish settlements in the West Bank, or impact of Latin American and South African Jewish communities on new immigration patterns, all become central considerations for those charged with rethinking democratic premises in American Jewish organizational affairs. The special concerns of Israel must somehow be placed within a Jewish context so that policy choices are not reduced to Israel's impact on America, but rather the more complex issue of Israel's reflection of, no less than impact upon the so-called Jewish question.

The existence of Israel has led to a realignment of forces. Because of the compelling fusion of objective circumstances and subjective sentiments, the Jewish people are no longer the people they were between the Anschluss and Auschwitz. Jews no longer exhibit the same circumscribed commercial concerns or the same focus on survival. Whether or not this shift from economic survival to political participation is celebrated, the fact that the Jewish question has become central to international debates in the 1990s is incontrovertible. It is profoundly intertwined with problems ranging from energy supplies to military preparedness, to profound reconsideration of the Holocaust and the behavior of nations under stress. Within this global context, the Israeli issue is profoundly meaningful to all peoples and parties. Outside of that context, Israel is of special meaning primarily to the Jewish peoples.

Given the plural status of Jewish identification, what then should be the posture of the individual Jew toward the question of national allegiance to Israel and political participation in matters of importance to Israel? This question is specifically anguishing for the American, Canadian, and West European Jews (in that order) since there is only limited potential for full citizen participation in Latin America, South Africa, Russia, Eastern Europe, and portions of the Third World where Jews exist in large numbers. Past Jewish participation in these home countries of the Diaspora has been at the economic and social levels. As a result, the problem of dual or multiple political allegiance remains, for such people, largely an abstraction.

Diaspora participation in affairs of state in Israel is limited to rhetorical flourishes and editorial anguishes. It is true that certain key leaders in the American Jewish community have some marginal voice in Israeli life. But this is primarily a consequence of philanthropic and monetary power; not any special policy-making acumen that is essential to Israeli political affairs. Prominent wealthy American Jews have the same input into Israel as the International Monetary Fund does in any Third World country. A central problem in consequence is the extent to which Jewish solidarity, in times of Israeli military crisis, can or should be brought to bear on one's own country or countries. Jewish mobilization in support of Israel by no means violates their citizen obligations to the United States or anywhere else in which they have a vote as well as a voice; but the United States is particularly sensitive to large interest-group pressures.

The arguments which have raged concerning divided loyalties of American Jews are largely chimerical if not entirely fictitious. Certainly, throughout the relatively brief history of the state of Israel, Jews have never surrendered political loyalty to another state. If anything, Jewish communities have drawn closer to the American political mainstream as Israeli interests have become intertwined with those of the United States. In the absence of any impulses in the opposite direction, the issue of dual loyalties remains of marginal importance. Only in special circumstances, such as the Pollard spy case, are uncomfortable issues of any relevant sort introduced.

While conceptually possible, it is empirically unlikely to envision a condition under which American and Israeli interests diverge so sharply as to compel Jews to confront the pluralistic premises of this viewpoint with the monistic requirements of choosing between either the United States or Israel. At such a time, the very essence of the American commitment to pluralism or, perhaps, the Israeli commitment to democracy, would be sorely strained. And in such moments, abstract guidelines must yield to historical specifics; such is the character of decision making in times of national strife. The great advantage of Israel is its explicit commitment to limited democratic government and pluralistic outlooks, presumably a milder form of commitment than Americans have to the United States. If this delicate equilibrium breaks down on either side, a decision might be forced. But to presume so on *a priori* grounds would represent an extreme form of unwarranted historical pessimism.

Jews have traditionally lived in a partial, fragmented world. Tensions and polarities are built into the substance of Jewish lifestyle. Marginality is a consequence of a people dispossessed, displaced, and well traveled. More pointedly, marginality is also a condition that makes it possible to face world problems with a maximum amount of objectivity and a minimum amount of undiluted fanaticism or ideological investment. Perfect integration into any national system, even that of Israel, could well represent negation of positive Jewish values. It would also signal a collapse of the pluralistic sources of American politics and traditions. Presently, neither of these outcomes seem imminent. Jewish concerns can remain largely focused on positive solutions to practical issues; including the status of Israel. But as Charles Liebman has rightly pointed out, that given Israel as a state with a moral purpose, neither Israelis nor Jews can quite accept the theory—much less the practice—of unlimited democracy. As a result, conservative values coexist in uneasy alliance with liberal politics.

What seems to have taken place is a huge shift in cultural fault lines, a transformation of values that has seen the emergence of problems of secularization and national identity that are characteristic of emerging free societies the world over. While concerns about individualism and identity clearly enlist the sympathies of Jews the world over, they do not exhaust the *Geist* or *Weltanschauung* of the Jewish people at century's end. Varieties of specifically Jewish clerical belief, from pragmatic reconstructionism to cabalistic mysticism abound. If the current situation hardly permits euphoria or ecstasy, the processes underway in Israel do serve to refocus Jewish energies and enlarge its visions. That so much change has occurred in the past quarter century is a tribute to the maturation of Israel, but perhaps more generically to the survival capacities of Judaism as such. Israel is the preeminent example in our times on how political and emotional flexibility are special characteristics of small new nations and big historic peoples.

References

Ben-Gurion, David. 1962. "How is Israel Different?" *Jewish Frontier* 21 (Aug.), as quoted in Howard M. Sachar, *A History of Israel: From the Rise of Zionism to Our Time*. New York: Alfred A. Knopf, pp. 718–719.

Horowitz, Irving Louis. 1974. "Israeli Imperatives and Jewish Agonies," pp. 3–36 in *Israeli Ecstasies and Jewish Agonies*. New York and London: Oxford University Press.

Wheatcroft, Geoffrey. 1996. *The Controversy of Zion*. London: Sinclair-Stevenson Publishers, pp. 342–43.

Suggested Readings

Ben-Sasson, H.H. 1976. *A History of the Jewish People*. Cambridge, MA: Harvard University Press.

Dashevsky, Arnold and Howard Shapiro. 1974. *Ethnic Identification among American Jews*. Lexington: D.C. Heath.

Deshen, Charles, S. Liebman and Moshe Shokeid. 1995. *The Sociology of Religion in Israel: Israeli Judaism*. New York and London: Transaction Publishers.

Eisen, Robert. 1997. "Jewish Mysticism: Seeking Inner Light." *Moment, v*ol. 22, no.1: 38–43.

Eisenstadt, Shmuel N. 1992. *Jewish Civilization: The Jewish Historical Experience in a Comparative Perspective*. Albany: State University of New York Press.

Elon, Amos. 1971. *The Israelis: Founders and Sons*. New York: Holt, Rinehart, and Winston.

Ezrachi, Yaron. 1997. *Rubber Bullets: Power and Conscience in Modern Israel*. New York: Farrar, Strauss and Giroux.

Harrison, Bernard. 1996. "Talking Like a Jew: Reflections on Identity and the Holocaust." *Judaism, v*ol. 45, no.1 (Winter): 3–28.

Heilman, Samuel C. 1992. *Defenders of the Faith: Inside Ultra-Orthodox Jewry*. New York: Schocken Books.

Horowitz, Irving Louis. 1974. *Israeli Ecstasies-Jewish Agonies*. New York: Oxford University Press.

———. 1997. *Taking Lives: Genocide and State Power* (Fourth edition). New York and London: Transaction Publishers.

Liebman, Charles and Steven M. Cohen. 1990. *Two Worlds of Judaism: Israeli and American Experiences*. New Haven, CT: Yale University Press.

Sachar, Howard M. 1976. *A History of Israel: From the Rise of Zionism to Our Time*. New York: Alfred A. Knopf.

Scholem, Gershom. 1971. *On the Kabbalah and its Symbolism*. New York: Schocken Books.

Segre, Dan V. 1980. *A Crisis of Identity: Israel and Zionism*. New York and Oxford: Oxford University Press.

Sklare, Marshall. 1971. *America's Jews*. New York: Random House.

Seltzer, Robert M. 1980. *Jewish People, Jewish Thought*. New York: Macmillan, London: Collier Macmillan.

Sobel, B.Z. 1974. *Hebrew Christianity: The Thirteenth Tribe*. New York: John Wiley and Sons.

Urofsky, Melvin I. 1976. "Do American Jews Want Democracy in Jewish Life?" *Inter-Change*. vol. 1, no. 7: 1–7.

Waxman, Chaim I. 1976. "The Centrality of Israel in American Jewish Life: A Sociological Analysis." *Judaism,* vol. 25, no. 2.

Wheatcroft, Geoffrey. 1996. *The Controversy of Zion*. New York and London: Sinclair-Stevenson.

Part One

Sociological Analysis
of Jewish Identity

2

The Diaspora-Community-Tradition Paradigms of Jewish Identity: A Reappraisal

Régine Azria

Introduction

As a preliminary, I shall venture a personal remark about the title of this meeting. I was quite amazed by the pathos of its wording, especially by the use of the words Jewish survival. Using terminology like "Jewish survival" to debate the issue of Jewish identity, in the State of Israel over fifty years after the genocide, sounds quite paradoxical—particularly to a member of the postwar generation, born in Western Europe four days after Israel declared its independence. This way of putting it reveals a deep anxiety about the future, a lack of confidence in the inner resources of our contemporary fellow Jews. The reasons for such a fear, and the reasons for my expressing such amazement at this fear, are probably to be found in the different contents and meanings of being a Jew at the close of the twentieth century.

This remark on somewhat contrasting feelings over Jewish concerns demonstrates the usefulness of our meeting here today. It gives me an opportunity to express my pleasure at participating, and to thank the organizers of this workshop for their kind invitation to do so.

As a sociologist, my approach to this issue is deliberately non-normative and critical. I do not intend to formulate value statements on the many ways of being Jewish. I would rather try to understand and construct interpretative patterns for the facts I observe, from a specific field of observation: France and its Jewry, i.e., the largest Jewish community in Western Europe.

In order to serve that purpose, I propose to reappraise three core components, concepts or dimensions of traditional Jewish identity—*Diaspora, community,* and *tradition*—and suggest a pattern of interpretation congruent with the present-day reality. The task of inventing fitting instruments for the building of tomorrow's Jewish identities, I shall leave to the many Jewish men and women of good will—political, social, cultural, religious activists and community leaders.

The Diaspora Paradigm

Rather than contrasting the Jewish Diaspora to Israel, as is usually done, rather than considering them as two components of a structurally bipolarized entity, I suggest an altogether different approach implying a paradigmatic change: *that Judaism is basically and fundamentally a Diaspora construct;* the *reference* to Israel rather than Israel itself operates as a dynamic agent, as a catalyst of utopia, whether under a prophetic, a messianistic or a Zionist form. Before showing its implications for the identity issue, let me first develop this statement in a more substantial way.

Diaspora, as dispersion and exile, has been decisive in the structuring of Jewish identities—not only because the post-exile period was the longest one in Jewish history, but principally because the social and religious matrix out of which Judaism progressively emerged was elaborated and fixed within a Diaspora spatial, political, and cultural frame. Originally imposed by history, the frame and matrix were given a meaning through their elaboration by tradition. In that way, one may say that Judaism is the output of Diaspora.

This statement points to the fact that Judaism was not primarily shaped in order to meet the requirements of state politics. Until now, Judaism gave no satisfying answers to the many pragmatic, administrative, diplomatic, and ethical questions arising from state management (Weiler 1988). Judaism was never concerned with political power and state authority precisely *because* it is a Diaspora construct. Here lies probably one of the sources of the fierce resistance of Israeli society to the endeavors of the representatives of traditional Judaism to impose their view and to be accepted as a political force in this country, even though Israel is traditionally held to be the native and emblematic place of Judaism.

Now, from the start, the Diaspora condition has been intrinsically ambiguous, the ambiguity consisting in the fact that all over their dispersion, Jews never stopped thinking of and longing for an else-where, for a place they alternatively or simultaneously perceived in mythical, spiritual, religious, or political terms; to the extent that the very notion of Diaspora had to include among its stock of representations, memory and imagination, the image of this elsewhere, present and absent at one and the same time.

The question that comes immediately to mind is that of the nature of the link developed by Jews during their history, between their various Diaspora concrete places and the elsewhere they never stopped bearing in their minds—the elsewhere which never failed to follow them wherever they went or settled.

From the beginning, Judaism kept within its bosom the tension between these two levels of reality: an absent and/or imaginary else-where, and the many concrete territories of dispersion; elsewhere being at one and the same time the mythical and historical place of its foundation, and the virtual and/or real place of its homecoming; else-where being at one and the same time the place that nourished the memory, the one that kept expectations alive, while the territories of the dispersion were the many concrete places where the nostalgia of the origin and the effervescent or latent expectations of the return were daily experienced in an ever suspended present.

Thus, Diaspora means much more to Jews than a mere physical dispersion. It suggests the displacement and the off-centering resulting from dispersion. Far from being meaningless, this dispersion was initi-ated from a place whose presence had been kept vivid thanks to a tirelessly recalled, repeated, and commented narrative tradition that perceived it as the foundation as well as the ultimate fulfillment; and which assigned Jews to start an unprecedented spiritual and human life-experience, displaced from this particular place (which is the very meaning of Diaspora and exile) as well as off-centered from the world in which they were immersed (which is the very vocation of a people set apart from other nations, while living among them).

Diaspora is the historical and religious setting within which this primordial tension became knotted. Judaism owes its emergence in the form we know—distinct from the Hebraicism of the founding period—to this very setting and to this primordial strain. Thus, Diaspora was not a mere accident in Jewish history nor a contingent event. It wholly recomposed the Jewish world and opened the way to a totally new entity, Judaism, that immediately included in the one and same institutional, ideological and symbolic arrangement the very fact of Diaspora and the ongoing collective presence of Jews all over the world; together with the vivid thought of an elsewhere, mythical or real, and the structural strain between this dispersion and the thought of this elsewhere.

Why is such a demonstration important to us here?

If one is ready to consider Diaspora no longer as the alternative or complement to Israel but as the structuring element of Judaism, one measures how central such a statement may be to the understanding of the transformations at work in contemporary Jewish identities.

In spite of the genocide and in spite of the persistence of anti-Semitism, modernity has paradoxically contributed to de-dramatize the Diaspora condition of Jews. Secularization as well as political and socioeconomic integration have greatly contributed to that process. Yet, besides that, thanks to the achievements of modern technology, especially those performed in the field of communications and transportation, the traditional space/time framing through which Diaspora was traditionally thought of and concretely experienced, has become obsolete, no longer relevant. In this era of jet planes and the Internet, the traditional distance and space/time parameters have lost much of their consistence. Mobility and movement have become part of the everyday life of an increasing number of individuals who freely and easily circulate on the "Web" and/or in the air between Paris, Tel-Aviv, New York, Bangkok, and Tunis. Thus, today, some Jews are simultaneously Israeli Jews and Diaspora Jews without being concerned about either this or which passport they carry. They travel around the world simply because they feel like it, or because they need to, for professional, academic, family, or vacation purposes.

Yet, the very sense, if not the clear materiality of Diaspora, remains a necessity to Judaism and to the construction of Jewish identities, a necessity that transcends the mere factuality of everyday life. This appears to be true on different levels of analysis.

On a structural and symbolic level, it is essential for Jews, for their own perception of themselves as Jews and for their perception by non-

Jews, to have at their disposal a global structure of interpretation of the Jewish condition, that helps understand why it is legitimate for Jews, no matter where they live or come from and whether they travel or not, to perceive themselves as being simultaneously here and there; as being simultaneously part of a universal present shared with all the world, and part of a history, equally distant from myth and utopia, which they share with their brother Jews. It is essential for Jews to have it clear in mind that the specificity of the Diaspora/Jewish condition enjoins Jews to be involved, though on distinct levels, in many historical experiences simultaneously that of their own people and that of the nations (*goyim*).

Besides that, it is also essential for Jews to have at their disposal a global structure of interpretation of the Jewish condition making it clear that, far from being subordinate to the existence of a Jewish state, the persistence of a Jewish Diaspora (which is no longer considered as exile by a majority of Jews, but as a voluntary choice) rests mainly—I would say, even exclusively—on the persistence of Judaism as a whole. For, once again, it is the very nature of Judaism to be a Diaspora fact, if not materially, at least spiritually or symbolically. Let me elaborate on this.

On a symbolic and spiritual level, and owing to its structurally ambivalent character, Diaspora, or the spiritual sense of Diaspora, is *par excellence* the provider of utopia for Judaism. Owing to the historical and religious circumstances of its coming into being, Diaspora could not but embody the utopian dimension of Judaism, that is, its capacity to contemplate the future beyond the given limits of space and time. Utopia is thus the expression of the lasting expectations of an ever-delayed fulfillment, an endless process whose concrete realization is, by necessity, systematically postponed, never taken for granted. Jews never ignored the intrinsically asymptotic dimension of hope. They never ignored that, missing that point, mistaking their ancestral dreams with reality, would lead them to the end of their history, to disaster. Therefore, the persistence of the spirit of Diaspora is not only essential to Judaism; it is a prerequisite.

This position of physical and spiritual displacement and off-centering is fundamental to the perception of Jews as Jews. It was at the source, and it still has a tremendous creativity and imagination. But that ubiquitous, problematic natural disposition is not without complications, in particular since the transition to modernity.

In the premodern past, when Jews were still confined to the margins of their host societies, the Diaspora condition was experienced without any possible confusion and ambiguity. Jews were marginal, considered as temporary residents in these societies. Moreover, the frontiers between Jews and societies were clear-cut and nonambiguous. Since the transition to modernity and the twofold individual and collective emancipation (that gave Jews access to citizenship and to national sovereignty), the Diaspora condition and the double standard through which Jews determine their relation to the world has taken place in quite a different context and reality, where borders and thresholds are blurred, where self-representations and representations of the others are more and more intricate. The case of Israel offers a perfect illustration of this relatively newly created situation.

As Israel is confirming its unequivocal status as a sovereign State, its image is getting blurred and is becoming a source of confusion and misunderstanding in the eyes of a seemingly increasing proportion of Jews (and non-Jews). This observation is true concerning the Jews living outside Israel, as it is difficult to know the true nature of their ties to Israel—religious, historical, ideological, private, ethnic, political, or emotional? These ties are probably a mixture of these elements. But this observation is true also concerning the Jews living in Israel. One knows that, even in Israel, being born a Jew according to the rabbinical definition does not necessarily imply a clear content or meaning to being a Jew.

Actually, the uneasy feeling about Israel derives principally from the fact that the traditional original Diaspora image of a spiritual mythic Israel, the existence of which was due to the sole force of faith and tradition and of an ancestral imaginary, was partly hidden by the present statehood reality of Israel, a political reality traditionally and historically alien to Judaism. The confusion at work between these two visions of Israel has a terrible human, moral, and political cost (Greilsammer 1993; Leibowitz 1993; Weiler 1988). This severe identity crisis now prevailing among Jews—perhaps a justification for the epithet "Jewish survival"—illustrates the necessity of a thorough reappraisal, implying a paradigmatic change. This leads me to the second point, very closely connected with the first.

The Community Paradigm

In order to counterbalance the disintegrating effects of dispersion, Jews have lived gathered into communities. Most often, these communities were imposed by the local authorities, but they were also the collective expression of the Jews' will to live together, separate from the rest of the society, according to the requirement of their Law. Despite the many conflicting issues that may have conspired to undermine their group cohesion, Jews were condemned to live together within a system in which the individual was an integral part of the whole, was absorbed by the group and whose existence was worth-living only through the group.

Obviously, this community paradigm, which used to be the complement to Diaspora in the shaping of Jews' identities, does not work any longer in modern open societies. Individualism, secularization, social and geographical mobility, social, cultural and ethnic mixing, inherent in modernity and in the huge human gatherings of the modern metropolis, have accelerated the process of disintegration of the ancestral and traditional community ties, and have promoted the formation of new types of aggregations of people. Today's "community" has little in common with the community of premodern times. Apart from the fact that they are alternative, open, voluntary and freely chosen groups, which one may enter and exit whenever one wants to, these new aggregates concern and are attractive to only a small portion of Jews.

To a larger portion of Jews, the Jewish community is no longer the primary framework of their socialization process or their sociability. It is not taken for granted as their everyday human, social or cultural environment of immersion. They are no longer immersed in such communities. For more than a century, the social trajectories of Jews have unfolded outside of the Jewish community framework, outside of its sphere of influence and control.

These remarks indicate the depth of the changes that have occurred in Jewish life and identity-building:

1. They indicate that Jews' identities are no longer unified by the fact of being Jewish. In contrast to the holistic, all-embracing traditional perception of Jewish identity, Jews tend to consider their Jewishness as one dimension among the multiple dimensions of their identity; they no longer consider themselves exclusively as Jews. They employ other criteria, such as professional status, political or ideological affiliation,

cultural and aesthetic affinities, nationality, etc., to define themselves. Their identities are as fragmented as their lives, and their Jewishness is but one of these many articulated (or disjointed) fragments.

2. The second point to be stressed, is the fact that Jewish self-identification and community belonging are disconnected from each other. An increasing number of Jews no longer identifies with Jewish community institutions. This does not mean that they do not identify as Jews. Nor does it prevent them from occasionally participating in selected Jewish group activities—fund raising, demonstrations against anti-Semitism, solidarity with Israel or persecuted Jews, commemorations, and so on.

This last point invites us to introduce a further distinction among the many levels of signification of the word "community." In particular, it invites us to distinguish between its institutional/organizational level and its traditional/religious/mystical level. In modern times, the latter has been largely turned into a subjective/emotional/ideological level, that can be expressed in terms of a "feeling of belonging." This feeling is, to a great extent, independent of actual attitudes and behaviors. People may feel involved in some particular Jewish issues without necessarily feeling bound to a regular participation in organized Jewish life. They participate only on the grounds of affinity.

Thus, one has to be extremely cautious in considering contemporary Jewish reality exclusively from the point of view of the community paradigm, as many observers and actors of Jewish life still do. This paradigm no longer reflects mainstream Jewish society. It refers to a system of representation and to a pattern of collective organization no longer representative of the prevailing situation. Moreover, it hides the logic according to which Jews articulate and recompose their identities. Today, a large number of Jews act as autonomous individuals rather than as members of a community. This point has been acknowledged by most of the studies conducted on Jewish communal participation (Beit-Hallahmi 1992; Cohen 1988; Goldscheider 1986; Lipset and Rabb 1995).

In France as well as in the United States, one notices a sharp contrast between the ostentatious visibility of widespread and diverse Jewish institutional networks on the one hand and a proportionally poor participation on the other hand. Community leaders are unanimous in deploring an ongoing trend to desertion, especially on the part of the youth (Webber 1994).

Thus, the notion of community is polysemic, multilevel. It describes a whole range of phenomena. Yet, for most Jews, the Jewish community is virtual or dispersed while still connected (thanks to the many sophisticated long-distance communication tools); it is an intermittent reality coalescing only from time to time on significant, exceptional, highly emotional circumstances.

Actually, rather then being bound to an ascribed group, Jews prefer to create their own affinity groups, affinity being measured as much in terms of educational, socio-economic and professional status or in terms of ethical or political attitudes, as in terms of ethnic or religious origin. There are so many ways, converging and conflicting, of being Jewish today, that being Jewish is no longer a sufficient stimulus to feel the need to stay close to one another and form a community. This type of voluntary non-compelling aggregation is what I have elsewhere called elective ethnicity (Azria 1993).

These free-willed community groupings take various shapes. Among these, France and Israel have experienced, more than elsewhere, a particular form of community-making: communities recomposed on ethnic grounds (Azria 1996a; Ben Raphael and Sharot 1991; Krausz 1986). This phenomenon may be interpreted as a reinforcement of the Diaspora effect, or as a (re)diasporization of Judaism (Azria 1996b). In both cases the phenomenon has been initiated after a rather long period of latency. In both cases, it has followed massive waves of Jewish immigrations from Oriental countries into societies mainly grounded in Western values and criteria. In both cases, the integration of the newcomers has been achieved through the (re)construction and the reaffirmation of a sub-culture of their own, distinct from the respective mainstream cultures (Ben Raphael and Sharot 1991; Krausz 1986). One observes that the recent flows of Russian immigrants to Israel tend to give a newly oriented impulse to this type of ethnic re-identification.

More compelling are the new aggregations grounded in radical observance. Yet, as most of their members are neophytes, returnees initially socialized within secularized environments (Danzger 1989; Davidman 1991; Kaufman 1991; Podselver 1986) there is no doubt that neo-Orthodox communities are by-products of modernity, by-products of the disillusions generated by modernity.

This neo-Orthodox revival reverts to a holistic world vision challenging modern individualism. It reverts also to a holistic world vision of traditional Judaism according to which religious law is a determinant in all life circumstances: private, professional, political. To the individuals who make that life-choice, community life is central. The paradox of this revival though, consists in the fact that, rather than being a transmitted attitude, the acceptance of total obedience to Jewish law, in its most radical form, derives from a free individual decision and choice.

Among the many questions raised by these multifaceted Jewish identity re-compositions, we might ask whether contemporary Jews consider themselves rather as autonomous individuals than as the inter-dependent members of a would-be Jewish people? Obviously, there is no clear, unambiguous answer to this question. Most Jews consider themselves simultaneously as autonomous individuals and as solidarity-bound members of a collective history.

Through these few illustrations, one measures the ambiguities of the community paradigm, as well as the need for an in-depth reappraisal of its meaning and relevance for the present.

The Tradition Paradigm

The last point that I shall address—briefly—is the tradition paradigm. Jewish identities can no longer be analyzed through this paradigm, for tradition and the relationship between Jews and their tradition have both been thoroughly deregulated under the pressure of modernity, secularization and individualism.

To many Jews, tradition has lost its normative authoritative dimension. Tradition is no longer considered as the all-embracing frame and matrix of an inherited package deal, but rather as a mere pick-and-choose reservoir of symbols, as a supplier of cultural references, at free disposal and available for selective and temporary choices. If some Jews feel the need to reinsert themselves within a Jewish genealogy and tradition, they feel free also to select what suits them, from a range of significant ancestors and traditions. I have in mind the example of young North African newcomers to the Lubavitcher tradition, totally identifying with the Lubavitcher rabbi.

Actually—and probably more significantly—the thread along which mainstream Jews try to reappropriate their Jewish identity is that of memory rather than that of tradition. Memory practices have replaced regulated traditional rituals. Modern Jewish rituals consist more in celebrating the historical past through book-writing and/or reading, lectures or museum exhibition attendance, commemorations and fundraising than in keeping a kosher home or in observing the Sabbath.

Of course, the memory of the *Shoah* (Holocaust) is at the center of such memory rituals, but also the rediscovery of, and return to, significant places of the Jewish Diaspora past. Thus, for instance, one notices the development of a new kind of tourism, the tourism of memory; Tour-operators driving thousands of Jews to the sites of death-camps in Poland, to Holocaust memorials in Jerusalem, Paris, Washington, even Berlin, to pilgrimage places and synagogues in North Africa and Central Europe.

This new type of memory is supposed to fill the void left by the desertion of the traditional forms of Jewish life. This renewed concern for anything likely to be integrated into a collective Jewish memory is to be understood as a testimony and an affirmation, albeit through nontraditional channels, of the faithfulness to Judaism and to its heritage, as an attempt to restore a disrupted continuity, as an unprecedented way to replace the living tradition by the exhumation of its traces.

These attempts to save the remnants of a deserted Jewish past, to reappropriate a memory threatened by oblivion and apathy, are to be seen as substitute practices aiming at identity survival. They try to fill the void left by the desertion of traditional rites and scholarships, through giving new substance to Jewish identities in search of meaning. As such, memory is becoming a sacred duty on equal terms with tradition and *mitzvot* (commandments). Will that be enough to motivate the coming generations to be Jewish? This question, we leave unanswered.

And to conclude I shall ask yet another question: don't you think that, instead of the traditional definition according to which a Jew is the child born of a Jewish mother, a more appropriate definition would be that *a Jew is a person whose children are Jewish?* This sounds like quite a stimulating challenge, doesn't it?

References

Azria, Régine. 1996a. "Réidentification Communautaire du Judaïsme," pp. 253–267 in G. Davie and D. Hervieu-Léger (eds.) *Identités religieuses en Europe.* Paris: La Découverte.
———. 1996b. "Les identités diasporales" (Diaspora identities). Journée d'études, C.E.F.R.E.S.S., Université de Picardie–Jules Vernes, 16 Dec. 1996 (unpublished)
———. 1993. "France–États-Unis, 'terres promises' des juifs?" (France and the United States, the Promised Land of the Jews?) *Archives de Sciences Sociales des Religions* 84, 201–222.

Beit-Hallahmi, Benjamin. 1992. *Despair and Deliverance: Private Salvation in Contemporary Israel*. New York: State University of New York Press.

Ben Raphael, Eliezer and Stephen Sharot. 1991. *Ethnicity, Religion and Class in Israeli Society*. Cambridge: Cambridge University Press.

Cohen, Steven. 1988. *American Assimilation or Jewish Revival?* Bloomington and Indianapolis: Indiana University Press.

Danzger, M. Herbert. 1989. *Returning to Tradition: The Contemporary Revival of Orthodox Judaism*. New Haven, CT: Yale University Press.

Davidman, Lynn. 1991. *Tradition in a Rootless World: Women Turn to Orthodox Judaism*. Berkeley and Los Angeles: University of California Press.

Goldscheider, Calvin. 1986. *Jewish Continuity and Change*. Bloomington: Indiana University Press.

Greilsammer, Ilan, ed. 1993. *Repenser Israel. Morale et Politique dans l'Etat Juif* (Rethinking Israel: Morals and politics in the Jewish state). Paris: Editions Autrement.

Kaufman, Debra Renee. 1991. *Rachel's Daughters. Newly Orthodox Jewish Women*. New Brunswick and London: Rutgers University Press.

Krausz, Ernest. 1986. "*Edah* and Ethnic Group in Israel." *The Jewish Journal of Sociology*, vol. 28, no. 1: 5–18.

Leibowitz, Yeshayahou. 1993. *Israel et Judaïsme: Ma Part de Vérité. Entretiens avec Michel Shashar* (Israel and Judaism: My portion of truth. Conversations with Michel Shashar). Paris: Desclée de Brouwer.

Lipset, Seymour Martin and Earl Raab. 1995. *Jews and the New American Scene*. Cambridge, MA: Harvard University Press.

Podselver, Laurence. 1986. "Le Mouvement Lubavitch: Déracinement et Réinsertion des Sépharades" (The Lubavitcher movement: Uprooting and reinsertion of the Sepharadi Jews) *Pardès*, vol. 3 : 54–68.

Webber, Jonathan, ed. 1994. *Jewish Identities in the New Europe*. London and Washington: Littman Library of Jewish Civilization.

Weiler, Gershon. 1988. *Jewish Theocracy*. Leiden and New York: E.J. Brill.

Bibliography

Deshen, Shlomo, Liebman, Charles S. and Moshe Shokeid. 1995. *Israeli Judaism*. New Brunswick, NJ: Transaction Publishers.

Goldscheider, Calvin and Alan S. Zuckerman. 1984. *The Transformation of the Jews*. Chicago: The University of Chicago Press.

Krausz, Ernest, ed. 1985: *Politics and Society in Israel*. New Brunswick, NJ: Transaction Publishers.

Liebman, Charles S. and Eliezer Don-Yehiya. 1984. *Religion and Politics in Israel*. Bloomington: Indiana University Press.

Medam, Alain. 1991: *Mondes Juifs. l'Envers et L'Endroit* (Jewish worlds: The other side and the place). Paris: PUF.

Sobel, Zvi and Benjamin Beit-Hallahmi, eds. 1991. *Tradition, Innovation, Conflict, Jewishness and Judaism in Contemporary Israel*. Albany: State University of New York Press.

Trigano, Shmuel. 1994. "Le concept de communauté comme catégorie de définition du judaïsme francais" (The concept of community as a defining category of French Judaism) *Archives Européennes de Sociologie* 35: 48–71.

3

Quasi-Sectarian Religiosity, Cultural Ethnicity and National Identity: Convergence and Divergence among *Hahamei Yisrael*

Eliezer Ben-Rafael

Who Is a Jew: A Matter of Identity

What is meant by Jewish identity has become quite a complex matter since secularization and emancipation have revolutionized the Jewish condition. Until recently, Jewish identity referred to three simple and complementary principles that remain valid only for a restricted constituency of traditionalists. As set down by Rabbi Kook (see Isch-Shalom 1990), the first principle consists in adherence to *Am Yisrael* (the People of Israel), an affirmation of the Jews as a people, a nation. The second principle is the belief in *Elohei Yisrael* (the God of Israel) and the commitment to *Torat-Yisrael* (God's Teaching). The third principle is the aspiration to *Eretz Yisrael* (the Land of Israel), both the original and the promised land of the Jew; according to this principle, any other place in the world where Jews live is exile. These centuries-old truths were transformed into questions during the eighteenth and nineteenth centuries. People began asking what the notion of *Am Yisrael* meant—a community, a nation, a public of believers; whether Torah is still the necessary basis of the Jewish faith; whether the notion of exile means a geographic concept, a moral position or a metaphor, and if non-exile refers only to Israel, a cultural autonomy anywhere or a state of mind. Different schools of thought, from Reform Judaism and the Haskala movement to the Bund and Zionism, have answered these questions in different manners, responding to the growing number of Jews who could no longer endorse the requirements of traditional Judaism (see also Eisenstadt 1992).

The concept of Jewish identity gained further complexity with the creation of Israel. The existence of a sovereign Jewish state has, indeed, made the issue of who is a Jew a matter not only of intellectual and ideological debate among scholars, but also a question of legislation in an existing state. Moreover, because this state is the only Jewish state in the world, and it happens to be located in the biblical land of the Jews, the discussion in Israel of who is a Jew is necessarily a political problem involving world Jewry. It is a discussion about the Diaspora, and the *a priori* right to obtain Israeli citizenship upon immigration. On the other hand, the importance attached by Jews in the world to Israel's attitude toward who is a Jew is a measure of their own interest in Israel.

Judaism has been studied primarily by means of opinion surveys, both in Israel and in the Diaspora. To cite but a few examples, Herman (1970; 1988) shows that Israelis see Judaism in terms of their own Israeliness, and the respect for Jewish symbols (see also Levy 1996). Lipset and Raab (1995), indicate the centrality, in U.S. Jewry, of both religiosity and commitment to Israel as the Jewish state (see also Goldstein 1992). Liebman and Cohen (1990) compare Israelis and Americans and find differences in emphasis among these two categories: Israelis insist on the Land of Israel as a factor of identification, and the Americans focus on the Jewish community. These works ask similar questions—questions that mark the elaboration of secularized Jewish identities: (1) the extent and significance of Jews' attachment to fellow Jews; (2) the values, symbols and practical requirements subjects perceive in Judaism; (3) the allegiance subjects feel vis-à-vis Israel as a land, a society, and a state.

The notion of collective identity points to sameness, continuity, and membership (de Levita 1965). It focuses on the collective self (Erickson 1963), and includes "sub-identities" (Klineberg 1967). It may be perceived as primordial (Geertz 1965), but its importance fluctuates with circumstances (Barth 1969). It is legitimized by values and symbols

(Weber 1968; Dumont 1977; Levi-Strauss 1961), and implies a concept of boundary and obligations to fellow members, images of cultural particularism, and an understanding of the collective's location in the world and in society. Like language (Ferguson 1966), it is uttered by individuals in daily speech, yet elaborated by codifiers (scholars, intellectuals, and writers).

The object of the current study is to investigate the extent to which, nearly two centuries after the emancipation, and in the aftermath of the Holocaust and the creation of the State of Israel, one may receive consistent answers to the question of who is a Jew. Given the diversity within modern Judaism, we expected a range of answers, but our intention was to ask whether or not these answers are consistent with one another, or, on the contrary, are mutually exclusive. In other words, is contemporary Judaism a pluralistic field or a plurality of fields? Even if one Judaism does not refer anymore to one Jewish people, do the various Judaisms, so to speak, refer to the same Jewish people, or do they circumscribe different Jewish peoples?

The student of these questions confronts numerous enigmas. Not the least of them concerns the legislative debate in Israel. For obvious reasons, the Orthodox and ultra-Orthodox lead the fight in favor of legislation inspired by the *halacha* (Talmudic law). While this camp is a minority not exceeding one fifth of the Israeli polity, one can hardly discern vigorous efforts by a secular coalition to oppose it. At best, one hears voices "in search of compromise," with the intention of accommodating both the Israeli Orthodox and ultra-Orthodox, on the one hand, and the non-Orthodox denominations of the Diaspora, on the other. What is more, the secular majority of the Israeli public does not show any combativeness in this respect, even though many express sympathy for the non-Orthodox. The relative passivity of the Israeli secular majority on a crucial constitutional issue is certainly intriguing, and increases the interest in the question of the unity, pluralism, and plurality of contemporary Judaism.

Our research turned to the most in-depth inquiry ever conducted regarding who is a Jew: the inquiry led by Ben-Gurion, Israel's Prime Minister, in 1958, spurred by the need of the civil authorities to register all citizens according to their religious affiliations.[2] As far as the Jewish population was concerned, these dispositions were difficult to define when it came to marginal cases where national and religious criteria might conflict. It is here that Ben-Gurion decided to ask, following endorsement by the government, dozens of Jewish intellectuals, scholars and writers in the world and in Israel, to address the who-is-a-Jew problem. The question was formulated as a judicial inquiry on one specific issue in one specific case: whether a child who does not belong to any other religion and who was born of a Jewish father and a non-Jewish mother should be registered in Israel as a Jew, when this is the desire of both parents. An additional question was asked, whether a religious conversion ceremony is necessary in such a case. In fact, what was at issue was the relation between nation and religion in Judaism, and the validity of traditional conversion to be considered a Jew, in a secular Jewish state like Israel.

To answer this query, Ben-Gurion selected fifty *"Hahamei Yisrael"* (Wise Men of Israel) belonging to all major trends of Judaism and degrees of religiosity—from the ultra-Orthodox to the free-thinker—in the Diaspora and in Israel. This was meant, not to be a representative sample of the Jewish people, but rather a significant group of Jewish intellectuals in world Jewry. This was effectively achieved even though the sample did not comprehend assimilated Jews nor individuals identified with non-Jewish organizations and movements. The sample numbered thirty Diaspora scholars and twenty Israelis, composed as follows: seventeen ultra-Orthodox (12 Diaspora Jews and 5 Israelis); sixteen Orthodox (7 Diaspora Jews and 9 Israelis); nine non-Orthodox (5 Diaspora Jews and 4 Israelis); eight free-thinkers (6 in the Diaspora and 2 in Israel). Thus, while the ultra-Orthodox and Orthodox constituted thirty-two of the fifty respondents, non-Orthodox and free-thinkers were only eighteen—an apparent indication that Ben-Gurion was primarily interested in learning the outlooks of religious scholars and how far differences divide them. He did, however, also wish to learn the opinion of prominent non-Orthodox but committed Jews.

In the manner of ethnomethodologists Garfinkel (1986) and Cicourel (1981), we investigated Ben-Gurion's results with the intention of learning how Jewish identity is interpreted by preeminent figures of the Jewish world. Accordingly, we followed Ben-Gurion's own methodology, following the twofold categorization by degree and style of religiosity, and Israel versus the Diaspora.

The Range of Jewish Identities

The Ultra-Orthodox

Diaspora respondents. Ultra-orthodox respondents present a unified and uncompromising front. They believe that *halacha* is the only basis for addressing the issue of who is a Jew. In a collective letter sent by members of the London High Rabbinical Court,[3] a deep disappointment is expressed regarding the approach of the prime minister, who felt it necessary to consult with anyone other than the chief rabbis of Israel. The London rabbis felt that the chief rabbis of Israel were more than competent to convey to Israel's government the unambiguous and certified position of Judaism and Jewish law (that is, the Talmudic *halacha*). What, in the Rabbi's opinion, was even worse, was that the prime minister also sought the opinion of individuals who "share nothing" with *halacha* and the Torah. Although the Rabbi's letter emphasizes that they respect Prime Minister Ben-Gurion's desire to work for the benefit of the unity of the Jewish people in the world, it is precisely for this reason that it is inconceivable that individuals could register as Jews in the Jewish State solely on the ground of their own statement, and independent of the traditional criteria. Employing subjective criteria would divide the Jewish people and encourage the assimilation of Jews to non-Jews.

Along the same lines, Aharon Kotler of the Beit Hamidrash Hagavoah (in the United States) points to the *halachic* criteria for Judaism, being born of a Jewish woman, or traditional conversion. In Kotler's view, only *halacha* can determine who is a Jew; its power resides in the fact that for Jews no distinction has ever been possible between religion and nation. Any alteration of this principle implies the greatest danger for the unity and existence of Judaism. There is no alternative to traditional beliefs, and nothing will fill the void left by the Torah, if it ever disappears from Jewish life. Jews are an unique people; they themselves are their only reference. Any attempt to deviate from this rule means denying the people's essence.

Following the same line of argument, Menahem Mendel Schneersohn, head of Habad Hasidism, answers Ben-Gurion from Brooklyn in two separate letters. The first letter is a brief formal reply to Ben-Gurion which states the essentials of Jewish tradition. It concludes that any statement by parents has no relevance regarding the registration of their child as Jewish. There is no point inventing a new concept of Judaism which would only confuse its significance. Schneersohn's second letter addresses Ben-Gurion directly as the "man who determines" the fate of the people of Israel. In this position of supreme leadership, Ben-Gurion must understand that it is unthinkable that the Jewish religion, which has been the most crucial aspect of the Jews' existence in exile, would loose its significance in its own land. For it is now, in the State of Israel, that the Jewish religion receives its most profound meaning as the essence of Judaism. It is also here that the abandonment of Jewish faith represents the greatest danger ever undergone by Jews, that is, the danger of collective assimilation to the world of the non-Jew. By this, Schneersohn meant what Zionism calls the "normalization" of the Jewish people—a danger that will increase when a generation will mature without any Jewish education or identity.

Joseph Dov Soloveitchik of Boston, and Hayyim Heller of New York, both prominent representatives of Lithuanian non-Hasidic ultra-Orthodoxy, and as such, competitors of the Lubavitcher, answer Ben-Gurion's query in quite the same way as the Habad leader. Addressed separately by Ben-Gurion, they compose their answer together because they share the same view. This answer is not less unambiguous than Schneersohn's. They, too, assert with firmness, that the *halacha* is the only legitimate source for determining who is a Jew, and that the ruling of *halacha* has remained unchanged ever since it was formulated. This position needs no clarification or interpretation. In any rabbinical court, any time and anywhere, this answer has always been the only one. It is from this outlook that the authors ask, "Would the State of Israel be built on the destruction of Judaism?"

A.R. Toaff, chief rabbi of Rome, is also angry at Ben-Gurion for having turned his query to "unauthorized" individuals who are not scholars of the Holy Scriptures. For him too, it is obvious that there can be no other answer to the query of who is a Jew than the answer given by the Talmud. No "declaration of parents" is able to turn a *goy* into a Jew. Shabtai Toaff, rabbi of Livorno and the father of A.R. Toaff, agrees. The very act of asking who is a Jew is out of place. Toaff senior repeats that, for any *halachic* question, Ben-Gurion, like any other Jew, must turn to rabbis; and in Israel, he must ask the chief rabbis. In any case, any rabbi one might ask would give the same answer. The Diaspora aspires to maintain strong links with Israel and its people because it sees the State of Israel as the source of Torah. As the guide for the Jews throughout the world, Israel has no right to alter traditional definitions. For if it does so, this will contribute to the assimilation of Jews everywhere.

Yehiel Yacov Weinberg, a former head of Berlin's Beit Hamidrash who lives in Montreux, is less angry than his colleagues about Ben-Gurion's inquiry. However, he cannot refrain from expressing his surprise that the question of who is a Jew has arisen. Only a confusion of notions could possibly lead to this kind of inquiry. It is clear to the author that there is no other Judaism than the Judaism of Torah and *mitzvot* (religious commandments). Any form of so-called liberal Judaism is a falsification of Judaism and is doomed to fail, both as identity and morality. Morality without religious support is an illusion, and, following Saadia Gaon, it is Weinberg's position that the Jewish nation is a nation only through Torah. Even the most dedicated patriot, one who resides in Israel for years, pays his taxes as an upstanding citizen, serves in the army and fights all Israel's wars—even this kind of Jew will exclude himself from the people of Israel if he converts to another faith. Weinberg points out that Ben-Gurion himself specifies in his query that it concerns an individual who has not embraced another faith. Hence, Ben-Gurion understands the essence of the special relationship of nation and religion in Judaism. From this it follows that a non-Jew cannot become a Jew except by converting to Judaism. Religious matters, he says, have their own rationale. Conversion to Judaism is as old as Judaism itself, and goes back to Abraham. It cannot be rephrased under the influence of circumstances. It is on this basis that Judaism defines its own notion of "race" in moral and spiritual terms and does not relate it exclusively to blood. God receives anyone into His alliance, and conversion to Judaism is not just a conversion to a new religion. It means taking part in an alliance with God by means of becoming one with the Jewish people. Hence, for the Israeli government there are only two options regarding the issue raised by Ben-Gurion. The first is to go on with traditional conversion; and the second to suppress it altogether, thereby breaking with Judaism. Compromises are not possible. This is why both Israeli and Diaspora rabbis would not approve of a certificate of Judaism issued by a clerk of the state, where "Jew" is stamped on the basis of the wishes of a non-Jewish mother. Any kind of Judaism based on less than the traditional rite would definitively divide the people into religious and non-religious Jews.

Israeli respondents. The Israeli ultra-Orthodox are not less opinion-
ated than their Diaspora counterparts. Yichya Yitzhak Halevy is a
dayan (judge) in the Tel-Aviv-Jaffa Rabbinical Court. His response
demands that the prime minister accept the rabbis' opinion, since this
is the response of Torah. Israel's religion, *Dat Yisrael*, says Halevy,
was born before the people of Israel, *Am Yisrael*. Abraham, the nation's
forefather, adhered to the religion of Israel before he himself founded
the people. Hence, religion will remain Israel's primary mark of dis-
tinctiveness forever. The people of Israel has remained faithful to this
religion through centuries of exile, and it is this devotion that has kept
it alive. The Yemenite Jews (whom Rabbi Halevy represents), for
example, stuck to their faith during the worst persecutions, as well as
when offered the most attractive inducements to convert to Islam.
Drawing an analogy from the Return from Babylonia, Halevy recalls
that Ezra obliged the people to send away their non-Jewish wives and
children. Such women, who give birth to, and educate non-Jewish
children (since they are not Jewish themselves) are the greatest danger
of assimilation and loss of holiness for the people of Israel. This is not
to deny legitimacy to those who want to convert to Judaism and become part of the Jewish nation. Such people should be welcomed, for
we see in them the image of Ruth, who proclaimed, "Your people is
my people and your God is my God." The Bible tells how Naomi,
Ruth's mother-in-law, refused to allow Ruth to become part of the
nation without embracing its faith. Following this example, non-Jewish women who want their children to become Jews should aspire to
become Jewish themselves. This identity has been sanctified by history, and may help ensure the unity of the Jews even now.

Yosef S. Kahanman, head of the Ponevizs Yeshiva of Bnei-Brak,
also understands that Ben-Gurion's query is not addressed to him
personally, but to the Torah. Like his colleagues, his answer is clear
and sharp. This question already arose, unavoidably, with two earlier
waves of immigration of Jews to the Land of Israel: the establishment
of the Children of Israel in Canaan under the leadership of Joshua, and
the return from Babylonia under Ezra and Nehemya. Jews never were
eager to accept neophytes, but for those who comply with all the
requirements, they should be ready to receive them with good will.
For Kahanman, the major Jewish problem of the time is the question
of *geula* (salvation). In Kahanman's view, Jews must now dedicate
themselves to moral adherence to the Almighty in view of precipitat-

ing the coming of Salvation; this is not the time for changing *halacha,* or for revising procedures for conversion.

Yehuda Leib Maimon, a pillar of the Rav Kook Yeshiva of Jerusalem, also belongs to those who are shocked by the very fact of Ben-Gurion's asking this question. There can be no other answer than the *halacha,* and this answer should be given by the chief rabbis of Israel. The whole investigation is completely incongruous. Yechezkel Sarna, the head of the Yeshiva of Hebron, agrees with Maimon. The Jews' Bible is eternal, he says, and its commandments cannot be altered. This is the way things will stand until the end of time. No argument in the world is powerful enough to change even a single letter of the Torah and the *mitzvot.* To confound one who is a Jew with one who is not, whether a child or an adult, means no less than the destruction of the Jewish people.

Yosef Zevin is also offended by the fact that a government or a committee of ministers may presume to make decisions regarding the national identity and religion. Such matters, says Zevin, are neither political nor administrative, and civil authorities have no power to alter even one letter of the *halacha,* or turn a non-Jew into a Jew. Judaism, we learn again, does not permit any separation between religion and national identity. What is more, Judaism, according to Zevin, does not recognize mixed marriages: a union of a Jew with a non-Jew is a non-union. A Jew who marries a non-Jew and gives birth to a child, gives birth to a non-Jewish child. Hence, by no means can it be accepted that someone who merely claims, "I am a Jew and I do not belong to any other religion" should automatically be registered as a Jew.

In conclusion. The who-is-a-Jew discourse of the ultra-Orthodox reflects the dominant notion of a collective that constitutes a whole, independently of its individual elements. Hence, a new member is not just to be socially accepted but to become a part of an integral whole. This whole has a Torah and is bound to the Divinity. The set of symbols, beliefs and *mitzvot* that constitute Israel's faith is not only one of the codes of Jewish identity, but its principal one. This principle has preceded the emergence and formation of the Jewish nation, and, actually, has been the creator and perpetuator of the people.

Here the geographic dimension is of little importance. Some of the respondents emphasize the point that Jews look to Israel and recognize that Israel is special for all Jews. This, however, derives more from a view of Israel as "a state of Jews" rather than as "the Jewish State."

The ultra-Orthodox respondents request that Israel conform to Talmudic law, applicable to Jews everywhere.

It is interesting to note that several of Ben-Gurion's Israeli respondents remind us of the biblical stories of Ruth and Naomi, and Ezra's expulsion of non-Jewish women. These arguments emphasize the role of *"Eretz Yisrael"* in Judaism, and the norms of purity and holiness that it requires of its Jewish inhabitants. They reflect an attitude that tends to see in Israel a Jewish reality that is special because it exists and develops in the Land of Israel, and to recognize in Israel the embodiment of a non-Diaspora dimension of Judaism. This very attitude also means that, from an ultra-Orthodox point of view, Israel as a Jewish state, cannot avoid the exigencies of the Jewish faith.

The Orthodox

Diaspora respondents. The Diaspora Orthodox respondents are more divided, some aligning themselves with the ultra-Orthodox position, others taking a more flexible stance. Jacob Kaplan, the grand rabin de France, belongs to the former category. He reacts like many ultra-Orthodox respondents, finding it "strange" that the government of Israel should ask for the opinion of anyone other than the state's chief rabbis. For Kaplan, what is essential is that a secular government cannot install itself as an authority in any but purely secular matters. The government must fight with all its power against mixed marriages, and follow the *halacha* with regard to the registration of Jews. Shlomo Perera, the Sephardic Chief Rabbi of Holland, approves this approach. Israel's chief rabbis have the authority to answer Ben-Gurion's query, and it is not clear why other rabbis—let alone secular individuals, and above all, Reform Jews—were asked for their views.

Shaul Lieberman of New York contends that a parent's will does not make a child a Jew. When a non-Jew likes Israel, Israel must reciprocate. Yet such feelings are not enough to make anyone a Jew. If the non-Jewish mother is willing to have her child become a Jew, then she herself ought to convert; the child will then automatically be Jewish. If the mother is not willing to convert, then there is no alternative but the religious conversion of the child. Lieberman does have reservations about converting a person who has not reached the age of consciousness, and suggestions postponing the conversion until the child has matured.

Alexander Altman of Brandeis University understands that the parents described in Ben-Gurion's query do not see themselves as religious Jews, but only as national Jews. Otherwise, they would, upon their own initiative, have their child converted. Yet, says Altman, one cannot ignore that Judaism implies a religious component along with the national component. The religious component has always been the vehicle of the Jewish national identity; these two aspects together embody the notion of Israel as "chosen." The only option is to ease the entry passage, and demand that rabbis make the conversion procedure more appropriate to the spirit of the time, and show openness and tolerance toward candidates for conversion. Great respect indeed should be accorded to those who aspire to become a part of the Jewish people.

Andre Neher of Strasbourg University worries about the danger of widening the gap between Israel and the Diaspora, and between Israel and Judaism. One cannot deny, he says, that Jewish identity is religious and that there is no entry into Judaism but by using the procedures defined by the traditional law. This, of course, is not to deny that once one is inside, one may disregard the religion, for this would not affect one's status. But by no means is the government entitled to determine criteria of its own regarding who is a Jew. Religion is inseparable, in Judaism, from national allegiance, just as the soul is inseparable from the flesh. Neher criticizes the opinion of Yeshayahou Leibowitz, who advocates drawing this distinction within the framework of a secular state. Neher's reply is that such a separation might be an ideal solution to prevent tensions between the state and the religious authorities, but it would be a blunt attack on the essentials of Judaism. On the other hand, Neher is also conscious that a problem does exist, and proposes that a special assembly be convened which would include representatives of the government, secular figures, and rabbis. This assembly should discuss the issues at stake in the relationship between religion and state. The government would present issues, the assembly would discuss them, and the rabbis would decide.

Avraham Heshel, a New York scholar of Judaism, points out the vulnerability of the Jewish people, at least in the Diaspora. It is only by retaining the strongest bond between the people and the Torah that Jews will be able to overcome the dangers of assimilation. A people without Torah, and a Torah without a people, are doomed to failure. Heshel knows that many Jews are not religious but for the Jewish people there is no possibility of surviving on the exclusive basis of a secular culture. The danger of assimilation exists everywhere, including in Israel, despite the holiness of the land. Yet, now that the State of Israel exists, the government should sponsor an in-depth investigation to clarify the role of religion in the state. This role cannot be just instrumental: the Torah is an objective and not just an instrument of survival for the people. Heshel, however, understands that some people might encounter difficulties in forging a secular existence for themselves without religious belief in Judaism. These reflections bring Heshel to sustain the idea of defining an intermediary status—"Hebrews"—for those who identify with the Jews but not with the Jewish faith.

Tsvi Wolfsohn of Harvard University supports this kind of position. There is no notion of Jewish identity independent of religious identity, he says, but secular Jews continue to be Jews. This is the work of the religious Jews who maintain the community and its *raison d' être*. Hence, for Wolfsohn it is obvious that one cannot depart from the religious rulings on conversion. To Ben-Gurion's query, he responds that Jews cannot go back to Paul's position among the first Christians that ritual circumcision and the religious commandments have become obsolete. If there are still individuals who do not want to be religiously Jewish, the only solution for them consists in inventing an in-between concept like "Hebrews." The main thing is not to mess with the notion of "Jew" which has its own long-standing significance, both nationally and religiously.

Israeli respondents. The Israeli Orthodox respondents are close to their Diaspora counterparts, but seem, at the same time, more unyielding. Shmuel J. Agnon, a prominent writer in Jerusalem, relies completely on the ruling of the Torah and *Hazal*.[4] He acknowledges that religion and state may clash on some issues, but in no case are we allowed to "mend" the Torah. Politicians should concentrate on affairs of state, and leave religious matters to the jurisdiction of rabbis. Regarding the problem of conversion, Agnon contends that because a convert can claim no privileges due to his ancestors' religious and moral achievements, he should be even more observant than other Jews.

Zaharya Cohen, the Yemenite rabbi of the cooperative village of Nahalal, shares the same traditionalist view. The very first Commandment that the Torah imposes on Jews, he recalls, is that the nation have one God. This is the very foundation of the "holy people" concept. Cohen's letter is long and involved, and abounds in illustrations and quotes from Talmudic scholars. The long history of the Jews has brought Jewish blood in the veins of many non-Jews and vice versa, but this is of no religious significance. What is important is whether or not individuals have gone through the *halachic* rituals required to render them Jews.

Shlomo Goren, the chief rabbi of the armed forces, discusses Ben-Gurion's query by focusing on the mother-child relation as elaborated by the Bible and the Talmud. He pursues the topic by considering further texts which lead to the conclusion that the mother, indeed, is the one to determine the affiliation of her child, and that this is true for non-Jewish mothers as much as for Jewish ones. Though, when the child of a non-Jewish mother and a Jewish father does go through conversion, this child is seen as if he or she sprung from Israel. In other words, as if the child has come from two Jewish parents, meaning practically that in this case affiliation follows the father's. Moreover, for a child, says Goren, conversion offers the status not of a convert, but of Israel itself. Goren recalls that conversion signifies the acceptance of *mitzvot* in the presence of three witnesses, as well as ritual immersion and ritual circumcision (for boys). No one is allowed to change this process. But children retain their right to cancel their conversion when they grow up. In this sense, Goren appears to consider the conversion of the child positively, in contrast to other respondents who would prefer to postpone the conversion to young adulthood. His position is less dissimilar to that of the other respondents, when he re-asserts that the Jewish history and the *halacha* demonstrate that one cannot separate religion from nation among Jews. Hence, a secular regime, he repeats, has no authority whatsoever to interfere with who is a Jew. On the other hand, Goren also sustains the creation by the state of a kind of intermediary status like "Judaizer," that is, a category referring to youngsters considering conversion but who are not yet prepared to undergo the conversion process. This relatively flexible conclusion is quite exceptional among the Israeli Orthodox respondents.

More normative is the position of Yitzhak Halevy Herzog, Israel's Ashkenazic chief rabbi, who reiterates that the *mitzvot* are the source of Jewish life. He recalls a Talmudic story which describes a dialogue between Jews and God, at the hour of Salvation. When God wonders "how you were able to wait all these years," the Jews answer, "God

Almighty, without your Torah that you gave us, we would have disappeared among the nations." The power of Judaism is the Torah, and any governmental regulation regarding who is a Jew which would contradict the Torah is a violation of Judaism, and creates a danger of division and confusion among Jews, which might destroy the foundation upon which the State of Israel rests.

Yosef Kapach, a scholar of Yemenite Judaism, also insists on a definition of the Jews that is grounded not in race or in tribalism—Jews belong to many races and tribes—but in religious faith and national identity. Jew is a noun and any other quality relating to it is an adjective. There is no Jewish Englishman or Jewish Spaniard, but an English Jew and a Spanish Jew. In a same manner, there is no Jewish Jerusalemite or Tel-Avivian, but a Jerusalem or a Tel-Aviv Jew. To be a Jew is the primary fact which consists in a link to a particular faith, even when one does not follow the *mitzvot*. Even then, a Jew does not run away from Judaism. And if someone wants to become a Jew, he cannot do this except through the traditional channels.

Yechezkel Koifman, a Hebrew University scholar of Talmud, reiterates that the People of Israel and the God of Israel cannot be separated. A Jew is not defined by personal conviction, but by a belonging to an entity—a membership that is determined only by birth or by conversion. Hence, the law of civil registration is not a secular law because it refers to the registration of Judaism, and Judaism is not a secular matter. The creation of the State of Israel has changed the condition of the Jew but not the definition of Jew. The Jewish religion and nationalism are one, the link between them indelible. It is true, Koifman acknowledges, that since many Jews are not observant, the rabbis who deal with conversion should demonstrate openness, tolerance and willingness to ease the process.

Efrayim A. Orbach, a Hebrew University scholar of Judaism, cannot refrain from reacting as many other Orthodox and ultra-Orthodox respondents did, by expressing his regret that the government of Israel feels justified in interfering in a matter that is essentially religious. It is not acceptable, in Orbach's view, that who is a Jew be submitted to a public discussion where secular Jews participate with the same status as religious authorities. On the other hand, Orbach also contends that in a state which promises not to discriminate between citizens according to religion or national identity, there is no need to register the citizens' religious or national identity on citizenship documents. The only factor which may justify this practice is the problem of security, and he requests that this aspect be carefully considered. Orbach stresses that in Israel personal status is regulated by religious law, and falls within the jurisdiction of Orthodox rabbis. Hence, individuals officially registered as Jews for their national affiliation but not their religion, will be turned away when they register for marriage, since for the rabbis they are not Jews. This raises the question of mixed Jew-Gentile marriages. Some say, Orbach argues, that in Israel, such marriages do not encourage assimilation of Jews to non-Jews, but on the contrary, of Gentiles to Jews. This has not been proven, yet, but what is more certain is that it will legitimize mixed marriages in the Diaspora, and thus surely contribute to the assimilation of Jews to non-Jews.

Moshe Zylberg, a member of the Supreme Court in Jerusalem, agrees with Orbach. There is no hope that guidelines on the who is a Jew issue will meet the wishes of all streams of Judaism. Zylberg sees three possibilities: (1) *Halachic* criteria; (2) integrating without reservation those non-Jews who want to become a part of the Jewish people; and (3) imposing a "light-style" conversion, in the manner of Reform Judaism. Israel is a secular state but the *halacha* has an official status regarding personal status. Hence, in the existing conditions, alternatives (2) and (3) are not realistic, and *halacha* criteria must be retained.

Shay Shalom, a writer, poet, and college teacher, makes an additional point. For him, the suffering of the Jews throughout history because of their loyalty to the symbols and practices of Judaism has sanctified these symbols and imposed on all further generations the duty to retain them as their dearest legacy. It is therefore justifiable to demand of anyone who wants to join the Jewish people, that he accept and identify with the symbols and practices of Judaism, that is, in particular, traditional conversion. Rabbis who assist conversions are acting on behalf of the Jews as a whole—including the nonreligious. It is only after converting that neophytes may decide whether or not they will be observant or nonobservant Jews. It is interesting to note, however, that Shalom recommends that circumcision be performed by doctors under strict medical supervision, demonstrating that the author, like other respondents in this category, but unlike many ultra-Orthodox respondents, is willing to show openness to universal values.

In conclusion. The respondents do not propose any reform of the traditional law regarding who is a Jew, and the procedure for entering

Judaism, but they show more consideration of, and sensibility to, universal considerations. Many respondents emphasize the need for tolerance and openness on the part of rabbis. The general tune is one of Beit Hillel (*kula*, making things easy), rather than Beit Shamai (*khumra*, making things hard). Moreover, several respondents speak of the possibility of instituting an in-between category of "Judaizers" or "Hebrews." Interestingly enough, openness is more apparent on the part of the Diaspora respondents than on the part of the Israelis. The latter may be inclined to view the problem as a question of state-institutional arrangement.

The Non-Orthodox

Diaspora respondents. Diaspora non-Orthodox respondents show versatility, though they, too, refer to religious tradition as their starting point. Henri Baruk, a Sorbonne professor of psychology, agrees that Judaism does not distinguish between religion and nation. Judaism, he also emphasizes, is not willing to expand like the other religions which it engendered. Judaism is a way of life which expresses values and beliefs: to become a Jew signifies accepting a heavy burden of work and study. It is an organic whole bound together by the notion of God's compact with Abraham. By no means is genetic heritage a sufficient condition for belonging to this People. Many born-Jews have assimilated, and, today especially, Jews experience a difficult conflict between Judaism and Hebrew culture, on the one hand, and Western culture, on the other. Jews confront the difficulty of adjusting Judaism to the circumstances of their daily lives. For Baruk, the unalterable essence of Judaism consists in: (1) the concept of moral responsibility implied by the notion of justice; (2) a total opposition to any fetishism; (3) a humanistic view of human life and liberty; (4) a veneration of cultural sources and traditions; and (5) a respect for the *mitzvot* and the Torah which warrant cultural and social uniformity and coherence. This Judaism accepts non-Jews as converts, but only those who accept that, once Jewish, they cannot easily escape this identity. This explains why many who have left Judaism have joined the anti-Semites and turned against Judaism with virulence. Baruk is, however, in favor of some changes, notably changes in the rules of conversion. He thinks, for instance, that the mother-link should not be the only basis of religious affiliation, and that a convention of rabbis should revise their approach to the issue. And Baruk reminds his reader that Jews may not alienate those who were persecuted as Jews by the Nazis, and should find a way to ease their entrance into Judaism, if this is their desire.

For Eliezer Finkelstein, a Cincinnati Conservative rabbi affiliated with the Schechter Seminary, any change in traditions is doomed to invite acrimonious debate. These traditions have always distinguished the Jewish nation. Finkelstein remarks that mixed marriages commonly involve a non-Jewish woman; this is obviously the most problematic since it is effectively the mother that raises and educates the child. And children who enter Judaism without religion may be viewed as receiving the rights without endorsing the obligations. Hence, the idea that the parents' wish is enough to determine the child's status as Jewish is unsustainable. But rabbis should make efforts to ease conversion, especially the conversion of children.

Solomon B. Freehof, a prominent figure in American Reform Judaism, emphasizes that rabbis have always been able to adapt to circumstances, and that their attitudes toward the conversion of children has always been particularly tolerant. With children, the basic difficulty concerns the child's lack of understanding; the answer to this objection is that conversion may be seen as a favor which is done for the child. It is permissible to bestow a favor upon someone, even if the person does not know the meaning of the favor. Freehof warns, however, that rabbis have often tended to adopt hard-line positions from which they had trouble turning back later on. Moreover, Freehof notes that the modern era has witnessed growing demands for conversions, which has caused many rabbis to be hesitant. Notable exceptions have been societies like the United States or Australia which were frontier countries and where Jewish women were outnumbered by Jewish men. In these societies, mothers actually often followed their children in conversion. Freehof also notes that Judaism is unclear about the basic attitude to adopt toward conversion on a large scale. He finds in *Shulhan Aruh*, the basic compilation of the codifications of Judaism, contradictory perspectives. Reform rabbis, he notes, take an open and positive approach to the acceptance of children into Judaism. They generally prefer that the candidate undertake preparatory studies rather than undergo a formal ceremony. Basically, Freehof proposes (1) that the State accept and recognize the existence of three Jewish religious communities; (2) that each community decide on its own conversion regulations. Those who will be converted by the more liberal will not be recognized by the less liberal and will thereby constitute a stratum of half-proselytes. This stratum will enjoy full citizenship rights, but will inevitably lack full acceptance in Jewish society because of the reservations of the Orthodox. This status will resemble the notion of "converted resident" that existed during the period of the Second Temple. One might then expect that, in a Jewish society, these individuals will tend to assimilate to Jews.

Menahem Kaplan, the founder of Constructionist Judaism, expresses his opinion thus: It is not yet possible to speak of a single Jewish tradition, and it is unfortunate that the State of Israel does not accord religious freedom to all Jews, and instead grants the Orthodox a monopoly on religious services and the regulation of personal status. This runs counter to the development of liberal society everywhere, of which Jews are an integral part. The State of Israel must reappraise its approach in this respect. Because of the Law of Return, the State's relation to Judaism is a public and political matter of prime importance. On the other hand, Israel is also a modern state that aspires to be a homeland for all Jews. This means that Israel cannot object to registering as a Jew the offspring of mixed marriages; this would contradict the spirit of the time and express the influence of but one kind of Judaism, *halachic* Judaism. We live in an era in which we have to find compromises; to this end, this respondent too suggests adopting a notion of "resident Jew," to be applied to the child of a Jewish father and a non-Jewish mother. If this child is willing eventually to undergo conversion, he or she will then become a regular Jew. Dante Lattis, a writer and journalist in Rome, takes this reasoning further yet. He suggests that state registration cannot be dependent on religion. To qualify for civilian registration in a Jewish country like Israel, it is enough that children of mixed marriages do not share any other faith, are *bona fide* Israelis, learn in a Hebrew school, and receive a Jewish education. ID cards would contain a notation that the designation "Jew" in such cases is not valid for any purpose that involves Rabbinical Law.

Israeli respondents. When it comes to Israeli non-Orthodox respondents, their opinions are, here again, generally less liberal than among their Diaspora counterparts. At the same time, they are also often more sensitive to the status of Israel in the Jewish world. Hayim Hazaz, a major writer, says that religion has kept the Jewish people alive for generations. It is unfortunate that it is being abandoned by the younger generation, especially in Israel where the State is secular and where *halacha* has no status. On the other hand, Hazaz also asks: if tomorrow thousands of mixed couples arrive and settle in Israel, will we reject them? Will we oblige them to embrace a religion that is alien to them? Seeing these difficulties, if a mixed couple wants their child registered as a Jew, the State should accept this child, and grant it the status of convert. Many of the greatest of Israel were converts, he notes. Hazaz is, however, quite an exception here to hold this position.

Yehuda Burlah, a prominent Sephardic writer in Jerusalem, holds the view that circumcision is the only important rite that applies to a Jewish boy. It is the primary expression of Judaism, and it is, and should remain, the rule for any form of conversion. Burlah, who is not religious himself, is against any other rite as well as anything that expresses religious coercion. Modern life, he says, is not appropriate to the imposition of countless laws such as those decreed by the Talmud. Rabbis should diminish the weight of these laws, and adapt them to contemporary values.

Joseph Schechter, a philosopher and educator in Haifa, starts his answer to Ben-Gurion by confessing that he does not know much about Judaism. He understands, however, that Jewish law has brought the people to the present era, in spite of the tenacious discrimination and poverty which they met everywhere. Schechter is opposed to those who preach the adaptation of Judaism to the modern world. Modernity has brought humanity near to total destruction. What does it mean to adapt to modernity? Despite the fact that he does not belong to the Orthodox world, Schechter is convinced that the sign of divinity is with the Torah.

Ernest Simon, a professor of philosophy at the Hebrew University of Jerusalem, offers a systematic presentation. He first discusses the relationship of the issue under discussion to problems of national security. Simon suggests that this aspect should be reconsidered, given the heavy price in terms of democracy which the registration issue represents (he has in mind the institutionalized differentiation between Jews and Arabs). Furthermore, the arrangement has nothing to do with the Law of Return[5], since the operation of the law takes place before the individual receives identity papers from the Israeli Authorities. And since the state has transferred its authority in matters of personal status to religious bodies, it has given up the right of determining the religious affiliation of the citizens. This is another reason why it is superfluous to indicate national or religious allegiances on identity papers. Simon turns then to the essence of the problem, noting that even non-observant and non-believing Jews practice many *mitzvot.* Despite modernization and secularization, Jews have continued to practice circumcision, with very little resistance to the practice. Simon remembers only the Association of Reform Amateurs, in Frankfurt am Main, in 1842, which proclaimed that the practice of circumcision should be abandoned. The founder of the Association, Theodor Kreitzner, finally converted to Christianity after he incurred protest from every strand of German Jewry. The Liberal synod of 1871 in Augsburg took a middle-of-the-road position by endorsing the practice of ritual circumcision, while rejecting the boycott against those who would not comply with it. Yet, even in Reform communities, the practice of circumcision was continued. This general attitude, which contradicts the spirit of modernization, is due, according to the author, to the fact that circumcision has always been the sign of adherence to the Jewish nation, and doing away with it would signify stepping outside the boundaries of Judaism. In conclusion, the mere declaration of parents cannot create a Jewish identity. A religious ceremony and circumcision are required. One may request of those who come to join this nation that they adopt the marker that has always symbolized its historical continuity and unity.

In conclusion. Non-Orthodox respondents exhibit a variety of opinions. The general tendency is to seek compromise, either by instituting an intermediate category as a precursor to full assimilation into the Jewish people, or by abolishing the specification of religious and national allegiance on identity documents. Ultimately, however, none of the non-Orthodox respondents is willing to consider the declaration of parents as sufficient to register the child of a mixed marriage involving a non-Jewish mother, as a Jew in the ordinary sense of the word. Likewise, no one advocates the abolition of the rite of circumcision. The notion of Torah is less present here than among the Orthodox and ultra-Orthodox respondents—the Israelis, in particular, tend to evince with special vigor the view that the Jewish character of the state may stand in tension with other values such as modernity, secularism and democracy.

The Free-Thinkers

Diaspora respondents. Among Diaspora free-thinkers, quite a few do not hesitate to look for new approaches regarding who is a Jew. Isaiah Berlin, an Oxford political philosopher, questions the appropriateness of asking Jews from abroad to answer a query which is the Israeli government's exclusive responsibility. As far as the issue itself is concerned, Berlin emphasizes that one must consider a number of cultural, religious, and national aspects which can hardly be distinguished from one another. To simplify the discussion, he differentiates two senses of the notion of Jew. In the narrowest legal sense, the definition of a Jew is delineated by the *halacha*. In a wider sense— less clear but more widely acknowledged in daily life—"Jew" describes every person who is bound to, and identifies with, the Jewish community. In this sense, one may even speak of an atheist Jew. As a Jewish state, Israel requires a legal definition of its own, even though as a secular, liberal, and democratic state, citizens should be allowed to marry, to be buried, and to educate their children according to their own preferences. Religiosity should by no means be a basis of discrimination between citizens, and individuals who are known as Jews but who do not qualify as such according to *halacha* should still be accepted as a part of the Jewish nation. These newcomers, it is true, would not be recognized by the rabbis, and would thus need a kind of ad hoc mechanism to determine their eligibility for the status of "political Jews." To fulfill this function, Berlin envisages a special committee operating as an organ of a government ministry or as an independent institution. In any case, it would be unacceptable that individuals who are considered Jews abroad would become non-Jews here and be obliged to go through conversion. If a Jewish father wants his children to be raised as Jews and his non-Jewish wife accepts this, it should by all means be agreeable to the authorities. In any case, Berlin agrees with a number of other respondents, that, in a Jewish country like Israel, these children will very likely assimilate to Jewish society. This, obviously, will not be acceptable to rabbis for religious purposes, but eventually these "political Jews" will succumb to pressure to undergo a religious conversion. To the extent that such a solution is not accepted by Israelis, and awakens a *kulturkampf*, it should still be possible to adopt a temporary solution such as the creation of categories like "Jew from Jewish father" or "spouse of Jew." This no-man's land, however, should not, by any means, become definitive for anyone, otherwise there is the danger that it will create a kind of inferior class of half-Jews. Berlin is convinced that, over time, the State of Israel will achieve strict separation between religion and state; this will lead to a "normalization" of the Jewish people.

Moshe Meizels, editor of the New York Zionist Hebrew weekly *Doar*, is of the opinion that things cannot be decided definitively in these early years of the State of Israel. Meizels recalls that the former Return to Zion, from the Babylonian exile, was also beset with problems of definitions of allegiance. In Israel today, moreover, the *halacha* has received an official status with respect to personal status regulations. It is thus implausible that definitions should be different with regard to the registration of citizens. It is inconceivable that citizens be considered half Jewish and half non-Jewish (that is, Jewish nationally and non-Jewish religiously). The link between religion and nation is fundamental to Judaism, and there is no escaping this reality, at least not today. It is Meizels's contention that the State of Israel is not just a Zionist continuation of Jewish life but a form of Jewish life of its own. Hence, Israel is not the prolongation of the Zionists' struggle against traditions and traditionalism anymore, and it shares a relation to the Jewish religion that goes back to pre-Zionism.

Hayim Perelman, a legal philosopher at the Free University of Brussels, considers it obvious that individuals who receive the right to immigrate to Israel by virtue of the Law of Return, and thus to join the Jewish nation, cannot be denied the right to register as Jewish citizens. It is not less obvious that the religious authorities should be in charge of the regulations concerning who is a Jew. Perelman is convinced that there is room in Israel, as among other cultivated peoples, for a distinction between nation and religion. It is important that the State of Israel achieve complete secularization, including in the area of personal status. Historically, this distinction has been impossible and inconceivable, and even now, the State of Israel is unable to recognize as a Jew a person who has embraced another faith. The religious law is rigid because it refers to a public of believers. Once there is both a state and state law, a different criterion applies. Even if one does not separate state from religion, the state has the obligation to decide for itself what its interests are. Perelman's proposal is thus to set up a special court composed of members of Knesset, representatives of the

Jewish Agency and religious authorities that will work out together a new modus vivendi between religion and state in Israel.

Aharon Zeytlin, a Hebrew and English writer in New York, distinguishes the concept of "Israeli" from the concept of "Jew." Israeli, says Zeytlin, is a secular concept, unlike the notion of Jew which carries both religious and national meanings. Only one people in the world, he says, adheres to the Jewish religion, and only one religion marks this people. A non-Jew who wants to become a Jew has no alternative but to convert. It is absurd, says Zeytlin, to think of an "administrative Jew" who would not be a Jew in the eyes of religious authorities. It is also clear that a secular government has no power to decide who a Jew is. Any nonreligious definition of who is a Jew will create a gap between Israel and the Diaspora, where abstracting religion from Judaism is unthinkable. Zeytlin recalls here the poet Elisheva Z. Yrkova who confessed in her old age, after a life of Hebrew poetry, that she never felt really Jewish because she did not convert to Judaism.

Leon (Arye) Simon , a London writer who settled in Israel, takes exception to the notion that "Jew," when applied to citizens of Israel, could differ from historical Judaism. He warns that adopting a new definition of who is a Jew would open a breach between Israeli and non-Israeli, and between religious and nonreligious Jews. This conflict may well be unavoidable but it should be delayed as far as possible, until the Jews of Israel get accustomed to their reality, in their new State. Abandoning the *halacha* at this point will be supported by only a small minority of Jews worldwide. In the meantime, it is reasonable to solve the issue raised by Ben-Gurion, by defining a kind of provisional status for children of non-Jewish mothers who wish to integrate into Jewish society. Simon calls this in-between stage "persons of Jewish father." Such a status would be valid for a limited number of years, permitting either the parents to emigrate, or to the child to proceed with conversion. Any other solution would engender disagreement and conflict. But one should also insist, says Zeytlin who echoes here many other respondents, that Beit Hillel rather than Beit Shamai should prevail among the rabbis who are in charge of conversions.

Simon H. Rifkind a New York lawyer and public figure, states his opinion succinctly: he is not able to discuss the who-is-a-Jew issue. He has never dealt with this kind of problem, and his experience in the realm of law is thoroughly irrelevant to the type of question that Ben-Gurion raises.

Israeli respondents. As for the two Israelis who belong to this category, they differ substantially in the tack taken by their arguments, but resemble one another in terms of their conclusions. Hugo Bergman, a philosopher at the Hebrew University of Jerusalem, believes in the holiness of the people of Israel, and in the unshakable relation between Jewry and Judaism. On the other hand, one cannot ignore that among immigrants to Israel, many have no Jewish roots whatsoever and present a wide diversity of specific situations. In this reality, there is no other way than to define two categories of Jews, one on the basis of declaration and one on the basis of *halacha.* Between these two categories one may find but partial overlapping. Bergman recalls Edith Shtein, a nun who perished in Breslau in the Holocaust and who was a Jew according to the *halacha* but not according to declaration. The secular state must operate on the basis of the declarative principle, irrespective of religious affiliation. We may hope that in the future the two categories of Jews, the declarative and the religious, will again coincide.

Hayim Cohen, the government's legal adviser, is the most incisive. The parents are their offspring's guardians and it is their right to declare the identity of their children as they wish. The clerk of the Population Bureau should register the children's identity as the parents declare it; he has no right to register children otherwise than as specified by parents. When both parents declare the child Jewish, this declaration signifies that the child is legally Jewish. The declaration may not fit the *halacha,* but the legal power of the parents is sufficient. To the extent that the mother does not agree with the father about the identity of their child, and seeing that mothers and fathers are of equal legal status, the child will be registered under the terms "identity unknown." Who is a Jew cannot be settled by the State in religious terms in any case since these terms are the exclusive responsibility of the religious authority. Cohen refers to additional examples of similar juridical contradictions. Among other cases, he notes that a woman may be considered as married, on the basis of the *halacha,* but divorced, under secular inheritance laws. Cohen also recalls Rabbi Yehuda's invalidation of the conversion of a man who converted "by himself," that is without a court or rabbi. Rabbi Yehuda invalidated the conversion but not the Jewish identity of the convert's sons, which attracted criticisms of other rabbis. This, according to Cohen, shows that there may be different approaches toward conversion, even re-

garding the *halacha*. In Israel, says Cohen, there is no need for looking with precision into the Judaism of individuals because the majority
is Jewish and the general tendency of the minority is to follow the
majority. The main thing is not whether children of mixed marriages
are converted according to the *halacha*, but whether they mix with,
and behave like, Jews.

In conclusion. Nearly all the free-thinkers search for compromises;
they review the alternatives and ponder them on the basis of rational
considerations. The compromises proposed include instituting intermediate categories of Jews, and changing the rabbis' approach. Some
propose that new rules be defined. Virtually no one suggests that the
religious dimension of who is a Jew be disregarded, or that rabbis be
excluded from the discussion. What is important to respondents in this
category is the notion of nation, and the integrity of Judaism as a
social and cultural reality. It is widely accepted that Israel is a special
setting where Jews are the dominant group and thus a focus of assimilation for the non-Jew. In this sense, there is a recognition that Israel is
different from the Diaspora for Judaism. Interestingly enough, the two
Israelis in this category focus on the civil/administrative aspect of the
issue—on the right of the state to establish a mechanism distinct from
the religious authorities—while the Diaspora respondents demonstrate
more sensitivity to what happens to the individuals involved, and the
moral problems implied.

Three Syndromes

Our investigation delved into the similarity, continuity, and fragmentation of formulations of Jewish identity as elaborated by intellectuals, scholars, and writers living in the Diaspora and in Israel. The
type of response received by Ben-Gurion can be analyzed according to
Ben-Gurion's original methodology, which distinguished respondents
according to religiosity and the Diaspora-Israel dichotomy.

Religiosity

For the *ultra-Orthodox*, the Torah and the *mitzvot* designate the
ultimate significance of the Jewish people, and it is this kind of collective that a new member is to become a part of. Conversion requires no
less than a genuine personal transformation. The *Orthodox* speak more

moderately of their religious devotion and show more understanding of the special problems which a Jewish secular state encounters with respect to who is a Jew. Some acknowledge that innovations and an inventive mind are needed, and propose defining new relations between religion and state; some go so far as to suggest the creation of an intermediate category between Jews and non-Jews. The *non-Orthodox* are less respectful of the *halacha* and view conversion as an entrance into the Jewish People more than into Judaism. Judaism is viewed, not as a static body of commandments, but as a dynamic and pluralistic civilization. The *free-thinkers* tend to be more willing to differentiate between Judaism as a religion and Judaism as a nation. Remarkably enough, virtually no one proposes to completely ignore the religious dimension, or to accept as Jews individuals who belong to other religions.

Diaspora versus Israel

Wider differences emerge among the Diaspora respondents than among the Israelis. The former seem more polarized between the ultra-Orthodox and Orthodox who insist on the role of the faith, and the non-Orthodox and free-thinkers who emphasize conceptual, cultural, and individual aspects. The Israelis, by contrast, are less spread-out, and less polarized. They tend to take for granted that Israel represents a Jewish condition essentially different from Jewry in any other place, and that as such, the Jewish State has to endorse leadership responsibility for the Jews as a whole. They thus tend to be less flexible on the issue under discussion, often rejecting Jewish pluralism, and aligning themselves on *halachic* requirements.

When considered as a whole, the attitudes of Diaspora versus Israeli respondents of different degrees of religiosity reveal a picture where convergence and divergence intermingle. We may speak of convergence regarding the who-is-a-Jew issue in a threefold sense. For all respondents, individuals born of a Jewish mother or who have converted to Judaism according to *halacha* are Jews. These individuals make up the large majority of Jews even according to the most liberal formulations of who is a Jew. The differences among trends and perspectives are negligible. Another convergence among all respondents concerns the fact that all speak of tradition or traditions by indicating the same texts and symbols. The greatest differences may exist between the interpretations of, and attitudes toward, those texts and symbols, their validity and authority. But all respondents draw their own tokens of speech, metaphors, historical examples, and literary references from the same reservoir—what Eisenstadt (1992) designates as "Jewish civilization." Finally, nearly all groups endorse the special importance of Israel as a Jewish state—or at least as a state of Jews—in the evolution of world Jewry. In the eyes of a large majority of the respondents—Israelis as well as non-Israelis—whatever is done in Israel regarding the status and institutionalization of Judaism is of direct consequence to the Diaspora and its relationship to the Jewish State.

On the other hand, one finds large differences among respondents, both in general and within each category and subcategory, in the aspects which respondents choose to emphasize or ignore. Yet one principally discerns tendencies that are more pronounced among respondents of given categories than among others. Thus, we may speak of three divergent approaches emerging from the interplay of religiosity and location in Israel versus the Diaspora.

Quasi-sectarian Religiosity

Among the ultra-Orthodox and the Orthodox, especially in the Diaspora, the strongest tendency is to repeat the traditional exigency of subordinating the notion of people of Israel to its collective divine mission. This tendency focuses on God and Torah. This approach diminishes, without disregarding it, the significance of Israel versus the Diaspora. It pays attention to this dimension mainly by laying the requirements of *halacha* upon the State of Israel and presenting their fulfillment as the condition of Israel's leading role in world Judaism. Failing this, Israel would serve as a source of division. This orientation that sets the belief in God and the practice of *halacha* at the center of the Jewish endeavor, might be termed "sectarian religiosity" if it applied only to the Orthodox. But instead it aspires to mobilize all Jews and return them to righteousness. By remaining preoccupied by this wider circle on behalf of an all-Jewish calling, this orientation is best depicted as *quasi-sectarian religiosity*.

Cultural Ethnicity

Among many non-Orthodox and free-thinking Diaspora respondents, the notion that emerges most strongly is community. This notion evinces, in new terms, a traditional facet of Jewish identity: individuals who qualify as Jews embody values, symbols, and attachments that mark them as a special collective. This attitude is best depicted as *cultural ethnicity*. Its proponents are often ready to consider nonritualistic forms of access to Judaism, and to draw the boundaries of Jewry quite loosely; they also most often contemplate favorably the creation of an intermediary layer which would confuse the collective boundary even more. This tendency includes Conservative and Reform Judaism, which, within their explicitly religious and not less unequivocally innovation-oriented discourses, emphasize social and moral aspects, and as a rule view *halacha* rulings as obsolete.

National Identity

Among Israelis, one finds a Judaism that is best understood in terms of *national identity*. This attitude focuses on the territorial-geographic dimension which is set in relation to a population and state institutions. It is, one may say, a new formulation insisting in its own way, on the Land of Israel facet of traditional identity. This orientation is conceived in a two-level scheme where the designation "Israeli Jews" corresponds to what is meant by "Israeli nation," and "Jewish people" includes both Israeli and non-Israeli Jews, and refers to a culture where religion plays an acknowledged and important role. Many Israelis emphasize the importance of the Israeli nation and see as crucial the role it presumably plays as the center and leader of the Jewish people. On the other hand, they are aware of the fact that the reference to common religious symbols has remained a major thread that keeps the link between Jews alive worldwide. Hence, even when they themselves are not religious, the supporters of this orientation endorse the institutionalization of *halachic* norms, since this points to a concept of Jewish affiliation that is valid for all. This, in turn, explains why Israeli respondents, whether religious or secular, are not eager to back anti-Orthodox positions when it comes to who is a Jew.

These three syndromes do not interact easily. It was just mentioned that Israeli respondents who elaborate the national-identity syndrome also tend, often, to endorse the sort of *halachic* criteria of membership evinced by the quasi-sectarian religiosity syndrome. Yet, the supporters of the quasi-sectarian syndrome "reciprocate" mainly by formulating *halacha*-inspired exigencies which, in their mind, condition the role of the Jewish State vis-à-vis world Jewry. In parallel, both quasi-sectarian and the national-identity partisans remain aloof from the cultural-ethnicity syndrome evoked by secular and non-Orthodox Diaspora respondents, which favors pluralism and stands for the legitimization of non-Orthodox criteria of membership. But—and here lies a major paradox—it is the Diaspora non-Orthodox Jewry referred to by this cultural-ethnicity syndrome, that is targeted by the national-identity syndrome when it proclaims the centrality of Israel for world Judaism.

We must, however, acknowledge that the respondents of Ben-Gurion's inquiry all belong to an exceptional generation of Jews. It is a generation of individuals who were between fifty-five and seventy years old in 1958, and who witnessed in their lifetimes, a multifarious and far-reaching transformation of the world as well as of the Jewish people. The transformation of the world was marked by two world wars, relentless ideological strife, the start of a protracted global cold war, and the unprecedented development of Western capitalism and civilization. Against this background, a series of events in Jewish history—among others, the huge demographic movement from the East toward the West, the destruction caused by the Holocaust, and the creation of a Jewish state in Israel—thoroughly transformed the Jewish people. This uncommon experience of that particular generation of Jews gave these thinkers an overwhelming interest in this topic and in their reflections on Judaism. Moreover, the relative stabilization of the conditions of life of world Jewry ever since the 1950s,[6] also means that reflecting about who is a Jew has not only shown us what Judaism was in the aftermath of that great transformation, but also for many years to come.

This extraordinary experience notwithstanding, those *Hachamei Yisrael* who were questioned by Ben-Gurion definitely assert their affinity to the past. They all refer more or less to the same collective; they all confirm the connection between nationhood and religion in Judaism; they extract their symbols from the same source, and feel concern for the existence of Israel, the "Land of the Jew." This is the best confirmation of the firmness and intrinsic power of Judaism itself.

Yet, *Hahamei Yisrael* also evince different emphases and different perspectives. The Israeli experience expresses itself in a new version of Judaism which becomes national. Non-religious or non-Orthodox Diaspora Jews reiterate the necessity of synthesis between Judaism and universal values. Orthodox thinkers demonstrate the velleity to discard any part of what they think is essential. Notwithstanding their proximity, these perspectives represent the possibility of mutual estrangement and alienation because of the different styles of Jewish life which they dictate. The sameness and continuity of these versions of Judaism, in light of the great differences between them, cannot but remind Wittgenstein's notion of *air de famille* (1958), which he uses to describe the variety of language games which make up a language. We may also use this analogy to depict the differences of interpretation and function of the same identity in the midst of rivalry, competition, exclusivity, and reciprocal demands—a patchwork of visions which differ, yet are drawn from the same sources and experiences, and thus really do resemble one another, in the very contradictory manner of a *real* family.

Notes

We would like to thank the Ben-Gurion Center of Ben-Gurion University of the Negev, Sde Boker, and the Ben-Gurion Archives of Tel Aviv, for making possible this work on the 1958 *Hahamei Yisrael* letters to Ben-Gurion.

1. The governance of personal status issues by the religious courts was not challenged at that time.
2. The letter was signed by Rabbis A.L. Grosnas, A. Rappoport, M. Lew, M. Shteinberg, and S. Swift.
3. Hebrew acronym for "our wise ones, blessed be their memories," referring to the scholars of the Talmud.
4. According to the law, individuals are considered Jews if they were born Jewish or have converted to Judaism. The kind of conversion is not specified, and has repeatedly become a subject of parliamentary debate, with the Orthodox factions pleading for recognition only of Orthodox conversion.
5. With the notable exception of some Middle Eastern, Soviet, and Ethiopian Jewry; for these were yet to undergo major changes between the 1960s and 1990s. These Jews inherit the dilemmas of Jewish identity, and contribute to the solutions which Prime Minister Ben-Gurion began seeking in the late 1950s.

References

Barth, F., ed. 1969. *Ethnic Groups and Boundaries.* Boston: Little Brown.
Cicourel, A.V. 1981. *Advances in Social Theory and Methodology.* Boston: Routledge and Kegan Paul.

De Levita, D.J. 1965. *The Concept of Identity.* New York: Basic Books.

Dumont, L. 1977. *Homo Hierarchicus—Le Systeme des Castes et ses Implications.* Paris: Gallimard.

Eisenstadt, S.N. 1992. *Jewish Civilization: The Jewish Historical Experience in a Comparative Perspective.* Albany, NY: State University of New York Press.

Erickson, E., ed. 1963. *Youth: Change and Challenge.* New York: Basic Books.

Feguson, C.F. 1966. "National Sociolinguistic Profile Formulas," pp. 309–315 in W. Bright (ed.) *Sociolinguistics.* The Hague: Mouton.

Garfinkel, H., ed. 1986. *Ethnomethodological Studies of Work.* Boston: Routledge and Kegan Paul.

Geertz, C. 1965. *Old Societies and New States: The Integrative Revolution.* New York: The Free Press.

Goldstein, S. 1992. "Profile of American Jewry: Insights from the 1990 National Jewish Population Survey." *American Jewish Yearbook 1992:* 75–173.

Herman S.J. 1970. *Israelis and Jews—The Continuity of Identity.* New York: Random House.

———. 1988. *Jewish Identity: A Social Psychological Perspective.* New Brunswick, NJ: Transaction Publishers.

Isch-Shalom, B.1990. *Harav Kook: Ben ratzionalism lemistikah* (Rabbi Kook: Between Rationalism and Mysticism). Tel-Aviv: Am Oved (Hebrew).

Klineberg, O. 1967. "The Multinational Society: Some Research Problems." *Social Science Information* 6: 81–99.

Levi-Strauss, C. 1961. *Race et Histoire.* Paris: Gonthier.

Levy, S. 1996. *Values and Jewishness of Israeli Youth.* Jerusalem: Guttman Institute (mimeograph).

Liebman, C. S. and S.M. Cohen. 1990. *Two Worlds of Judaism: The Israeli and American Experiences.* New Haven, CT: Yale University Press.

Lipset S. M. and E. Raab. 1995. *Jews and the New American Scene.* Cambridge, MA: Harvard University Press.

Weber, M. 1968. *Economy and Society.* New York: Bedminster Press.

Wittgenstein, L. 1958. *Philosophical Investigations.* Oxford: Basil Blackwell.

4

Collective Jewish Identity in Israel: Towards an Irrevocable Split?

Eva Etzioni-Halevy

Introduction

What are the prospects for the survival of collective Jewish identity in Israel at the end of the twentieth century and into the next century? In this chapter I argue that Jewish identity is still strong at present, but is headed for a split into at least two separate identities, with increasing hostility between them. This split is apt to create increasing difficulties in the functioning of the democratic political arena in Israel. As yet, however, the split is not yet irrevocable, and much will depend on what the spiritual and intellectual leadership in the two camps say and do.

Background

The Place of Collective Identity in Contemporary Society

The preceding statement is based on the assumption that collective identity by choice is a legitimate way of coping with the problem of self-realization in a pluralistic and increasingly individualistic society, and that collective identity serves as a basis for solidarity—and hence as an integrative force, essential to society and democracy. This integrative force helps bridge the rifts and smooth the conflicts that are manifested in the political arena—rifts and conflicts so crucial to the function of a democracy. These assumptions arise from a broad consensus of theory in the social sciences today.

There is, firstly, a convergence between the modernist and the postmodernist schools of thought. Thus, several prominent representatives of both schools of thought have emphasized that one of the main features that characterizes the globalizing postmodern society (in the words of the postmodernists) or the hyper-modern society (according to the modernist school), is the multiplicity of options for self-realization, and the ability of people to choose and construct their own identities (Bauman 1992; Beck 1992; Touraine 1997). It is further agreed among such theorists that it is precisely in this situation of wide-ranging pluralism and unbounded multiplicity of choices, that many people seek self-realization neither exclusively through individualism nor through globalism. Rather, they also—legitimately—opt for a collective identity, through tribalism by choice (Bauman 1992: 199) or for socially constructed primordiality (Eisenstadt 1997).

Another facet of this broad theoretical convergence is between the neofunctionalist and conflict schools of thought. Thus, while the father of neofunctionalism, Jeffrey Alexander (1985), believes that sociological analysis must focus on social conflict in addition to solidarity and consensus, the Marxian-Weberian conflict theorist Pierre Bourdieu (1990) holds that in every field of struggle and conflict, there is also a certain degree of consensus among the actors.

Finally, even analysts of the democratic political arena hold converging views. They generally concur that the political arena is inherently rife with conflict, and that such conflict is essential to democracy. But there is also widespread agreement (see, e.g., Dye and Zeigler 1996; Higley and Burton 1989; Kaase 1996; Etzioni-Halevy 1997) that beyond the controversies and conflicts there must also be a measure of consensus on the most basic rules and values.

Collective Jewish Identity in Israel

There are three collective identities, relevant to three partially overlapping publics in Israel: (1) Israeli identity, which is somewhat different for Arabs and Jews; (2) Jewish identity; and (3) Arab/Palestinian identity, which is somewhat different for Arabs in Israel and in the territories. Of these, I shall address the issue of collective Jewish identity only, which applies to 80 percent of the country's population.

In the literature, we find two conceptions, which form the basis of two complementary definitions of Jewish identity: a substantive one, and a subjective one. For the substantive definition, we look to Smith (1992): Jewish identity may be conceived of as a collective identity based on a common culture, values and symbols that, in turn, have their roots in:

- a shared sense of common descent;
- collective historical memories;
- a shared affinity to the Jewish religion; and,
- a common attachment to a homeland.

The second definition is subjective and concerns collective Jewish identity as conceived, not by the observer, but by the subjects for whom it is relevant, that is, by Jews. This conception is frequently used by researchers, when they ask respondents (in variously worded questions) whether they feel a weak or a strong sense of Jewishness. It was used, for instance by Herman (1970), by Etzioni-Halevy and Shapira (1975), and in a recent survey by the Tami Steinmetz Center for Peace Research, conducted in autumn 1996, which will be discussed in more detail below.

The Central Thesis: From Collective Jewish Identity to Two Separate Collective Identities

There exists a strong collective Jewish identity common to Jews in Israel, but it is gradually disintegrating. Instead, two separate collective identities (with several sub-identities) are emerging: an increasingly stringent and separatist religious Jewish identity, and a secular identity in which the Jewish element is becoming progressively weaker. Also, the bearers of these identities are increasingly divided into distinct camps, with growing hostility between them.

Thus, there is a gradual enfeeblement of a central integrative mechanism, which until now has been crucial in bridging conflicts within the common, democratic, political arena. The difficulties generated by this progressive weakening are likely to be exacerbated in the future.

The gradual split of the common collective Jewish identity can be explained by two factors. The first is that the common bonds which have served as foundations for the collective Jewish identity are gradually eroding. The second factor is that large parts of the spiritual, ideological, and intellectual leadership (the elite) in both the religious and the secular camps are encouraging the growing rift, and fanning the animosity between the two camps.

The Erosion of the Common Bases of Jewish Identity

Today, collective Jewish identity in Israel is still strong. In a survey of a representative sample of Jews in Israel (Steinmetz 1996), respondents were asked to indicate the strength of their feelings of Jewishness by placing themselves on a five-point continuum, from a very weak sense of Jewishness to a very strong sense of Jewishness. Seventy-nine percent of the respondents expressed a very strong sense of Jewishness, almost all the rest a strong sense of Jewishness, and only 3 percent expressed a weak sense of Jewishness.[1]

However, most of the common bases of this identity are eroding:

A shared sense of common descent. There is no reason to believe that this sense will disappear in the foreseeable future. However, its significance for Jewish identity is likely to diminish, as the other bases of the common identity are gradually becoming more tenuous.

Collective historical memories. Collective Jewish identity has long been based on shared historical memories, especially those of persecution in the Diaspora, and the sense of a shared destiny emanating from them. Today these collective memories are focused in particular on the Holocaust—but they are receding, and will recede even further with the passing of time. In this context, I argue that recent visits of Jewish youngsters to "Holocaust sites" do not testify to the strength of collective memories. Rather, they represent a last-ditch attempt to revive memories that are already fading.

Apart from memories of persecution in the Diaspora, collective Jewish identity in Israel has also been based on shared memories of the history of Jewish settlement in Palestine, the establishment of the state, and the various struggles and wars that accompanied these developments. These memories have had a unifying effect that has strengthened collective Jewish identity, in that they have been anchored in the Zionist ideology—whereby Zionism is conceived of as the national liberation movement of the Jewish people—shared by the entire Jewish community in Israel, with the exception of the *Haredim* (ultra-Orthodox).

However, the ability of such memories to form a common basis of Jewish identity has been weakening, because of the growth of the *Haredi* community, that does not share the Zionist ideology. At the same time, the capacity of these memories to serve as a basis of shared collective identity has also diminished because of systematic endeavors by "the new historians" to destroy the myth of Zionism as a movement of Jewish national liberation: instead, the Zionist movement is viewed as belligerent colonialism, intent on exploiting and repressing another people. Not surprisingly, then, the unifying potential of the shared memories connected with the history of Zionism has been gradually eroded.

A common attachment to a homeland. Jewish identity of Jews in Israel has also been anchored in a common attachment to the homeland, the land of Israel. This has been expressed, in part, in the ideology of Zionism, based on collectivist values, wherein the requirements of building and defending the country for the sake of the entire nation take priority over the needs and achievements of the individual.

Yet, as a variety of research (e.g,. Shapira and Herzog 1989; Ben Rafael 1996: 71–75) has shown, collectivist values are receding, and are gradually replaced by individualist values. These increasingly individualist values indicate an erosion of collective attachment to the country among a large part of the Jewish community in Israel.

Concomitantly, we are also witnessing an increasingly fierce attachment to the land of Israel in the religious-biblical sense. This attachment, however, is common to the religious only, and is not shared by the secular Jewish community. At the same time, part of the secular left has been developing what may be termed a post-Zionist ideology, whereby the State of Israel no longer has legitimacy as a Jewish state, but should rather be the state of all its citizens, Jews and Arabs alike.

Thus, individualist, non-Zionist, and post-Zionist values are all being strengthened at the expense of Zionism, and the common attachment to the homeland has become weakened. Hence, Zionism is less capable than it was in the past of serving as a basis of common Jewish identity, and the trend toward the weakening of this common denominator may be expected to progress even further in the future.

A shared affinity for the Jewish religion, as expressed in the

Pentateuch, the Talmud, and the Rabbinical literature, and by the acceptance of Rabbinical authority and of the traditions and customs flowing from all of these. Jewish identity has been, and still is, based in part on a common affinity to this religion, since even many nonreligious Jews have harbored some vague positive sentiments towards this religion, or at least towards its customs and traditions. Or, as Amnon Dankner (1997) expressed it, today "the depths of the collective Israeli soul are intertwined with Jewish contents, symbols and rituals." But recently this common affinity has progressively disintegrated.

Among the religious, commitment to the above has been strengthened in recent years (see below). But among secularists, the positive sentiments towards the Jewish tradition are growing weaker. This is so because the secularists' sympathetic affinity with the Jewish tradition has been anchored largely in childhood memories from the parental, or the grandparental, home. But today, there are more and more people (and particularly young people) who are third- or fourth-generation secularists, and thus no longer have such memories.

It is true that neither the religious nor the secular are static categories: some secular Jews have undergone a process of a "return" to religion, or of a growing affinity to it. And there is an even larger number of religious people who have undergone a process of secularization. But there is an even larger proportion of people who have remained either religious or secular over the last two or three generations. So, it is still true that the proportion of third- and fourth-generation secularists is growing from generation to generation, and will become even larger in time.

In view of this, it is significant that Jewish identity is not only weaker among secular than among religious Jews, but is also weaker among third- or fourth-generation secularists than it is among first-generation secularists. This has been shown by a previous research project on Tel-Aviv University students (Etzioni-Halevy and Shapira 1975), and by Steinmetz (1996) with regard to the general population. The results of the latter survey show that some 95 percent of religious Jews, but only 65 percent of secular Jews, evinced a very strong sense of Jewish identity. Also, among secularists whose parents are/were religious, 90 percent expressed a very strong sense of Jewish identity. By contrast, among secular Jews whose parents were also secular, only 60 percent harbored such a strong sense of Jewishness.

Thus, with the secularists' intergenerational distancing from the Jewish religion, Jewish identity as a common denominator to both religious and secularist Jews is eroding, and separate identities are emerging.

The Emerging Identities

All of this raises the question as to the nature of the two emerging identities. In my assessment, they will become increasingly bifurcated because one is becoming more stringently religious and separatist, while the other is becoming more and more secular, and less and less Jewish.

The first part of this assessment is based on the fact that among large parts of the religious community there is a trend towards an intensification of religious observance (see Friedman 1993a, 1993b). And an identity based on an increasingly stringent religious observance is necessarily (even if not intentionally) separatist, for it increasingly alienates secularists who do not share the observant way of life.

Secondly, there is the intergenerational distancing of the secular community from the Jewish religion, and from the conglomeration of symbols, customs, and traditions anchored in it. Instead, the secular collective identity is based more and more exclusively on a secular Israeli culture. It is not my intention to determine whether this culture is or is not authentically Jewish. However, on the basis of the previously cited data on the intergenerational diminution of the secularists' Jewish identity, one must conclude that it forms a weaker source of Jewish identification than does the culture that is anchored in the Jewish religion.

Thus, as the religious Jewish identity is becoming more strongly— even radically—religious, and as the secular identity is becoming less and less Jewish, the two identities are becoming more and more alien to each other, and the rift between them is growing.

The Internal Rifts in Each Camp

The trend toward a growing divergence between the two collective identities is somewhat mitigated by internal cleavages in each camp. In the religious camp, this is a controversy between the *Haredi* and the rest of the religious (that is, between the Orthodox and the ultra-Orthodox community). In this controversy, the *Haredi* accuse the religious of banding with the secular, while the religious accuse the *Haredi* of exploiting the State of Israel by parasitically accepting its bounty while eschewing the fundamental civil duty of military service.

Yet the Orthodox and the ultra-Orthodox also converge on many issues, for instance on the issue of increasing stringency in religious observance, and religious attachment to the Land of Israel; moreover, many educators in Orthodox educational institutions are drawn from the ultra-Orthodox camp. The Orthodox and the ultra-Orthodox also band together politically whenever the enforcement of Jewish law (*halacha*) is at stake.[2]

By the same token, the secularists are also divided into the fiercely anti-religious, the religiously indifferent, and those who are sympathetic toward religion. However, they are united in their resentment of what they conceive of as religious coercion by the religious camp.

Given that each of the camps is divided on some fundamental issues, but remains united on other issues, internal divisions can only slightly mitigate the overall rift between the collective identities in the two camps.

The role of "traditional" Jews. The trend toward growing divergence between the two identities is also somewhat mitigated by the existence of a relatively large number of "traditional" (neither religious nor secular) Jews. Even though traditionalists are not meticulous in their religious observance, their Jewish identity is almost as strong as that of the religious. Thus, Steinmetz (1996) showed that 95 percent of the religious, and 90 percent of traditional Jews (compared with 65 percent of secular Jews) evinced very strong Jewish identity.

At the same time, it is doubtful that the traditionalists will have that same ability to mitigate the growing rift between religious and secular identities in the future, because traditionalists are—virtually by definition—moderates. And, by virtue of being moderate, they are also quiescent. Moreover, unlike the religious and secular camps, traditional Jews do not form a distinctive community with its own leadership to represent its point of view. As the split between the religious and secular identities grows, traditional Jews may find themselves in a progressively difficult situation with respect to the definition of their own identity, in between the two more articulate camps. And the greater their difficulty in defining their own identity, the more difficult it will become for them to mediate between the two antagonistic camps. Thus, their moderating influence may be expected to become weaker over time, and this is likely to become yet another factor that exacerbates the split.

The Role of the Leadership

An additional explanation for the growing rift between the religious and secular collective identities lies in the role which the leaders of both camps have played in encouraging and enhancing it. In the religious camp, these include politicians of the religious parties, rabbis, *admorim* (*Hasidic* leaders) and heads of yeshivas, heads of the religious youth movements, as well as journalists, particularly in the *Haredi* press. In the secular camp, these include politicians of left-wing parties, intellectuals, and journalists in the secular press.

For several years, but in particular before and after the murder of Prime Minister Yitzhak Rabin, several such personalities have led campaigns of mutual denigration. Thus, some secular leaders have accused the religious of fanaticism, extremism and a propensity for violence; while on their part, several religious leaders have accused the secular of abandoning Jewish tradition and values, even of being devoid of values altogether.

Thus the leaders of the two camps have engaged not only in a campaign of mutual vilification, but also in an attempt at mutual delegitimization. The problem in the formation of the two identities, however, lies not in the fact that one or the other of them is not legitimate, but rather in the fact that the growing mutual hostility of the leaders in the two camps increasingly jeopardizes the proper functioning of Israeli democracy. Thus, the elite who celebrate and encourage this mutual hostility do not merely exacerbate the problem, but indeed form an integral part of it.

Implications for the Democratic Political Arena

All this raises the question, whether our democratic political system can continue to function, in light of the growing split and rising animosity between the two major camps.

As I see it, ever since this political system came into being in the Yishuv era at the beginning of the century, it has been held together, to a large extent, by "the elite connection"—a relationship between the secular elite of the ruling government party and the elite of the religious parties. That is to say, it has been held together by the circular flow of resources, funds, appointments, and organizational infrastructure in return for political support, between them (see Etzioni-Halevy 1993, 1997).

This elite connection has always been questionable from an ethical point of view. But, at the same time, it has made possible the establishment and survival of coalitions over the years, coalitions in which religious parties have joined secular governments, despite controversies over religious issues between them; thus it has had a stabilizing effect on Israeli democracy.

However, as major analysts of democratic politics have emphasized, beyond the controversies and conflicts, a certain amount of consensus on basic values is also necessary for the proper functioning of any democratic political system. It follows that even an Israeli-style elite connection can function only so long as there is some minimum consensus between the rival camps, which this elite connection brings and holds together.

Hence, as the rift between the collective identities of the religious and the secular communities grows, it may be expected to become increasingly difficult to justify the mutual concessions and flow of resources between them, which are necessary for the functioning of the democratic political system. Hence, the difficulties in maintaining this system, even with the aid of the elite connection, will gradually increase.

Is the Split Irrevocable?

In my estimation, a certain progressive erosion of some of the common denominators between religious and nonreligious Jews is likely to continue. However, the tendency of the leadership in both camps to exacerbate these developments and fan the animosity between the two camps certainly is not irreversible. Also, it is not inconceivable that a religious, spiritual and/or intellectual leadership will arise that will look for unifying, rather than for divisive, elements in Judaism, so that new foundations for a new collective Jewish identity based on values and symbols common to both religious and non- religious Jews in Israel—and in the Diaspora as well—may be laid.

The political leadership may be obliged to promote divisiveness, as this is necessary for the proper functioning of the political process in the Israeli democracy. But the same is not true for religious leadership, or for secular intellectual leadership. What is needed is a leadership in both these camps that will work toward a reversal of the spiraling animosity. Failing this, political conflicts may well become unmanageable, and the next century may see Israel turn into a mire of separatist movements.

Notes

1. For instance, in the autumn of 1997, with respect to the promotion of legislation designed to exclude representatives of Conservative and Reform Judaism from religious councils, and with respect to the promotion of legislation denying state recognition to conversions to Judaism performed by Conservative and Reform rabbis abroad.
2. The question on Jewishness was included in the survey at this author's request.

References

Alexander, Jeffrey C. 1985. "Introduction," pp.7–18 in Jeffrey C. Alexander (ed.) *Neofunctionalism*. Beverly Hills, CA: Sage.

Bauman, Zygmunt. 1992. *Intimations of Postmodernity*. London: Routledge.

Beck, Ulrich. 1992. *Risk Society*. London: Sage.

Ben Rafael, Eliezer. 1996. *A Non-total Revolution*. Ramat Ef'al: Yad Tabenkin (Hebrew).

Bourdieu, Pierre. 1990. *In Other Words*. Stanford, CA: Stanford University Press.

Dankner, Amnon. 1997. "The Internal Grammar." *Ha'aretz* (9 June).

Dye, Thomas R. and Harmon L. Zeigler. 1996. *The Irony of Democracy*. Belmond: Wadsworth.

Eisenstadt, Shmuel N. 1997. Keynote Speech to the 28th Annual Conference of the Israel Sociological Association, Tel-Aviv, 9–11 February.

Etzioni-Halevy, Eva. 1997. *A Place at the Top: Elites and Elitism in Israel*. Tel Aviv: Cherikover (Hebrew).

———. 1993. *The Elite Connection and Democracy in Israel*. Tel Aviv: Sifriat Poalim. (Hebrew).

Etzioni-Halevy, Eva and Rina Shapira. 1975. "Jewish Identification of Israeli Students—What Lies Ahead?" *Jewish Social Studies* 37: 251–66.

Friedman, Menachem. 1993a. "The Lost Kiddush Cup," pp. 175–86 in Jack Wertheimer (ed.) *The Uses of Tradition*. New York: The Jewish Theological Seminary.

———. 1993b. "The Market Model and Religious Radicalism," pp. 192–215 in Laurence J. Silberstein (ed.), *Jewish Fundamentalism in Comparative Perspective*. New York: New York University Press.

Herman, Simon N. 1970. *Israelis and Jews*. New York: Random House.

Higley, John and Michael Burton. 1989. "The Elite Variable in Democratic Transitions and Breakdowns." *American Sociological Review* 54: 17–32.

Kaase, Max . 1996. "Consensus, Conflict and Democracy in Germany." Paper presented at the 12th Germany-Israel Foundation Meeting, on Conflict and Extremism in a Democratic Society. Israel, December.

Shapira, Rina and Hanna Herzog. 1989. "A Dark Secret," pp. 137–57 in Rina Shapira and Rahel Peleg (eds.) *Sociology of Education—A Reader.* Tel-Aviv: Am Oved (Hebrew).

Smith, Anthony D. 1992. "The Question of Jewish Identity, " pp. 219–33 in Peter Y. Medding (ed.) *A New Jewry.* Oxford: Oxford University Press.

Steinmetz, Tami. 1996. Unpublished survey of Jews in Israel, conducted by the Tami Steinmetz Center for Peace Research.

Touraine, Alain. 1997. Keynote Speech to the 28th Annual Conference of the Israel Sociological Association. Tel-Aviv, 9–11 February.

5

Building Jewish Identity for Tomorrow: Possible or Not?

Samuel C. Heilman

I should like to explore three questions crucial to any conference that seeks to address the matter of building Jewish identity for tomorrow. The first is why identity in general, and Jewish identity in particular, has of late become such a dominant concern in the contemporary life of our people. The second seeks briefly and operationally to define the nature of contemporary Jewish identity. And the third is to question whether Jewish identity can indeed be built, fashioned, for a future about which we know very little.

The answer to the first of these questions is tied to the matter of social change that has become an essential feature of those societies and cultures in which most Jews, and particularly Jewish youth, find themselves. These are societies characterized by high degrees of technological change, and, as Kenneth Keniston long ago correctly noted, "the primary motor of social change is technological innovation" (1965: 194). These are societies that place a high premium on innovation and change, arguing that the new is always improved. In such societies where change *per se* is desirable, stability is perceived as an unacceptable constraint, and its champions are considered as overly conservative at best, reactionary at worst. In such a time, *socialization*, the process by which the young are shown how to fit into known and stable roles, in institutions that provide a sense of continuity between the past and the future, is undermined. One result of this is that people of one generation believe that they are not easily able to prepare those of another to fit into and take over the institutions of the society. Phrased differently, at a time when innovation and change are endemic, parents and teachers cannot easily or with much confidence guide their children and students, for the world in which those children and students mature is likely to be significantly different from the world in which the parents and teachers grew up.

In this "new world," not only are there a new science and technology, but social norms, cultural expectations, aesthetics, and patterns of behavior have been radically changed. In less than a generation, almost every aspect of sociocultural existence seems outdated. Nothing seems to be forever. This is behind the concept of "future shock" (Toffler 1970). This is also what is implied in the common lament of parents in the modern societies of the West, the primary locus of Jewish youth: "I just don't know how to raise my children any more."

Keniston concluded that "in a rapidly changing society…, identity formation increasingly replaces socialization in importance" (1965: 212). Certainly, Jews have overwhelmingly been part of societies that have undergone rapid change. In North America, where so many Jews live today, change is persistent. Moreover, Jews have remained in the forefront of that change by virtue of their high rates of mobility—both geographic and social. With regard to the former, we find, most Jewish children are likely to have lived and grown up in a community and neighborhood different from the one in which their parents lived and matured. Moreover, most also do not intend to remain in that same location as they launch their own adult lives—a transition facilitated by the fact that most go away from home during their college years, and even in youth they are sent away to summer camp. Calvin Goldscheider has noted "the nonrootedness of the young generations and the[ir] movement away from centers of Jewish concentration— regionally and within metropolitan areas," as well as the fact that "early residential independence coupled with later family formation is…a more dominant feature of Jewish than non-Jewish males" (1975: 132; also Goldscheider 1986: 78).

As for social mobility, as Nathan Glazer has argued: "integration and upward social mobility are what Jews have wanted" (1987: 13; see also Jaret 1978: 9–20). Sidney Goldstein found already in the 1960s—the era when this mobility became a dominant feature of American Jewry—that Jews "increasingly enter[ed] occupations whose nature requires mobility because of the limited opportunities available in particular areas" (1970: 37). Thus Jews became far more cosmopolitan than parochial, mobile rather than stable, socialization into traditions or a community of habituation became difficult, if not impossible.

For Jews in Israel, the other great Jewish population center, change has been no less endemic. Endless waves of immigration created a population that was constantly having to readapt itself and its national identity. A rapidly expanding nation undergoing both geographic and cultural changes among its native-born led to a youth culture in which—much as was the case in America—immigrant parents felt disadvantaged in their capacity to draw on their own childhood experiences in order to guide the socialization of their own children. In a pioneer and immigrant society, socialization is replaced by identity formation as well. This is even more intensified when one of the goals of that pioneer society is to create a new national identity as was and remains the case in Israel. For Israel was in a very concrete sense as much about redefining what a Jew was as it was involved in nation building.

The Holocaust and the decisive break that it assured with generations of past Jewish identity, and the formation of the State of Israel, only exacerbated that sense of breach from the past. Yet, paradoxically, this put even more pressure for some overarching Jewish identity that could help overcome both history and geography. As technology has made it possible, moreover, for Jews to move from their home to other Jewish communities, as travel between Israel and all other Jewish communities on earth becomes not only easy but common, even those who have a sense of what being a Jew is find this identity battered by the sense of relativism that comes from the decline of purely local experiences. Even among the most traditionalist Orthodox—whom one often presumes to have some transcendent and historical notion of what Jewish identity is and demands—there is a sense of flux as, for example, American Jewish Orthodox youth find their Jewish identities transformed by prolonged cultural contact with Israel and vice versa. Indeed, in some quarters there are misgivings and anxieties about the relativism that this inserts into the hearts and minds of the Orthodox so that, for example, some yeshivas that cater to both Diaspora and Israeli Orthodox youth try increasingly to separate these two groups from each other for fear that if they do not do so, even these tradition-directed Jews will develop a pluralistic Jewish identity. This sort of pluralistic identity, a kind of other-directed identity, runs the risk of engendering doubts and a sense of a soft identity core. The fear here is that Jews will "find it difficult to locate a fixed position on which to stand" (Keniston 1965: 203).

In America and Israel, therefore, with their premium on change, where the past seemed ever more distant and the future increasingly unpredictable, the pressures on identity-formation became correspondingly greater. Here Jewish identity began to take on a far more salient character. This identity was conceived as something that transcended neighborhood and community, went beyond ethnic origins or family history, and was understood as a more universal concept that could act to unify all Jews in all places and all times. Jewish identity, it was hoped, could provide what all identity is supposed to: "a sense of self that will link the past, the present, and the future" (Ibid.: 212). This was particularly the case in America with the rise of the unmeltable ethnics in the last twenty-five years. Here, "for better or worse," as Daniel Bell has noted, "the very breakup of the cultural hegemony of the WASPs and the growth of ethnicity as a legitimate dimension of American-life...'forced'..[Jews] to maintain an identity, and to define themselves in ethnic terms" (1986: 17). "Ethnic identity and religious identification have become in large part expected norms of individual identification" (Glazer 1987: 17). Specifically, being a Jew today and into the future seems a necessary way of being an American. Jewish identity seems to have moved increasingly toward ethnicity or heritage and culture, while being a "good Jew" has been defined in vaguely moral terms (see e.g. Bell 1986; also Cohen 1991). As Nathan Glazer sums it up, "Less and less of the life of American Jews is derived from Jewish history, experience, culture, and religion. More and more of it is derived from the current and existing realities of American culture, American politics, and the general American religion" (Glazer 1985: 36).

This sort of Jewish identity is largely a matter of symbolic heritage. Moreover, for most Jews, divorced from what being a Jew in the past had been, the content of this symbol, this ethnocultural Jewish identity lacks substance. Thus, an interest in a Jewish identity is, for most American Jews, "not a very strong desire" and "it adapts itself to the needs of integration in the United States....It makes few demands and is largely cut off from historic Judaism in terms of belief and practice" (Glazer 1987: 18). To many contemporary Jews, the old models, whether based on religious ideals and ideology or ethnic customs and traditions, seemed increasingly irrelevant to the present and the imagined future. American Jews see themselves as Americans perhaps as much if not more than they see themselves as Jews. To maintain this bicultural identity with the least discomfort and cultural conflict, many if not most American Jews have made these two cultures interchangeable.

Israelis often have in a parallel fashion replaced Jewish with Israeli identity, making the two interchangeable. Religious identity, moreover, seems often to be given to the province of the *Dosim* or *Haredim* who make up a kind of class apart in the minds of most contemporary Israelis. But these two culture pairs—Jewish and American, Jewish and Israeli—are not interchangeable. Judaism, for example, does not set democracy as an ideal above all others, while America—and to some extent Israel—does. Or, to take another example, Judaism places a premium on the community above the individual, whereas America places the individual's life, liberty, and pursuit of happiness above all else. Israeli civil society also includes non-Jews, so being an Israeli cannot be identical with being a Jew.

For those who do put much store in their search for Jewish identity, who want an identity with content and direction, who want something more than a symbolic identity, the instability that characterizes contemporary culture has added a sense of urgency to the search. It is these people whose quest for a serious and content-driven Jewish identity—not those who are satisfied with a watered-down symbolic one—that surely is the concern of this conference.

Yet, given all the instabilities and changes that are an endemic part of contemporary life, does it make sense to talk about building a Jewish identity for tomorrow? Does this not assume that the skills of one generation (1) can be transmitted to the next generation, and (2) will be appropriate for it? Does it not assume some absolute truth unaffected by time or space, history or culture? And at a time when the relations between generations have been weakened by the constancy of change, when new is always improved, how likely is it that the youth will be ready to accept the notion of an absolute truth from their elders? Identity building in some sense requires what Keniston called "paternal exemplars" (1965: 204). But they are just what is missing in most places and cases. That is not to say that youth do not sometimes wish they could find people who would be models and guides, who would tell them what they should be. As Erikson has

correctly pointed out, identity formation requires just this sort of guidance, offering a way to bind together the past, present and future into a
coherent whole.

That this is of concern to serious young Jews is dramatically illustrated in the following address given by a young, essentially committed Conservative Jewish young high school senior (whose words I
draw from my own forthcoming ethnography; Heilman, in press).

Identity? A definition? To actually be someone. To maintain certain characteristics
that make you a unique individual. While "identity" is not an extraordinary word
in the English language, it is, I would venture to say, a word to which many
adolescents my age cannot relate. The question is, Why? Why do so many youths
have a problem finding their identities?

High school is a time of inner struggle. Speaking from personal experience, my
struggle was intensified when I was forced to begin the search for my role as a
member of the Jewish society, alongside the secular one. For thirteen years I had
been raised in a Conservative household. I knew no other aspects of Judaism other
than what I had been living. Then, in September of my freshman year, I began to
attend an Orthodox yeshiva. I was faced with a new lifestyle, one that I had never
before explored. The first few months of that year were strange for me. I was
taught to pray differently, dress differently, and open my mind to new possibilities.
And this is where my inner conflict began.

Throughout that year, I was in school from 7:50 in the morning until 5:00 in
the evening. I barely had time to sit and talk with my family, let alone think about
my new experiences. Yet as the months continued, I realized it was time to open
my eyes. I needed to sit down and think about the dramatic changes I was going
through. I remember one day I spent an entire morning in the office of my rebbe
[spiritual leader and teacher], crying. I was so confused and did not know how to
deal with my frustration. I felt as though I was living inconsistently. For nearly
nine hours every day, I would go to school to learn and act like an Orthodox Jew.
However, when I would return home at the end of the day, I had to switch gears
once again and resume my usual lifestyle. As I utilized an entire box of tissues, I
told my rebbe about this conflict I was facing. And the entire time I spoke, he just
sat there, listening, with a subtle smile stretched across his face. Then he began to
speak, and the words that followed were ones that will remain with me for the rest
of my life.

"Elisheva," he said, "nothing is wrong with you. In fact this is a very good
thing. You have shown me that you are thinking, something most kids your age do
not know how to do."

I heard these words yet I had no response.

I spent the next couple of weeks thinking about what my rebbe said, his
voice ringing in my ears. I never did come up with any definite answers to the
problems I was facing. Even now, almost three years later, I often stop to think
about what I am doing.

Everyone wants to have an identity. Feeling lost can be a very scary thing.
And I know that while things may be hard for me now, they do not become easier
next year when I leave home. Without anyone telling me how to observe Judaism,
I am not sure which path I will choose to follow. Yet throughout all of my

grappling, I have learned one thing. That is, for right now, I do not need to have a label. As long as I continue the search for my identity as a Jew in society, I am well on my way. As my rebbe said to me, I have begun to think, and sometimes that is what is most important. (Heilman, in press)

In this brief sermon, which was part of a teen Shabbat program during which adolescents led the service in a large suburban American synagogue, we discover many of the issues raised in the earlier part of this chapter. First is the admission that many youths have problems finding their identities; at the same time, the young woman admits that the whole issue of identity is something adolescents may not be able to relate to. This ambivalence perfectly expresses the search for identity coupled with the feeling that there is not really anyone around who can provide the required guidance, and therefore it is better to simply avoid the issue. Yet, there is no avoiding it, for this is a time of intensifying inner struggle to find an identity. And finding a way to be Jewish enters into this struggle.

The specific problem reported by the adolescent in this passage arises from the fact that she moves from one Jewish world to another each day. The cultural, ideological, and religious diversity and change that is a continuing part of her daily existence makes it very hard for her to reach any transcendent coherent Jewish sense of self. This is no small matter to her; it is "dramatic" as she put it, able to bring her to tears, leading to confusion and fear rather than coherence.

And when at last she bares her soul before her teacher, an Orthodox rabbi, even he does not feel able to give her any absolute direction. Instead, he offers her a kind of vague endorsement that essentially says: "You're to be congratulated for thinking about this but you're on your own." And as she herself admits, it will be even harder when she leaves the shelter of the yeshiva—harder because even more change is coming and she is uncertain who and what kind of Jew she should be in the next setting in which she will find herself.

Can one build an identity for her future? Well, her rebbe, at least as she has perceived his message, seems to say she will have to do it herself, accepting inconsistencies as she has learned to do through high school. Nor is Elisheva unique; she is perhaps only more articulate and concerned than many others, who share her predicament or something like it.

Another speaker, a young man also on the verge of leaving high school and home, reflected on many of the same concerns about Jewish identity. Although sounding more self-assured, he too expressed much of this same dilemma. For him a sense of rootedness in the congregation serves as the touchstone of his identity; but even more important is "the ideological basis I have to form my own opinion about God and about Judaism." Like Elisheva, he tells the congregation that as a Conservative Jew he has been taught to think, to form his own opinions. That independence he implies is also a hallmark of the movement, its essential core and most important contribution to his Jewish identity.

But independence in identity formation, while surely valuable in a culture that emphasizes democracy and youth—as the modern secular societies in America and Israel do—makes "building" an identity a far more uncertain and equivocal prospect. Being on your own may give a sense of autonomy, but it also suggests the possibility that anything goes in that identity. And being able to make the identity choice on one's own does not necessarily insure that the youth making the choice will have the necessary foundation on which to base that choice. As Elisheva reminds us, the issue of a *Jewish* identity is something to "which many adolescents my age cannot relate." In a sense Jewish identity remains for many young people—to say nothing of their elders—a kind of *terra incognita*.

If we are willing to concede a fluid and changing definition of being Jewish, then this sort of autonomous model of identity building and formation is the ideal. But if we wish a Jewish identity that is transcendent both historically and territorially, that serves as a link that will bond Jews to one another and a single people, the autonomous and independent approach may not work too well.

To be sure, there may be no choice. Each age creates the characters best fitted to survive in that age. We in America, where religious or ethnic identity and activity is essentially a matter of one's choosing, have evolved a Jewish identity out of our particular history and circumstances. As Will Herberg explained almost a half-century ago, "it [had] become 'normal' for Jews, and even for synagogue members, to believe in and observe nothing in particular," and thus for the content of their Jewish identity to be equally empty (1950: 323). But American Jews, while feeling a need for such an identity, do not have the wherewithal to construct one. In many if not most cases, they suffer from what some have called "asemitism"—an indifference to or unawareness of Jewish identity. Indeed, to many of the young, Jewish attachments are often incomprehensible and not very important, residues of a past age at best. Moreover, they grow increasingly discomfited by, or more likely oblivious to their Jewish identity the older they get. For many of these young people the Jewish identity they build is simply one that stresses that they are *not* Christian (Bellah 1987: 228). ("I was born Jewish" or "I grew up as a Jew" were the key phrases here.) This sort of a Jewish identity does not have to be raised constantly to the level of conscious awareness. Moreover, to sustain this sort of Jewish identity, it is enough to remember one's feeling of solidarity with other Jews and Jewish history at certain moments: family passages, weddings, funerals, occasions of anti-Semitic assaults, or when Israel or some other Jewish population is in distress. Steven M. Cohen notes that by the end of the 1980s: "a large majority of Jews (roughly two-thirds) feel committed to Jewish continuity and to their identity as Jews. Only about a fifth to a quarter, though, are committed to a particular Jewish content...." (1991: 5).

This sort of Jewish identity is a matter of little more than symbolic heritage. It is not the invigorated and powerful Jewish identity that the young active Jews I have quoted seek. They want something more that will provide them with continuity and stability but also provide direction and compass. That is what they want the "parental exemplars" to build for them. When Jews were not free to assert an individual identity, choose where to live, or with whom to marry, when their right to select a career or to pursue any kind of education was systematically blocked, Jewish identity remained essentially a matter of fate. But in the rapidly changing environment of today, this is no longer the case. That is why the young must ask for help in building an identity. But all we can say to them is, echoing Elisheva's teacher, is: it is good that you are grappling with this; keep it up.

If they can create a vital and active Jewish identity for themselves, maybe that will sustain the entire people. But can they?

That we believe that we might successfully intervene and change what these vicissitudes have wrought is either extraordinarily courageous or audacious. Some will argue that it is possible only when we put people in an environment when we control change, when today and tomorrow are no different from yesterday. This is, I believe, how yeshivas and comprehensive institutions sometimes succeed. They teach youth to disregard the changes around them, and to accept and be satisfied with the old- time religion. But for the rest of us outside those sheltering walls, for those of us who have wandered from the precincts of tradition even slightly, we may just have to go it alone.

References

Bell, Daniel. 1986. "Where Are We?" *Moment* (S): 15–22.
Bellah, Robert N. 1987. "Competing Visions of the Role of Religion in American Society," p.228 in Robert N. Bellah and Frederick E. Greenspahn (eds.) *Uncivil Religion: Interreligious Hostility in America*. New York: Crossroad.
Cohen, S.M. 1991. "Content or Continuity?" *The 1989 National Survey of American Jews*. New York: American Jewish Committee.
Glazer, Nathan. 1985. "On Jewish Forebodings." *Commentary* 8: 36.
————. 1987. *New Perspectives in American Jewish Sociology*. New York: American Jewish Committee.
Goldscheider, Calvin. 1986. *Jewish Continuity and Change*. Bloomington, IN: Indiana University Press.
————. 1975. "Demography and Jewish Survival," p. 132 in M. Himmelfarb and V. Baras (eds.) *Zero Population Growth: For Whom?* New York: American Jewish Committee.
Goldstein, S. 1971. "American Jewry, 1970: A Demographic Profile." *American Jewish Yearbook 1971:* 37.
Heilman, Samuel C. In press. *Synagogue Life: A Study in Symbolic Interaction*. New Brunswick, NJ: Transaction Publishers.
Herberg, Will. 1950. "The Post-War Revival of the Synagogue." *Commentary* 9: 323.
Jaret, C. 1978. "The Impact of Geographical Mobility on Jewish Community Participation: Disruptive or Supportive." *Contemporary Jewry* 4 (Spring/Summer): 9–20.
Keniston, Kenneth. 1965. "Social Change and Youth in America," in Erik H. Erikson *The Challenge of Youth*. New York: Doubleday Anchor.
Toffler, Alvin. 1970. *Future Shock*. New York: Random House.

6

Judaism and Jewish Ethnicity: Changing Interrelationships and Differentiations in the Diaspora and Israel

Stephen Sharot

Descent versus Consent

One feature of what many call postmodernism, and what others call late modernity, is that cultural identities are no longer structured and regulated by the constraints of descent but are structured and transformed by the freedoms of consent. The language of descent—of hereditary qualities, liabilities and entitlements—is being replaced by the language of consent—of agents who choose freely not only their occupations and spouses but also their religions and even their ethnicities (Sollors 1986: 5–6). The transition from traditional to modern societies included the change from ascription to achievement, but this affected mainly occupations, classes, and socioeconomic statuses. Modernization also included the process of nation-building, which involved distinguishing groups in terms of descent. Terms such as "American," "French," and "German" were understood to signify unified cultures to which minority religious and ethnic descent groups might acculturate, and dominant groups into which the minorities might assimilate.

The multiplicity of differentiations in extensively pluralistic postmodern societies, together with processes of globalization, have weakened these distinctions. Cultural diversity (both religious and ethnic) has obscured the notion of a dominant culture associated with purportedly nonethnic carriers; in the absence of a normative standard or reference group, cultural identities come to be perceived as freely chosen and constructed by consent.

The change from descent to consent has not affected all cultural identities in equal measure. One cultural identity which has undergone considerable transformation in the direction of consent is religion. An identity previously passed on, in most cases, from one generation to another has become in some Western societies, especially the United States, a matter of consumer freedom, of private preference and taste (Roof and McKinney 1987; Greer and Roof 1992). Two interrelated changes have contributed to the religion of consent. One change is the substitution of the autonomous self or inner spirituality for the external voices of authority. The other is an ever more extensive religious pluralism, providing the religious consumer with a wide range of choices.

Nowhere is there more emphasis on the right of the individual to choose his or her religious preference than in the United States, and nowhere are the number of religious alternatives so great. The triple melting pot of Protestant-Catholic-Jew, which appeared to be entrenched ever since the 1950s, has been superseded by a religious pluralism which also includes Islam, Eastern religions, and New Age religions (Sarna 1991). Religious privatism is occurring in other societies, but making the self the locus of religion has fewer implications for religious choice if the choice is made within a society with few religious alternatives. Such is the case for Jews in Israel where the high social boundaries between national groups associated with Judaism and Islam and the state-supported near monopoly of Orthodox Judaism serve to restrict choice among religious traditions.

Ethnic identities are also undergoing a transformation from descent to consent, but this is a slower process and is not yet so encompassing as in the area of religion. The very definition of ethnicity includes references to descent or inheritability, and the development of ethnic choice is likely to depend more than religious choice on intermarriages. An increasing number of ethnic intermarriages produces multiple ancestries from which children can choose their preferred ethnicity (Alba 1990).

In the past, the constraints of descent meant that a religious intermarriage was often accompanied by one spouse's adoption of the other spouse's religion; but the understanding of ethnicity as inherited made the adoption of a spouse's ethnic identity problematic. The principle of religious preference has made partners in intermarriage feel less obligated to adopt the religion of their spouses—but conversion of one spouse to the other's religion is still more likely than the adoption by one spouse of the other's ethnic identity. Where religious and ethnic identities are associated with each other, one spouse may effect a differentiation of religion and ethnicity by choosing to adopt the partner's religion without the accompanying ethnic identity. I argue in this chapter that there are signs of this occurring among American Jews.

In comparison with religious identities, which may even become more salient when adopted, the choice of ethnic identities provided by multiple ancestries is likely to be accompanied by a decline in the salience of ethnicity. Recent studies of white Americans have shown that, although most Americans desire a sense of ethnicity, this identity is of middling salience, without a deep commitment to special behaviors or social ties (Alba 1990). Where ethnicity and a particular religious tradition are associated, the decline in the salience in ethnicity may affect loyalty to the religious tradition. Hammond and Warner (1993) present evidence that appears to show that, among Catholics, a decline in ethnic religious loyalty followed a decline in ethnic identity, and that in the past the same process may have occurred among Protestants. The relationships of ethnic and religious identities among most Catholics and Protestants are thought to be different than those among most Jews, and the question arises as to the effects of ethnic intermarriage and religious choice in case of the latter.

Hammond and Warner (1993) follow Abramson's (1980) categorization of three patterns of ethnic-religious relationships in the United States. Jews are given as an example of the first pattern, a fusion of religion and ethnicity, together with other groups such as the Amish and the Mormons. In the second pattern, religion may be one of several bases of ethnicity so that ethnicity extends beyond the religion as, for example, in the cases of Greek Orthodox and Dutch Reformed. In the third pattern, a number of ethnic groups are linked to the same religion so that the religion extends beyond ethnicity as, for example, in the cases of Irish or Italian Catholics. In the second pattern, it is possible to claim an ethnic identity without the religious, whereas in the third pattern the religious identity can be claimed without the ethnic. Such differentiations are claimed to be exceptional in the first pattern, where there is a fusion of religion and ethnicity: denial of either religious or the ethnic identity involves the denial of the other.

Ethnic versus Religious Identity among Jews

Since the entrance of Western Jewry into modernity at the end of the eighteenth century, the number of Jews and Jewish movements claiming a religious or an ethnic identity without the other are too numerous to be designated as exceptions to the pattern of religious-ethnic fusion. Placing the Jews in a category together with the Amish and the Mormons as a case where "religion is the major foundation of ethnicity" is problematic. A person born and brought up as Amish or Mormon who refutes the religion does not remain an Amish ethnic or a Mormon ethnic. A person born Jewish who refutes Judaism may continue to assert a Jewish identity, and if he or she does not convert to another religion, even religious Jews will recognize the person as a Jew. Unlike the Amish and the Mormons, Jews may differentiate between religion and nationality or ethnicity on the basis of their core sacred book, the *Tanach* or Old Testament. A history-cum-mythology tells of a people who became the exclusive carriers of a religion through their covenant with God, and because the religious ceremonies recall and celebrate the history of a people, they lend themselves to secularized reformulation.

According to tradition, the Jewish people existed to serve the Torah, the Jewish religious law, and because there was no other people who subscribed to that law in all its essentials, it was evident that Judaism could not survive the disappearance of the Jewish people. However, by contrast to Christianity with its focus of the life and teachings of the founder, the *Tanachic* focus on the history of a people meant that, once the process of secularization began, it became possible for Jews to identify with the people without the religion. The traditional formulation could then be reversed: the Torah existed to serve the Jewish people. Within secularized contexts, Jews might better be categorized with such groups as the Greek Orthodox, among whom ethnicity extends beyond the religion, than with the Amish or Mormons.

Apart from the secularist ethnic identity, there are also Jews, such as Jewish Christians, who claim that their adherence to another religion does not invalidate their Jewish identity. On the other hand, there have been many Jews in the modern period, primarily during the period preceding World War II, who have identified religiously as Jews and claimed a non-Jewish national identity. Both of these types of differentiation have been associated with persons who are recognized as having been "born Jewish." What is new in recent decades, especially in the United States, is the number of people recognized as "not born Jewish" who have converted to Judaism or participate in Jewish religious ceremonies. This development opens up the possibility of different ethnic identities becoming co-joined with Judaism, somewhat similar to Irish, Italian, and Polish Catholics. A brief historical summary will provide perspective on the differences between Jewish ethnic and religious identities that have emerged in recent decades, and those that emerged in the late eighteenth and nineteenth century.

Beginning toward the end of the eighteenth century, new patterns of Jewish identity developed in Europe and North America in response to secularization and the construction of new collective identities of the modernizing nations. The construction of boundaries of citizenship and identity involved formulating terms for the Jews' inclusion or exclusion. Where secularization was accompanied by a willingness to include the Jews—often conditioned upon the Jews' adoption of the dominant culture and national identity—many reinterpreted their Jewish identity as a purely religious one and eschewed any Jewish national, or what came later to be known as Zionist, identity. Proclaiming that they differed from their non-Jewish compatriots only in terms of religious persuasion, the Englishmen, Frenchmen, Germans, and Americans of the Jewish or Mosaic faith developed forms of Judaism which they believed would allow them both to participate in the wider society and to retain an identity associated with Judaism. Such self-designations indicated a break from the past and a separation from coreligionists who still embodied the characteristics associated with the term "Jew" in the public mind. Although identity was attributed with a differentiated religious meaning, in most cases involvement in Judaism was limited to rites of passage, infrequent visits to the synagogue, and a few yearly observances in the family setting.

In Eastern Europe, where the construction of national and ethnic identities involved marking the Jews as unassimilable outsiders, the inroads of secularism and the breakup of traditional communities led to many Jews' adopting a nonreligious national, ethnic, or cultural Jewish identity. This type was, in some respects, the converse of the type that had become common in Central and Western Europe and the United States. A greater proportion of secularized Eastern European Jews believed that their problems required radical solutions (a socialist revolution or an autonomous Jewish state), and religion was seen as an irrelevance or obstacle to the achievement of such solutions (Sharot 1976; Goldscheider and Zukerman 1984).

The ideologically secularist Jewish movements attracted only a minority of Eastern European Jews, but a number of the secularists joined the mass migration to the West beginning the 1880s, and transplanted their socialist, nationalist, and Yiddish cultural movements to those communities. In the United States the secularist movements of these Eastern European immigrants continued to find support among the second generation, in the years between the two World Wars; secularist ethnic identities remained the preference of a minority, in the 1920s and 1930s there were still anti-religious Zionists, secularist Yiddish culturalists, and a number of anarchist, socialist, and communist Jewish organizations (Glazer 1957; 1990).

Secularist nationalists, especially socialist Zionists from Eastern Europe, were prominent in the first modern waves of Jewish migration to Palestine, and the construction of the national identity of "New Hebrews" or "Israelis" involved attempts to make a clear differentiation between nationality and religion. The emphasis on nationality rather than religion was signaled by substituting the "people of Israel" for God when drawing upon biblical and traditional literature. The dissociation from Judaism in formulations such as "Canaanite," was intended to contrast between the "Hebrew" and the "Jew," the latter being associated with the negatively evaluated condition of Exile (Diamond 1986; Zerubavel 1995).

Both the religious anti-national or a-national Jewish identity espoused by Reform Judaism, and the national, anti-religious or a-religious Jewish identity of secularist Zionism were expressions of an acute preoccupation with the boundaries of identity, and were cast in highly ideological terms. They were examples of modernist movements in their rejection of traditionalist religious societies, their conceptions of progress, and their reinterpretations of the Jewish past to legitimize their endeavors and visions of the future. Reform Jews found their values of social justice in the teachings of the ancient Jewish prophets, and secularist Zionists pointed to the Hebrew kingdoms of antiquity as expressions of the primary ties between the people and the land, and the importance of political autonomy. Finding an appropriate link with a distant past, and disburdening themselves of the dead weight of tradition, both Reform Judaism and secularist Zionism presented themselves as carriers of a mission which would bring further enlightenment and freedom in the future (Sharot 1982: 206–224; Sharot 1996).

A number of events and social processes have resulted in the decline of the modernist, ideological forms of the denationalized, religious Jewish identity and the dereligionized national Jewish identity. The exclusively religious identity that was given ideological and ritual expression in classical Reform Judaism lost its attraction in the face of vehement racial anti-Semitism, the Holocaust, the achievements of the Zionist movement, the establishment of the State of Israel, and the wars between Israel and Arab countries. The second generation tended to be drawn to Conservative Judaism, which combined religion and ethnicity and provided, in its ritual forms, an attractive middle road between the old society Judaism of their parents and the Reform Judaism of the more established American Jews. The third and subsequent generations have shifted more to Reform Judaism—but this brand of Reform Judaism no longer attempts to dispute the national component of Jewish identity, and places greater emphasis on Israel and Zion (Sharot 1976; Wertheimer 1993).

The Six Day War accelerated the decline of both non-national religious identity of the Diaspora and antireligious national identity in Israel. The American Council for Judaism, a Reform offshoot which represented the anti-Zionist position of classical Reform Judaism, virtually collapsed (Wertheimer 1993: 30) and in Israel ideological secularism was marginalized by the interpenetration of politics and religion that followed the war (Liebman and Don-Yehiya 1983). In addition to the Six Day War and its repercussions, two longer-term processes contributed to the decline of a secularist or antireligious Jewish ethnicity, both in the Diaspora and in Israel. One was secularization. Secularist Judaism had its high point at a time when the religious world view was beginning to lose its shared, taken-for-granted qualities, but religion still retained a strong influence over a large part of the community. Once the pervasive influence of religion came to be confined to a minority enclave (or a number of enclaves) which rarely impinge on the daily lives of the majority of Jews, secularist Judaism lost its appeal and was replaced by minimal religiosity (Sharot 1991). Ideological secularism may appear to have retained some importance in Israel, but it tends to take the form of opposition to the religious establishment and to the political power of the religious sectors, especially the *Haredim*, rather than to religion per se.

Another development which contributed to the decline of the anti-religious or a-religious Jewish identity, especially in the Diaspora, was the decline of ethnic cultural elements (especially the Yiddish language), which in the past provided a cultural basis for non-religious ethnicity, and the decline of communal and social structures, such as ethnic neighborhoods and industries where Jews provided the majority of both employers and employees. The destruction of Yiddish culture in Eastern Europe and the decline of its remnants in the West undercut the foundations of a Jewish ethnic identity which could draw upon rich cultural resources with little regard to, or in opposition to, religious heritage. Where an all-encompassing religion has lost its strength, and where non-religious ethnic cultural sources are no longer available, instead of rejecting religious symbols, secularized Jews tend to reinterpret them, extracting their supernaturalist meanings and making them suitable for familial and ethnic celebrations.

Ethnic versus Religious Identity among Jews in the United States

Ideological differentiation and oppositions between religious and ethnic forms of Jewish identity are now rarely made, but there are signs of the emergence of a non-ideological, de-ethnicized religious identity among American Jews. Before delineating and presenting the evidence for this identity, it should be emphasized that this is not the most common form of identity among American Jews, the majority of whom continue to mix religious and ethnic components in their identities. When asked in a 1990 survey what it means to be Jewish in America, 70 percent said it was a cultural group, 57 percent said it was an ethnic group, and 49 percent said it was a purely religious group (Heilman 1995: 105). It would be interesting to probe what American Jews mean by these labels; meanwhile, it is reasonable to assume that the label "cultural group" encompasses both religious and ethnic elements, and that those who said that Jews were an ethnic group did not necessarily mean that they were only an ethnic group. That there is a religious element in the identity of most of the American Jews who prefer the labels cultural, national, or ethnic to purely religious can hardly be doubted: four-fifths identify with one of the Jewish religious denominations, and many of the remainder who termed themselves "just Jewish" were no doubt stating the absence of a religious preference within the orbit of Judaism rather than a Jewish identity without a religious element. We may agree with Heilman (1995: 135) that most American Jews do not associate their identity exclusively with religion; but what is interesting is that nearly half stated that Jews in America were a purely religious group. The religious label is in accord with how most non-Jewish Americans identify Jewish Americans (Lipset and Raab 1995: 60).

American Jews are no longer under pressure to proclaim their Americanness by refuting an ethnic Jewish identity, but soon after Jews found that they could openly proclaim their ethnicity without damaging their Americanness, the very notion of what it was to be an ethnic group or involvement: the disappearance of a uniform, stable, single notion of what it means to be American causes the conception of what it means to belong to a specific ethnic group to lose its clarity. The emerging de-ethnicized religious American Jewish identity is not, as it was in the past, a consequence of discomfort in proclaiming dual loyalties, but rather accompanies the high level of intermarriage within a society which emphasizes religious choice and retains high levels of affiliation to, and participation in, religious institutions. Although the intermarriage rate of American Jewry is no higher than that of many European Jewish communities, the implications of intermarriage on Jewish religious identities are likely to be greater in the United States because organized religion, including organized Judaism, continues to thrive in the United States—more so than in most European countries. For this reason, and because it is the largest Diaspora community and likely to continue to provide the clearest contrast with Judaism in Israel, I will focus on American Jewry and will make only brief comparisons with European Jewry.

Until recently, there was little dependable data on the rate of intermarriage of American Jewry as a whole, but the sample design of the 1990 National Jewish Population Study ensured more accurate information than previous studies by including categories which had not been included in previous surveys: Jews in areas of low levels of Jewish concentration and persons born Jewish who had converted out. The core Jewish American population of 5.5 million, as delineated by the researchers, included 4.2 million who were born Jewish and currently identified themselves as Jews, 1.1 million who admitted to being born as Jews and who currently claimed no religion, and 185,000 "Jews by choice" who were not born Jewish, but identified with Judaism. Of the born Jewish adults in the survey, 31 percent had intermarried. The percentage of born Jews who married persons not born Jewish rose from 11 percent of those who married prior to 1965, to 31 percent marrying between 1965 and 1974, to 51 percent marrying between 1975 and 1984, to 57 percent marrying between 1985 and 1990. Thus, in recent years, for every one new couple consisting of two Jewish partners there are at least two couples in which only one partner is Jewish. The survey counted 1.35 million non-Jews who lived in households that had a Jew in them (Goldstein 1992; Heilman 1995:111–112, 135).

The majority of non-Jews who marry Jews do not convert or identify with Judaism. The calculations of some Jewish sociologists that the number of Jewish adults would increase, or at least not decline, as a consequence of intermarriage (Goldscheider 1986:11–12, 128; Cohen 1988:38–40), were not confirmed by the 1990 survey. One of every five spouses who was not born Jewish in the pre-1965 intermarriage cohort chose to be Jewish either by conversion or self-identification, but this declined to less than one out of every ten in the 1985–90 cohort. Few born-Jewish respondents had converted to non-Jewish religions, and it was evident that in the majority of intermarried households both husbands and wives retained their separate religious identities (Goldstein 1992).[1] In households where one of the marriage partners was a convert, most of the children were being raised as Jews, and in mixed-marriage households one-quarter of the children were being raised as Jews (Wertheimer 1993: 61).

The Reform movement's outreach to non-Jewish partners of Jews was a response to the low level of conversion, and it represented a remarkable break with the nearly 1,600 years Jewish tradition of discouraging conversion to Judaism. The Reform movement also made an important break with Jewish religious law by passing a resolution in 1983 proclaiming that a child born of a non-Jewish mother and a Jewish father would be considered Jewish as long as the child was raised as a Jew (Mayer 1985: 173–5, 232). A survey found that, whereas the great majority of Orthodox Jews would be "upset" if their children married someone Jewish only by patrilineal descent, only one-third of Conservative Jews and one-tenth of Reform Jews said that they would be "upset" (Wertheimer 1993: 176)

Although the majority of non-Jews who marry Jews have neither converted nor chosen to identify with Judaism in recent years, the rapid rise in the intermarriage rate has meant that there is a growing number of "Jews by choice" who make up an increasing proportion of the Jewish population and of synagogue members, especially in the Reform branch.[2] In 1990, 38 percent of American Jews identified with Reform Judaism, 35 percent with Conservative Judaism, and 6 percent with Orthodoxy. About half of the Jews by conversion identified with Reform, and of those mixed-marriage households who identify with any of the Jewish religious denominations, more than half identify with Reform (Wertheimer 1993: 53). The 1990 survey showed that 24 percent of the members of Reform synagogues were families in which one spouse was a convert to Judaism; this compared with 8 percent in the Conservative movement and almost none in the Orthodox movement. Projecting current trends, by the year 2010, 40 percent of Reform Jews will have been born to couples with one born-Jewish parent and one convert, and a further 5 percent will have been born to mixed couples (Lazerwitz 1993).

Thirty percent of Jews by choice have not undergone a formal conversion to Judaism, but in most cases this has not prevented them from participating in the religious and other activities of Jewish congregations (Goldstein 1992; Heilman 1995: 133–134). Data from a number of surveys, including the 1990 survey, indicate that Jews by choice and their children identify with a breed of Judaism which has little or no ethnic connotation. The 1990 survey found that, on most indicators of Jewish religious practice, Jews by choice tend to be either as observant or more observant than those born Jewish. It was reported that 56 percent of Jews by choice belong to a synagogue, compared with 39 percent of the born Jews who identify with a Jewish religious denomination and 5.6 percent of the secular Jews or born Jews who do not identify with any Jewish religious denomination. There was little difference between Jews by choice and born-Jewish religious identifiers in the observance of the two yearly rituals which the vast majority of Jews observe (participating in the Passover seder and lighting Hanukkah candles), but with respect to other practices there were significant differences: 72 percent of Jews by choice fasted on Yom Kippur compared with 58 percent of born-Jewish religious identifiers and 6 percent of Jews who identified themselves as secular; 40 percent of Jews by choice had separate meat and milk dishes compared with 20 percent of born-Jewish religious identifiers and 8 percent of secular Jews; and 68 percent of Jews by choice lighted Sabbath candles compared with 43 percent of born-Jewish religious identifiers and 11 percent of secular Jews. However, only 11 percent of Jews by choice had visited Israel (which may be considered more an ethnic than a religious expression of Jewish identity), compared with 31 percent of born-Jewish religious identifiers and 11 percent of secular Jews (Goldstein 1992).

The authors of a report on Jewish communities in eight large cities, based on data collected between 1985 and 1988, compared three marriage types: the inmarriage with both partners born Jewish, the conversionary marriage with one partner born Jewish and the other a convert, and the mixed marriage with one Jewish and one non-Jewish partner. Although the inmarrieds were slightly more likely than the conversionary to belong to a synagogue (60 percent and 56 percent respectively), the conversionary were somewhat more likely to attend synagogue regularly; 34 percent of the conversionary attended synagogue weekly or more, compared with 28 percent of the inmarried and 6 percent of the mixed. With respect to religious practices, such as the Passover seder, Hanukkah candles, fasting on Yom Kippur, and Sabbath candles, the level of practice of the inmarried and conversionary was identical. Inmarrieds were more likely than the conversionary to belong to a Jewish organization other than a synagogue, to have visited Israel, and to have more Jewish close friends. Reporting on the religion of their three best friends, 75 percent of the inmarried had either two or three best friends who were Jewish compared with 50 percent of the conversionary and 31 percent of the mixed married (Medding et al 1992).[3]

The meanings of Jewish ethnicity, which include tracing ancestry to common putative ancestors, and reference to a common history are not easily acquired among Jews by choice, and the question arises as to whether they are acquired by those with mixed ancestry—the children of intermarriage. Mayer's 1981–83 survey of 117 children of intermarriages found that children of conversionary marriage were more than three times as likely to identify with the Jewish religion than children of mixed marriages. However, although 84 percent of the children of conversionary marriages affirmed that their current religious identity was Jewish, only about one-half identified exclusively with the ethnic ancestry of their Jewish-born parent. Unlike their religious identity, they were prone to see their ethnic identity as an amalgam of two heritages. They were also likely to have a mixed group of Jewish and Christian friends and to reject particularistic notions such as that Jews have a greater responsibility to help other Jews in need than to help all people equally (Mayer 1985: 252–266).

The de-ethnicizing effects of intermarriage on Judaism are not likely to be confined to Jews by choice and their children. The patterns of religious observance of Jews by choice will affect their marriage partners as well, since most religious practices are observed by the family as a unit. The born Jewish partners and their children are not likely to deny the ethnic components of their identity, but it is likely to be of only moderate salience and without deep commitments to special non-religious behaviors or social ties. As Jews by choice come to make up an increasing proportion of Reform congregations, the relatively non-ethnicized Judaism of their families and offspring is likely to affect the congregations as a whole, as well as the movement. The resolution of the Reform and Reconstructionist movements proclaiming that children were Jewish if they were brought up as Jewish regardless of which parent had Jewish ancestry was a recognition of a non-ethnicized Judaism. According to the movements' decisions on patrilineal descent, the supposition of Jewishness conferred by birth must be authenticated by the individual's commitment to Judaism. Thus, the born-Jewish also become Jews by choice.

In moving toward the position of the majority of Americans, that religious identity is chosen rather than ascribed by birth, the Reform movement has also encouraged a personalistic approach to religion which permits each Jew and congregation to choose their own selections from the tradition and religious services (Wertheimer 1993: 191–2). The American Reform movement of the nineteenth and early twentieth century demonstrated its acculturation by rejecting many traditional practices which appeared inconsistent with the values of the Enlightenment and modern culture. Reform Jews today are no longer under pressures from non-Jews to reconcile Judaism with modernity, and there is no longer a self-conscious rejection of Jewish tradition. Since the mid-1960s the Reform movement has made both changes which represent radical breaks with tradition (such as the ordination of women, and patrilineal descent), and changes which draw upon tradition (such as the donning of yarmulkes and prayer shawls, Hebrew usages, and the affirmation of the importance of the *mitzvot* and religious study). In place of the former modernist ideology of religious change signifying progress and a break with tradition, the emphasis now is on congregations' and individuals' ability to choose those religious expressions according to their preferences and tastes. Many Reform temples have compiled their own liturgies, and in 1975 the New Union prayer book provided a number of optional services from which congregations and individuals could choose (Wertheimer 1993: 96–108; Eisen 1992). Jews by choice, many of whom display higher levels of religious observance than born Jews, may well be attracted to a tradition which is not presented as an obligatory system of religious laws, but as a rich source of religious behaviors from which members make selections according to what they find personally meaningful.

The selection of religious expressions by individuals and families can extend beyond the boundaries of a single religious tradition. The 1990 survey found that 10 percent of households in which the marriage partners were both born Jewish and one-third of the core Jewish households always or usually have a Christmas tree. Thirty-seven percent of American Jews stated that they went at least once a year to a non-Jewish religious service (Heilman 1995: 131). Interfaith synagogues, combining Judaism and Christianity, have appeared, as have humanistic synagogues which eschew theistic beliefs. There is also a movement which combined Jewish religious traditions with Eastern religions and self-actualization themes (Wertheimer 1993: 78–80).

Ethnic versus Religious Identity among Jews in Europe

Jews by choice, non-ethnicized Judaism, and movements combining Judaism with other religions are far less evident in Europe despite intermarriage rates that are as high, and often higher, than those in the United States. The changes within Judaism in the United States are made possible by the general features of religion in that society; the operation of religious movements within an open market, the constitutive pluralism and structural flexibility of institutional religion, and the individualistic tendencies in American religion are as evident in American Judaism as they are in American Christianity (Warner 1993). Judaism in Europe is far less pluralistic and flexible; Orthodox synagogues are the dominant type in most European societies, with a much smaller contingent of Conservative and Reform synagogues than in the United States. In the majority of cases Orthodox affiliation does not indicate Orthodox religious observance or a belief in even the most basic doctrines of Judaism (Miller 1994).

Jewish identity varies greatly among the various European communities, but apart from the small ultra-Orthodox communities, which continue the relatively unself-conscious fusion of religion and peoplehood, Jewish identity in Europe is likely to be expressed in secular ethnic rather than religious forms. This trend has been reinforced by the transformation of many Western and Central European societies from relatively homogeneous national societies—in which the Jews were often the most prominent religious or ethnic minority—to multiethnic and multireligious societies. In this context of ethnic pluralism and weak religious institutions and identity among the majority, very few non-Jews who marry Jews convert, and the vast majority of the children of mixed marriages are not raised within the Jewish religion. A de-ethnicized religious Jewish identity is not a likely development, and ethnic Jewish identities will decline in salience.

Ethnic versus Religious Identity among Jews in Israel

In Israel, intermarriage with non-Jews, which is largely confined to Russian immigrant couples, is not a factor in the transformation of identity among Israeli Jews, and the de-ethnicized Jewish religious identity which is emerging in the United States has no basis in Israel. A de-religionized ethnonational Jewish identity may be an appropriate designation for that part of the Israeli Jewish population who say that they are "totally unobservant" of the religious tradition (21 percent in a survey carried out in 1991) and also for some of those who say they observe the tradition "somewhat" (41 percent), as opposed to those who say that they observe the tradition to "a great extent" (24 percent) or "strictly, in all its particulars" (14 percent) (data from Levy et al. 1993: 121). It is true that ideological expressions of secular identity have lost their intensity and appeal, and that, especially after the 1967 war, there was an interpenetration of Jewish and Israeli identities, but these developments should not be taken to signify a strengthening of Jewish religious identity. The greater readiness among Israeli Jews to proclaim a Jewish identity probably reflects changes in the Israeli civil religion with its more extensive nationalization of traditional religious symbols after 1967. Very few Israelis have increased their religious observances and most continue, as before, to participate in highly secularized forms of popular observances, especially the Passover seder and the lighting of Hanukkah candles (Liebman and Don-Yehiya 1983; Liebman and Cohen 1990; Sharot 1990).

The 1991 survey found that average levels of religious observance among Israeli Jews are relatively high and that most, including those who define themselves as "nonobservant," carry out certain practices from the religious tradition. However, from the replies to questions on the reasons for their practices, it is evident that the "nonobservant" and many of the "somewhat observant" see themselves as observing national or family customs and ceremonies rather than religious commandments (discussions of the report are found in Liebman and Katz 1997). When asked to what extent various factors influence their feelings of being part of the Jewish people, the four highest ratings were given to the establishment of Israel, living in Israel, upbringing in parents' home, and the history of Jewish settlement in modern Israel. These were followed by participating in the Passover seder and celebrating Hanukkah, holidays whose traditional religious meanings have been superseded among many Israelis by their national historical meanings and as family gatherings. The "Jewish religion" received a lower rating, toward the bottom of the list. There were no significant differences between the religiously observant and the mildly observant or nonobservant with respect to their beliefs that the establishment of Israel influenced their feelings that they were part of the Jewish people, but only 8 percent of the nonobservant and 33 percent of the mildly observant said that the Jewish religion influences a lot their feelings of being part of the Jewish people compared with 72 percent of the greatly observant and 79 percent of the strictly observant (Levy et al. 1993: 133–136, C68)

Israeli Jews have not been untouched by the trends of religious self-determination and self-selection of postmodern societies, but in the Israeli context religious preference or the religion of your choice have little meaning in the sense of choosing among religious traditions or denominations. Many Israelis have, however, chosen to be clients of religious or quasi-religious cults such as Transcendental Meditation and "I Am" (Beit-Hallahmi 1992). These are client cults providing various forms of therapy and teachings which are believed to allow the clientele to come to a deeper understanding of themselves and the world, maximize their potentials, improve their social relationships, and advance in their careers. Client cults do not require formal membership or organization among the clientele, and participation, which for most is limited and temporary, is not seen to pose any problems for the participants' Jewish identity. Cult movements, which require far greater commitment and regular participation, are seen to pose a danger to Jewish-Israeli identity, and a movement such as Emin has a hard time trying to persuade other Israelis that there is no contradiction between Emin beliefs and Israeli identity. Such movements attract few Israelis, and those concerned with self-realization and self-expression are more likely to do their spiritual seeking among the ephemeral cultural forms of client cults. These can be constituted as their privatized religion, albeit of a fragmentary kind, whereas Judaism remains important for them in providing public expressions of their national identity.

Conclusion

To conclude, the disappearance of the ideological differentiations between religious and ethnic or national Jewish identities in both the Diaspora and Israel has not meant a convergence of Jewish identities. In the Diaspora, the boundaries of the Jews as a discrete ethnic group are breaking down, and in the United States there are signs of the emergence of a non-ethnicized religious Jewish identity. In Israel, public expressions of the religious components of Jewish identity are strong, but a large part of the population has a weak religious Jewish identity at the private level; and Jewish identity as a national identity tends to become encompassed by the Israeli national identity. It would appear that the two major centers of the Jewish population, the United States and Israel, will draw further apart from each other with respect to the differentiations between religion and ethnicity or nation in their Jewish identities.

Notes

1. A 1988 study of Jewish populations in a number of large cities found that the percentage of conversionary marriages (non-Jewish born spouse converting to Judaism) as a proportion of intermarriages declined from 28 percent before 1970 to 13 percent in the 1980s. Comparing the generations, the proportion of conversionary marriages increased from 2 percent of all marriages with Jewish members in the first generation to 6 percent in the fourth generation, but the proportion of mixed-marriages increased from 1 percent in the first generation to 38 percent in the fourth generation (Medding et al. 1992).

2. A survey of a number of Jewish communities in large cities found that 57 percent of conversionary marriages were Reform compared with 30 percent Conservative and 3 percent Orthodox; the respective figures for inmarriages were 43 percent, 39 percent and 9 percent (Medding et al. 1992). The 1990 national survey found that 51 percent of Jews by choice identified with Reform, 32 percent with Conservative Judaism, and 8 percent with Orthodoxy; the respective figures for born Jewish religious identifiers were 43 percent, 40 percent, and 7 percent (Goldstein 1992)

3. The Conservative conversionary married were almost as likely as Conservative inmarrieds to belong to a Jewish organization other than a synagogue, and were more likely to have visited Israel. Thus, for these indicators, the relatively low ethnic identification held only in the Reform camp, but with respect to Jewish friends, the differences between the Conservative inmarrieds and conversionary was just as great as between Reform inmarrieds and conversionary (Medding et al. 1992).

References

Abramson, Harold J. 1980. "Religion," in S. Thernstrom, A. Orlov, and O. Handlin (eds.) *Harvard Encyclopedia of American Ethnic Groups*. Cambridge, MA: Harvard University Press.

Alba, Richard D. 1990. *Ethnic Identity: The Transformation of White America.* New Haven, CT: Yale University Press.

Beit-Hallahmi, Benjamin. 1992. *Despair and Deliverance: Private Salvation in Contemporary Israel.* Albany: State University of New York.

Cohen, Steven M. 1988. *American Modernity or Jewish Identity?* Bloomington: Indiana University Press.

Diamond, J. S. 1986. *Homeland or Holy Land? The "Canaanite" Critique of Israel.* Bloomington: Indiana University Press.

Eisen, Arnold. 1992. "American Judaism: Changing Patterns in Denominational Self-Definition." *Studies in Contemporary Jewry* 8: 21–49.

Gans, Herbert J. 1979. "Symbolic Ethnicity: The Future of Ethnic Groups and Culture in America." *Ethnic and Racial Studies* 2: 1–20.

Glazer, Nathan. 1990. "American Jewry or American Judaism," pp. 31–41 in Seymour Martin Lipset (ed.) *American Pluralism and the Jewish Community.* New Brunswick, NJ: Transaction Publishers.

———. 1957. *American Judaism*, Chicago: University of Chicago Press.

Goldscheider, Calvin. 1986. *Jewish Continuity and Change: Emerging Patterns in America.* Bloomington: Indiana University Press.

Goldscheider, Calvin, and Alan S. Zukerman. 1984. *The Transformation of the Jews.* Chicago: The University of Chicago Press.

Goldstein, Sidney. 1992. "Profile of American Jewry: Insights from the 1990 National Jewish Population Survey." *American Jewish Year Book* 92: 77–173.

Greer, Bruce A., and Wade Clark Roof. 1992. "'Desperately Seeking Sheila': Locating Religious Privatism in American Society." *Journal for the Scientific Study of Religion* 31: 346–352.

Hammond, Phillip E., and Kee Warner. 1993. "Religion and Ethnicity in Late-Twentieth-Century America." *The Annals of the American Academy of Political and Social Science* 527: 55–66.

Heilman, Samuel C. 1995. *Portrait of American Jews—The Last Half of the Twentieth*

Century. Seattle: University of Washington Press.

Lazerwitz, Bernard. 1993. "Basic Characteristics of American Jewish Denominations." *Sociological Papers*, vol. 2, no. 1, Bar-Ilan University: Sociological Institute for Community Studies.

Levy, Shlomit, Hanna Levinsohn, and Elihu Katz. 1993. *Beliefs, Observances and Social Interaction Among Israeli Jews*. Jerusalem: The Louis Guttman Israel Institute of Applied Social Research.

Liebman, Charles, and Eliezer Don-Yehiya. 1983. *Civil Religion in Israel*. Berkeley and Los Angeles: University of California Press.

Liebman, Charles and Steven M. Cohen. 1990. *Two Worlds of Judaism: The Israeli and American Experience*. New Haven, CT: Yale University Press.

Mayer, Egon. 1985. *Love and Tradition: Marriage between Jews and Christians*. New York: Plenum Press.

Lipset, Seymour Martin, and Earl Raab. 1995. *Jews and the New American Scene*. Cambridge, MA: Harvard University Press.

Medding, Peter Y., Gary A. Tobin, Sylvia Barack Fishman, Mordechai Rimor. 1992. "Jewish Identity in Conversionary and Mixed Marriages." *American Jewish Year Book* 92: 3–76.

Miller, Stephen H. 1994. "Religious Practice and Jewish Identity in a Sample of London Jews," pp. 193–204 in Jonathan Weber (ed.) *Jewish Identities in the New Europe*. London: Littman Library of Jewish Civilization.

Roof, Wade Clark, and William McKinney. 1987. *American Mainline Religion: Its Changing Shape and Future*. New Brunswick, NJ: Rutgers University Press.

Sarna, Jonathan D. 1991. "Jewish Identity in the Changing World of American Religion." 91–103 in David M. Gordis and Yoav Ben-Horin (eds.) *Jewish Identity in America*. Los Angeles: University of Judaism.

Sharot, Stephen. 1996. "Traditional, Modern or Postmodern? Recent Religious Developments among Jews in Israel." In *Postmodernity, Sociology and Religion*, edited by Kieran Flanagan and Peter C. Jupp, 118–133. London: Macmillan.

———. 1991. "Judaism and the Secularization Debate." *Sociological Analysis*, 52: 255–275.

———. 1990. "Israel: Sociological Analyses of Religion in the Jewish State." *Sociological Analysis* 51: 63–76.

———. 1982. *Messianism, Mysticism and Magic: A Sociological Analysis of Jewish Religious Movements*. Chapel Hill: University of North Carolina Press.

———. 1976. *Judaism: A Sociology*. New York: Holmes and Meier.

Warner, Stephen R. 1993. "Work in Progress toward a New Paradigm for the Sociological Study of Religion in the United States." *American Journal of Sociology* 98: 1044–93.

Wertheimer, Jack. 1993. *A People Divided: Judaism in Contemporary America*. New York: Basic Books.

Zerubavel, Yael. 1995. *Recovered Roots: Collective Memory and the Making of Israeli National Tradition*. Chicago: University of Chicago Press.

7

On Theory and Methods in the Study of Jewish Identity

Stuart Schoenfeld

Introduction

In addressing the large topic of theory and methods in the study of Jewish identity, this chapter will use a particular recent development in the area as a structure upon which to hang observations about the field as a whole. Its point of departure is an article about the view of Jewish identity found in postmodern social theory. However, this chapter is not about how postmodern theorists understand Jews, but about how postmodern social theorists' interest in Jews acts as a challenge to our understanding of the work that we do.

The winter 1996 issue of *Judaism* contains an article by Michael Weingrad entitled, "Jews (in Theory): Representations of Judaism, Anti-Semitism, and the Holocaust in Postmodern French Thought." Weingrad writes, "Every major contemporary French theorist has made some study of, or pronouncement upon, the Jews and their place in the West. This means that in literature and cultural studies, where the influence of French poststructuralist thinkers is so immense, a strange sort of 'postmodern Jewish Studies' has become a central part of the scholarly discourse" (Weingrad 1996: 79).

Weingrad goes on to consider and to criticize three particular theorists. Jean François Lyotard writes of "jews" (with a small *j*)—those whose social status and self-awareness is based on being outsiders; those who don't fit into the modern social order and are the objects of conversion, expulsion, assimilation, and extermination (Ibid., 82–3). Julia Kristeva, building an interpretation of Judaism around a specific reading of Mary Douglas's interpretation of the (Hebrew) Bible, locates anti-Semitism in a call to return to pagan-feminine aspects of personality that have been repressed (ibid.). René Girard accounts for anti-Semitism as an indication that the human work of transcending the need for sacrificial victims—a task which he sees as the essence of the gospel of the New Testament—has not been completed. In assessing these various authors, Weingrad concludes that while Jews and Jewish identity are central to their theories, their accounts of Jews and Jewish identity are reductionist, ahistorical, and uninformed.

These three are hardly the only contemporary postmodern social theorists to write about Jews; in some ways Weingrad's choices are surprising. On the one hand, Martin Heidegger, a major philosophic source of this school of thought, was an enthusiastic Nazi; and Paul de Man, who popularized deconstruction, was exposed as a wartime collaborator who wrote anti-Semitic journalism. On the other hand, Emmanuel Levinas was a Talmud scholar and principal of a Jewish school; Jacques Derrida is Jewish; Zygmunt Bauman has in his theoretical project worked with at least a good chunk of the literature on modern Jewish identity. Other postmodern theorists are themselves Jews; they may be particular kinds of insiders, but they do write from inside the experience.

What can we make of this phenomenon of "postmodern Jewish Studies"? For those of us who try to connect our work with an abstraction called "Jewish identity" and who believe that over the past thirty years there has developed a small academic field in this area in which there are recognized paradigms of research and interpretation, this phenomenon offers a mirror in which our field is reflected in an unusual way. I would like to suggest four useful things that we may see by looking in this mirror.

1. The mirror may not allow us to see things which we must, in intellectual honesty, consider important; but it shows us central aspects of anti-Semitism and of the identity of Jewish intellectuals to which we may not be paying enough attention.
2. This unusual mirror suggests formulations of the central problem of Jewish identity that are somewhat different from the language we usu-

ally use. In particular, it may be helpful for those of us trying to understand the literature in our field to pay more attention to the concept of ambivalence and to be less exclusively focused on the concept of assimilation.
3. This perspective suggests the more explicit integration of ideological (cultural) issues to supplement the focus on (social) patterns of interaction.
4. Postmodernists are generally critical of social science as part of the "modern project" of social engineering. This critical stance encourages those of us in the field to remember the uncertain outcomes of history and historical trends, and to be cautious about the social engineering implications of our work.

The Significance of Anti-Semitism and Intellectuals to the Study of Jewish Identity

Some years ago, Heilman (1982) offered the observation that a body of literature on American Jews, in which Jewish identity is a central topic, had emerged within sociology, but that it was written and read almost entirely by Jews.[1] The literature to which Heilman refers—and to which those of us at this conference contribute—investigates the extent to which Jews remain a culturally and socially distinct group in those countries in which they are a minority, and the process of change and continuity in the sociocultural patterns of Jewish Israelis. A group of more or less standard survey research questions has been used in numerous studies, asking about affiliation, ritual practice, informal, familial and organizational social networks, and ties with Israel. The analyses of American Jewish identity based on the 1990 National Jewish Population Survey use this kind of data. In the social policy discussions within Jewish organizations, the discussions about Jewish identity most often focus on these survey results.[2] Survey research is supplemented by rich anthropological field studies aimed at explicating the experience of Jewish life (e.g., Goldberg 1987; Kugelmass 1988; Zenner 1988). Historians have examined social patterns, cultural debates, and institution building. There is even a corner of Political Science which focuses on governance, coalition building and policy making of the organized Jewish community (Elazar 1995).

By contrast, the field of "postmodern Jewish Studies" to which Weingrad refers is not interested in the question of Jewish continuity, but in developing a way of interpreting emerging sociocultural trends. Jews are interesting as a high profile case study of the emergence of postmodern identity. To some extent, there is also an interest in the role of Judaism, Jewish self-consciousness, and others' consciousness about Jews in the development of Western civilization and later world culture. In "postmodern Jewish studies," Jewish identity is a focus of theory because it intersects in important ways with the attempt to understand sociocultural transitions. The intersection takes place around interpretations of the Holocaust, of anti-Semitism, and of the cultural role of self-conscious intellectuals.

This rather stark contrast between those of us who study "Jewish identity," and the writing on the topic by "postmodernists" is not meant to suggest that postmodernists are pioneering the literature on Jewish identity and the Holocaust, on the identity of Jewish intellectuals or on the way in which power relationships produce unflattering representations of Jews. There are excellent studies on all these topics by sociologists, anthropologists, historians and those who study the literary and visual arts.[3] What is intended by this contrast is the recognition that this literature has been seen as separate from the topic of "Jewish identity" and that the postmodernists' view of them as central might provoke our own work. Some examples follow.

To begin with, there is the argument that the methodical, premeditated murder of millions of European Jews should be understood as a natural development of modern Western civilization, not an historical aberration or an outgrowth of a long history of anti-Semitism. This interpretation was not invented by postmodernists, but they play a vital role in keeping it current in intellectual discourse.[4] If an interpretation of this kind gains broad acceptance in the academic world, it must have consequences for our field. Most Jews are striving to accommodate their life strategies to the norms and values of modernity. How do they incorporate this view of the genocidal logic of modernity into their self-understandings and life strategies? How do they place it in the context of other interpretations to which they are exposed?

Postmodernists also emphasize the way power relations are deeply embedded in cultural images and within the individual personality. This emphasis returns the psychological response to anti-Semitism to a central place in the understanding of Jewish identity.[5] It is true, we can document a low level of violence or direct discrimination directed at Jews, and we can document the increasing presence of Jews—disproportionate to their representation in the population—in positions of political and economic responsibility. Nevertheless, if little is denied to Jews as individuals, the respectability of a life strategy based on Jewish culture remains under attack. The United States is getting ever farther away from Will Herberg's (1955) view of America as the country of the "three great faiths." In popular culture, Jews seem to be represented as either victims, neurotics, or exotics. Consequently, Jewish identity is either a curse, an illness, or something foreign—a source of shame. And one worries whether these images will merge with older but still enduring views of Jews as clannish outsiders disingenuously posing as insiders. The temptation to identify oneself as a "former Jew,"[6] or to be invisible as a Jew, or to maintain a strict Marrano-like division between being a person in public and a Jew in private,[7] must be enormous.

Postmodernists also pay particular attention to their intellectual heroes who are products of the Jewish encounter with modernity. There is a cottage industry on Freud's Jewish identity and its significance not only for psychoanalysis but also for the postmodern human condition. It has been argued that the Frankfurt school, and Walter Benjamin in particular, were able to see things not only because of their brilliance and training, but also because of their social position as Jews. The same, of course, applies to Franz Kafka. To think of this formidable group of intellectuals as a Jewish group developing a particularly Jewish view of the world is an energizing challenge to those of us who work in the field of Jewish identity studies. It challenges us to trace their influence on contemporary Jewish self-awareness (in contrast to the postmodernists' interest in their general cultural influence).[8] It is also a challenge to focus on the cultural as well as the social dimension of Jewish identity, a point which will be developed presently.

Lastly, if we can reject the temptation to see the postmodernists' interest in Jews as a form of narcissism or as a preference for identifying with dead Jews rather than live ones, the postmodern interest in Jews, their disclaimers to the contrary notwithstanding, contains an argument for Jewish exceptionality.

Ambivalence as a Key Concept Instead of Assimilation

As Himmelfarb has pointed out, the theory either implicit or explicit in most sociological studies of Jewish identity derives from American studies on the acculturation and assimilation of immigrant groups (1982: 62–66).[9] The model is one of gradual loss, over several generations, of distinctive behaviors and attitudes. Gordon's influential book, *Assimilation in American Life*, refined the concept carefully, indicating that assimilation could come in several varieties, that it could take place along separate dimensions and that the assimilating group could develop potentially stable compromise positions.

The postmodern theorist Zygmunt Bauman (1991) uses a rather different way of approaching diversity. Bauman, of course, is following in the steps of literature that critiques the theory of inevitable assimilation. *Beyond the Melting Pot* (Glazer and Moynahan 1973) is usually cited as the first challenge, followed by others. Like other postmodernists, Bauman is concerned with the many non-assimilating minorities around the world and the fragmentation of complex cultures into multiple life-worlds, which are not well understood by each other. It is unclear whether this movement towards fragmentation and disorder is a precursor of chaos, greater human freedom, or more subtle forms of control; but it is a phenomenon to be explained, and Bauman explains it in terms of the failure of assimilation. He presents assimilation as a modern phenomenon, part of the reorganization of the world into nation states with a common culture and an intentionally cultivated identity. Use of the word assimilation to describe a social process is Victorian. Bauman describes what he found in the *Oxford English Dictionary*:

> In the biological narrative of the sixteenth century . . . the term "assimilation" referred to the acts of absorption and incorporation performed by living organisms. . . . it was not before the middle of the eighteenth century that the meaning was generalized into an unspecific *"making* alike." The contemporary use, in which the onus is shifted toward the "absorbed material" and away from the converting organism ('to be or *become* like to . . .), came last, and became common currency only about 1837—exactly about the time when an invitation (or more precisely, *the command*) to assimilate was first sent around by rising nationalism. (Bauman 1991: 103)

Using the experience of Jews as a case study, Bauman finds the modern nation-state's offer/command of assimilation to be in bad faith. Bauman puts his conclusions in the past tense, describing German Jews, "For individuals aspiring to be admitted into the company of the elect, the world turned into a testing ground, and life into an extended trial period. They had confined themselves to a life under scrutiny, to a life-long and never conclusive examination" (ibid.: 112).[10] Moreover, to the extent that they were successful at playing by the new rules, they were more and more disliked as a foreign element threatening to "take over." In addition, if an enthusiast for assimilation took upon himself the task of working within his group to encourage its transformation, he was open to criticism as someone who identified with the minority and its needs. German Jews in the process of assimilation thus found themselves "suspended in the empty space between a tradition which they already left and the mode of life which stubbornly denied them the right of entry" (ibid.: 158). The Jewish intellectuals in which postmodernists are interested are the interpreters of this condition, a condition of "exile, displacement, ambiguity and non-determination [which] happened to be that of the Jews just before it turned into a universal human condition" (ibid.).

If we change the past tense in these sentences to the present, we have a language which is currently used to describe the position of other minority groups, and to explain why the choice/offer/command of assimilation is questioned and rejected. Moreover, in the contemporary politics of diversity, national assimilation is a much less attractive goal. Given the contemporary disenchantment with modernity in general and in particular with the project of building autonomous nation-states based on common culture, what is there to assimilate into? And so we have the current groping for an understanding of contemporary society as a global system moving towards multiple Diasporas.[11] These Diasporas are not "traditional" societies in the anthropological sense, but outcomes of contemporary power relationships. The cultural elements they contain are contested and unstable, but they are self-consciously outside of "the dominant culture" and critical of it. While under some conditions they are still thought of as minority groups on their way to assimilation (in Israel perhaps), this now appears to be unusual.

This is rather different from the cultural pluralism that Gordon and those who shared his perspective saw as one possible form of assimilation. In Bauman's formulation, pluralism is not a stable continuation of multiple cultural traditions. Instead, the failure of assimilation throws the members of a group back on themselves, but with the awareness of the inadequacy of the past culture as a way of life for the future. The social situation, and the social psychology, is one of deep ambivalence and uncertainty. The members of the group have decisively left their pasts behind,[13] without fitting in somewhere else.[14] In this context, debates among intellectuals about culture become central to the study of identity. As Sharot (1997) puts it, the focus for group identity is not descent, but consent.

Jewish Identity as an Ideological Rather than a Social Issue

In the field of Jewish identity studies, a focus on ambivalence as a central problem leads in four directions. Each of them emphasizes the cultural as well as the social dimension of Jewish identity.

First are studies of the relationship between what, for purposes of convenience, may awkwardly be called "intellectuals who are Jewish" and "Jewish intellectuals." The former are those intellectuals who think that the focus for group identity is not descent, but consent, and think of themselves as Jewish but address a larger audience; the latter consists of those who address themselves to specifically Jewish audiences and issues. The two groups overlap; their members know one another and speak to one another. The same person may belong to both, depending on the task at hand. The roles, though, are different, and there are many who fit into one group but not the other. The creative work of both groups is the construction of Jewish identity, one incidentally, the other as a central goal.

The second direction in which such studies lead focuses on the relationship between ideas and group action. The intentional, reflexive (Giddens 1991) construction of identity on the part of intellectuals has social impact when people pay attention to their ideas and act on them. The competition between Jewish ideologies and movements, each with its own intellectual leadership, was the burning question for nineteenth- and early twentieth-century Jews. This competition was never really resolved, and may be taking center stage again.

Third are studies which focus on diversity among Jews. Here the ethnographic descriptions of the multiple worlds of contemporary Jewry are helpful in demonstrating that pluralism is not a slogan but a reality, and that the reality of Jewish pluralism, despite the rhetoric about it, is not well understood.[15]

The fourth direction looks at the relationship of Jewish self-awareness to the complexity and fragmentation of contemporary culture. Within this general area, the shift from print to electronic media has special significance for Jews. Judaism and secular versions of modern Jewish identity have been strongly based on the study and interpretation of texts. Changing communications media, as well as their content, challenge not only the context but what has historically been the cultural process symbolic of the social construction of Jewish identity (Schoenfeld 1993).

Uncertainty of Outcomes in Encouraging Identification

Finally, postmodernists are generally critical of social science as part of the modern project of social engineering. The project of applying rationality to the improvement of the world has had mixed results. Confident predictions of irreversible historical trends have proved to be false. Social engineering has produced unintended, unforeseen, and unfortunate results.

It is also useful for those of us who study Jewish identity to be aware of this skepticism. Within the Jewish world, in contrast to the academic world, the study of Jewish identity is an applied field. Looking at this applied field in the unusual mirror of postmodern social theory suggests that the use of our work for social planning purposes has limitations about which we might want to be self-conscious and public. In significant ways, the change in the social environment between 1990 and 2020 may be as great a change as the change from 1890 to 1920. Planning strategies based on the premise that the future will be like the past, only more so, may be, as Marshall McLuhan put it "looking into the future through a rear-view mirror." Developments in technology and the struggle with ecological limitations may lead within the next generation to a sociocultural environment in which the question of Jewish identity appears in very different ways than it does now. The skepticism about social engineering also suggests that, if the cultural issues of Jewish identity are as central, or more central, than the social ones, we act responsibly by highlighting them rather than avoiding them.[16]

Conclusion

This chapter has used the interest of postmodern cultural studies in Jewish identity as an opportunity to support a theoretical approach to Jewish identity which emphasizes cultural rather than social issues. It has not been the intention of this paper to deny the importance of the study of the social base of Jewish identity. If a group does not support those social institutions which provide channels of communication about the meaning of shared fate—households, friendship networks, schools, synagogues, social services, federations, fraternal associations, newspapers, magazines, e-mail networks, etc.—it is rather difficult to sustain a debate over the meaning of the future of the group's identity or for there even to be a "group" which has an identity. It *has* been the intention of the chapter to promote a clearer theoretical articulation of cultural ambivalence as a central problem in Jewish identity studies, to investigate not just the social settings, but also the issues within them.[17]

Examining this problem may also help to bring into focus the difficult topic of "Jewish exceptionality."[18] Our field is concerned with a group which has been intimately involved in what global human society has become, and this involvement seems to be continuing. It is a rare night on which there is not some item in the evening news in which Jewish history and world history intersect. At least some Jews continue to believe that their high profile involvement with an uncertain, reflexive, and troubled world will continue, and that continuity is a matter of both fate and choice (Dawidowicz 1976).

Notes

The author wishes to thank the Melton Center for Jewish Education, The Hebrew University of Jerusalem, for its assistance while this paper was being written. Writing of the paper was supported by a sabbatical grant from York University.

1. The important early work in this literature, which set a pattern for much subsequent research, is Sklare and Greenblum's book, *Jewish Identity on the Suburban Frontier*, originally published in 1967.

2. The community surveys which follow the American Jewish Committee model are reviewed in Cohen, Woocher and Phillips (1984). This publication includes extensive questionnaire items and a comparison of findings from dozens of studies. There is no conceptual discussion of Jewish identity, but the notes to the inventory of frequently used standard questions (204–208) identify the ones that provide information about Jewish identity and identification, essentially the same ones used in the 1957–8 Lakeville study. Sklare and Greenblum's study also included an item asking people to describe what makes a person a "good Jew" by ranking a list of twenty-two characteristics (321–332). This evaluative item has not been as widely used.

3. Key word searches through Sociological Abstracts (on CD-ROM as Sociofile) and Psychological Abstracts (on CD-ROM as Psychlit) for "Jewish identity" and similar phrases reveals large clusters of papers on the effects of anti-Semitism on Jewish identity, on the Jewish identity of Holocaust survivors and the identity of Jewish intellectuals.

4. A scholar in the field could probably trace the interpretation back to somewhat different "vulgar" Marxist explanations and the more complex views of the Marxist precursors of postmodernism, the Frankfurt school; the argument is also found in Steiner (1971) and Rubenstein (1977).

5. For earlier work, see Lewin (1948) and Herman (1989); for suggestive current work, see Gilman (1986, 1991, 1995), Gold (1996, 1997) and Prell (1992).

6. This is a reference to a century-old joke that has recently become current again. A hunchback and an assimilated Jew pass a synagogue. The assimilated Jew says, "I used to be a Jew." The hunchback says, "I used to be a hunchback."

7. Marrano-like because of the fear that the private Jewish part is a source of public shame.

8. For example, the influence of Freud, Kafka, and the Frankfurt school on Gershom Sholem's and Shai Agnon's understandings of Jewish identity.

9. Himmelfarb distinguishes what he calls the study of Jewish *identification*, "the process of thinking and acting in a manner that indicates involvement with and attachment to Jewish life" (1982:57), from the study of Jewish *identity*, "one's sense of self with regard to being Jewish" (ibid.). In the study of Jewish identification, Jewish identity is operationalized through constructing a set of questions based on certain behaviors and attitudes which distinguished members of the immigrant group from other Americans. The retention or loss of Jewish identity is studied by asking these questions of a sample and analyzing the pattern of responses by generation and other variables.

10. The debt of this passage to Kafka is clear.

11. See Schoenfeld (in press), as this applies to Canadian Jews.

12. Liebman (1973) used the concept of ambivalence as a way of organizing his perspective on American Jewish identity. Whether he uses ambivalence in the same way as Bauman, and the extent to which his work may be seen as a precursor of the postmodernist view of diversity, requires a separate analysis. See also Heilman (1977).

13. If there were sufficient space, it would be possible to show that this applies to Orthodox as well as other Jews.

14. The reply, "that fitting into a stable cultural framework is and always has been an illusion" is an even stronger postmodernist argument than this chapter makes.

15. See Schoenfeld (1977) for an application of the themes of cultural reflexivity, ambivalence and uncertainty, to the study of Jewish identity. Exotic forms— *Haredim* and militant nationalist Jews—have been used as emblems of Jewish identity. In contrast, the forms characteristic of the large majority of Jews— moderate nationalism and not particularly devout religious identification—are generally neglected (Furman's 1987 ethnography is an exception). The life-worlds in which these forms of Jewish identity are considered plausible has been little studied. Similarly, we have some thoughtful and impressive first-person accounts by converts to the various branches of Judaism (e.g., Myrowitz 1995), but no ethnography.

16. It is possible to see Jewish identity as a discussion about moral and ethical issues, that has continued over generations within a historically defined group. Policy decisions are in reality based more on the values of those making them than on a belief in the usefulness, in terms of social engineering, of the studies we academics produce; and that is probably a good thing.

17. See also Schoenfeld (1997a).

18. See Eisen (1991). See also Berman, (1995: 270) who writes "I have been arguing that the Jews, forced by nature and history to be small, have survived and thrived by learning to think big."

References

Bauman, Zygmunt. 1991. *Modernity and Ambivalence*. Ithaca, NY: Cornell University Press.

Berman, Marshall. 1995. "A Little Child Shall Lead Them: 'the Jewish Family Romance,'" pp. 253–275 in Linda Nochlin and Tamar Garb (eds.) *The Jew in the Text: Modernity and the Construction of Identity*. London: Thames and Hudson.

Cohen, Steven M., Jonathan S. Woocher, and Bruce Phillips, eds. 1984. *Perspectives in Jewish Population Research*. Boulder, CO: Westview Press.

Dawidowicz, Lucy. 1976. "Jewish Identity: A Matter of Fate, a Matter of Choice," in *The Jewish Presence: Essays on Identity and History*. New York: Harcourt Brace Jovanovich.

Eisen, Arnold. 1990. "The Rhetoric of Chosenness and the Fabrication of American Jewish Identity," pp. 53–70 in Seymour Martin Lipset (ed.) *American Pluralism and the Jewish Community*. New Brunswick, NJ: Transaction.

Elazar, Daniel Judah. 1995. *Community and Polity: The Organizational Dynamics of American Jewry*, 2nd edition. Philadelphia: The Jewish Publication Society of America.

Furman, Frida. 1987. *Beyond Yiddishkeit: The Struggle for Jewish Identity in a Reform Synagogue*. Albany: State University of New York Press.

Giddens, Anthony. 1991. *Modernity and Self-Identity*. Stanford: Stanford University Press.

Gilman, Sander L. 1986. *Jewish Self-Hatred: Anti-Semitism and the Hidden Language of the Jews*. Baltimore, MD: Johns Hopkins University Press.

———. 1991. *The Jew's Body*. New York: Routledge.

———. 1995. *Jews in Today's German Culture*. Bloomington, IN: Indiana University Press.

Glazer, Nathan and Daniel Patrick Moynahan. 1973. *Beyond the Melting Pot: The Negroes, Puerto Ricans, Jews, Italians, and Irish of New York City*. Cambridge, MA.: M.I.T. Press and Harvard University Press.

Gold, Nora. 1996. "Putting Anti-Semitism on the Anti-Racism Agenda in North American Schools of Social Work." *Journal of Social Work Education* 32(1): 77–89.

———. 1997. "Canadian Jewish Women and Their Experience of Anti-Semitism and Sexism." Paper presented at the International Workshop on Jewish Survival—The Identification Problem at the End of the Twentieth Century," 18–19 March, Bar-Ilan University Sociological Institute for Community Studies.

Goldberg, Harvey E. 1987. ed. *Judaism from Within and Without: Anthropological Studies*. Albany, NY: State University of New York Press.

Gordon, Milton M. 1964. *Assimilation in American Life: The Role of Race, Religion and National Origins*. New York: Oxford University Press.

Heilman, Samuel. 1982. "The Sociology of American Jews: The Last Ten Years." *Annual Review of Sociology* 8: 135–160.

———. 1977. "Inner and Outer Identities: Sociological Ambivalence among Orthodox Jews." *Jewish Social Studies* 39(3): 227–248.

Herberg, Will. 1955. *Protestant-Catholic-Jew: An Essay in American Religious Sociology*, rev. ed. Garden City, NY: Doubleday.

Herman, Simon N. 1989. *Jewish Identity: A Social Psychological Perspective*, 2d ed. New Brunswick, NJ: Transaction Publishers.

Himmelfarb, Harold. 1982. "Research on American Jewish Identity and Identification:

Progress, Pitfalls, and Prospects," pp. 56–95 in Marshall Sklare (ed.) *Understanding American Jewry*. New Brunswick, NJ: Transaction Publishers.

Kugelmass, Jack, ed. 1988. *Between Two Worlds: Ethnographic Essays on American Jewry*. Ithaca, NY: Cornell University Press.

Lewin, Kurt. 1948. *Resolving Social Conflicts: Selected Papers on Group Dynamics*. New York: Harper and Brothers.

Liebman, Charles. 1973. *The Ambivalent American Jew*. Philadelphia: The Jewish Publication Society of America.

Myrowitz, Catherine Hall. 1995. *Finding a Home for the Soul*. Northvale, NJ: Jason Aronson.

Prell, Riv-Ellen. 1992. "Why Jewish Princesses Don't Sweat—Desire and Consumption in Postwar American Jewish Culture," pp. 329–359 in Howard Eilberg Schwartz (ed.) *People of the Body*.

Rubenstein, Richard. 1977. *The Cunning of History*. New York: Harper.

Schoenfeld, Stuart. In press. "Reluctant Cosmopolitans: The Impact of Continentalism, Multiculturalism and Globalization on Jewish Identity in Canada," in Steven M. Cohen and Gaby Horencyzk (ed.) *National and Cultural Variation in Jewish Identity*. Albany, NY: State University of New York Press.

———. 1997a. "Bar/Bat Mitzvah in Their Social Context: Late Modernity, Identity And Jewish Education." *Journal of Jewish Education* 63 (3): 11–16.

———. 1997b. "Recent Books on Jewish Identity." *Contemporary Jewry* 18: 150–158.

———. 1993. "Texts, Media and Jewish Identity." *Agenda* 1 (2): 14–19.

Sharot, Stephen. 1997. "Judaism and Jewish Ethnicity—Changing Interrelationships and Differentiations in the Diaspora." Paper presented at the International Workshop on Jewish Survival—The Identification Problem at the End of the Twentieth Century," 18–19 March, Bar-Ilan University Sociological Institute for Community Studies.

Sklare, Marshall and Joseph Greenblum. 1979. *Jewish Identity on the Suburban Frontier,* 2d ed. Chicago: University of Chicago Press.

Steiner, George. 1971. *In Bluebeard's Castle : Some Notes towards the Definition of Culture*. New Haven, CT: Yale University Press.

Weingrad, Michael. 1996. "Jews (in Theory): Representations of Judaism, Anti-Semitism, and the Holocaust in Postmodern French Thought." *Judaism* 45 (1, no. 177): 79–98.

Zenner, Walter, ed. 1988. *Persistence and Flexibility: Anthropological Perspectives on the American Jewish Experience*. Albany, NY: State University of New York Press.

Part Two

Jewish Community Boundaries

8

Jewish Identity and Survival in Contemporary Society: The Evidence from Jewish Humor

Christie Davies

Introduction

The survival of Jewish identity is one of the most remarkable socio-logical phenomena of the last two thousand years. Most peoples in exile, however brilliant their culture, disappear. They intermarry and adopt the language, religion, and customs of the host community that surrounds them. The ancient Greeks founded settlements that stretched from Marseilles to Peshawar, from Pontus to Alexandria. In their day these Greek foundations enjoyed a vigorous high culture and their citizens had a shared sense of superiority over their "barbarian" neighbors. Today they are but food for archaeologists.

By contrast the descendants of the Jews who were forced into exile by the Romans formed a permanent living Diaspora. Despite centuries of pressure to convert, assimilate, and intermarry and despite the persecution, expulsion, and murder of entire communities by anti-Semites there is a visible Jewish presence in every continent. A citizen of Tel Aviv visiting cities as far flung as Sydney, Johannesburg, Buenos Aires, Bombay, Moscow, Manchester, Montreal, or Miami knows that he can seek out a Jewish community with whose members he will have much in common. The Wends of Schleswig, the Welsh of

Patagonia, the Africans of Abercregan, the Ulstermen of the Appala-
chians, the Norwegians of Lake Wobegon are but museum pieces, but
the Jews remain.

The basis of the Jews' unusual survival in exile is twofold. First,
they were both a people and a religion, and secondly they had previous experience of surviving in exile, first during the period of bondage
in Egypt after which they received the Mosaic law, and later, in
Babylon, when the law was edited in the form we know it today
(Davies 1982; Porter 1976: 2–6). The law is almost a prescription for
surviving exile, for it emphasizes separation as the basis of holiness
(Douglas 1970, 1975). The rules governing everyday life such as the
dietary laws (Ibid.), the sexual prohibitions (Ibid.; Porter 1976: 82–93;
Soler 1973), the rule of *shatnes*, the keeping of the Sabbath in a
manner different from other days all emphasize the maintenance of
boundaries between categories that must be kept separate. As such
they act as a perpetual metaphor and reminder of the key boundary
that must be maintained at all costs, between Jews and Gentiles, so
that the integrity of the Jewish people may be preserved. The rules
also assist in the prevention of intermarriage with outsiders, a matter
of little importance to a host people absorbing and assimilating immigrants on their own ancestral territory, but vital to the survival of
a people in exile who lacked a homeland for nearly two thousand
years.

Today at the end of the twentieth century, nearly a half-century
after the foundation of the State of Israel, Jewish identity in Western
Diaspora communities does appear to be under threat. It is possible to
envisage a future in which these communities fade away through secularization and intermarriage, leaving behind only a small, highly Orthodox remnant. Rather than complacently seeing Jewish humor through
functionalist spectacles as one of the means of preserving and conserving Jewish identity and as an identifier and a source of esoteric
pleasure, it makes more sense under these circumstances to focus on
the way in which Jewish jokes reflect contemporary threats to Jewish
identity, and to the maintenance of the patterns of behavior that under-
pin Jewish identity. The two threats to Jewish identity to be considered in the context of an analysis of Jewish joking are those posed by
Jews who undergo conversion to another religion and by those Jews
who choose to marry out. The rules preserving Jewish identity that are
the main subject of humor are the dietary laws; such humor seems to

arise from situations where Jews have begun to break these rules, but where the rules nonetheless retain a degree of moral force.

Conversion and Assimilation

In the nineteenth and very early twentieth centuries the main threat to Jewish identity was the possibility that large numbers of Jews might convert to Christianity to obtain social or economic advancement. Baptism was the entrance ticket to many careers from which Jews were otherwise excluded, or as Heine put it, the "passport to European civilization" (Rosten 1970: 133). Benjamin Disraeli could never have become Prime Minister of the United Kingdom had not his father had his children baptized in the Church of England after a quarrel with his synagogue. The fathers of Heinrich Heine, Alfred Adler, and Karl Marx all went through conversions of convenience (Oring 1984: 24–74; Telushkin 1992: 134). According to Rabbi Joseph Telushkin "perhaps one-third of Berlin's Jews became Christians between 1800 and 1850" (1992: 134), and in the year 1900, 559 Viennese Jews from a Jewish population of 146,926 did so (Oring 1984: 70), though some of them in each case may have had other reasons for converting. Whatever the reason, such a hemorrhage must have been perceived as a threat to Jewish identity by the remaining Jews, particularly when some of the converts or their descendants also became anti-Semites. Apostasy is linked to destruction not only linguistically but historically.

Jewish humor in the face of this threat to Jewish identity has tended to play with two related themes. First, the depiction of the converts as having abandoned Judaism for Christianity for self-interested reasons that had nothing to do with religion. Second, the portrayal of the conversion as ineffective—the convert retains Jewish habits and characteristics and has failed to become a full-fledged, fully accepted Christian. He or she is neither one thing nor the other. As the proverb has it:

"A meshumed iz nit keyn goy un nit keyn yid." [An apostate is no gentile and no Jew] (Kumove 1986: 70)

Leo Rosten writes of an early example of such a joke:

Daniel Abramovich Chwolson (1879–1920), a Jewish professor under the Tsars, had been converted to the Greek Orthodox faith. When asked if he had done this out of conviction or expedience, he dryly replied, "I accepted baptism entirely out of conviction—the conviction that it is better to be a professor in the Imperial Academy in St. Petersburg, than a teacher in a *cheder* in Vilna." (1970: 133) Another version goes, "...than a *melamed* in Eyshishok." (see also Telushkin 1992: 133–34)

There are many later examples of jokes on these two themes of self-interest and ineffectiveness:

For the past five years Neidel had been a Christian Scientist. One Sunday morning as he was leaving the house to go to church, his wife seized his arm. "What's the matter with you?" she cried. "You're wearing a *yarmulkah*!" "Oy I forgot!", groaned Neidel. "It's my goyisheh kop!" (Wilde 1986: 167; also Telushkin 1992: 136)

A Jew converts to Catholicism and eventually becomes a priest. He is invited to speak in a church. After the service the local bishop congratulates him. "Everything was fine," he says, "only next time, maybe you shouldn't begin by saying, 'Fellow goyim.'" (Telushkin 1992: 136; Novak and Waldoks 1981: 94)

Three Jewish converts to Christianity are sitting in a country club, each explaining how he came to convert.
"I fell in love with a Christian girl," the first man says. "She wouldn't marry me unless I became a Christian. I loved her and so I did."
"I wanted to get promotion at my bank," the second man says. "I knew there was no point in even applying for a higher position if I was Jewish. So I converted."
"And I converted," the third man says, "because I became convinced of the greater truth of Christian theology, and of the ethical superiority of the New Testament's teachings."
The first two men glare at him: "What do you take us for, a bunch of goyim?" (Telushkin 1992: 136–37; also Novak and Waldoks 1981: 95)

It isn't often that an honest-to-goodness true anecdote is offered which is genuinely funny, but this one was reported in the staid *Catholic Beacon*. The ending fairly bursts with unconscious humor:

Arthur Feldman, formerly of the Jewish faith, has completed his training period and has taken the required Communion. He will shortly graduate from the Church of the Transfiguration. (Spalding 1973: 302)

American banker Otto Kahn was Jewish by birth but had converted to Christianity. He was once walking with a hunchbacked friend when they passed a synagogue.
"You know, I used to be a Jew," Kahn said.
"And I used to be a hunchback," his companion replied. (Telushkin 1992: 125)

All these jokes undermine either the sincerity or the effectiveness of conversions out of and away from Judaism. A real threat is turned into a source of ludicrous comedy. However, there is a sense in which the jokes have become dated, due to the decline in "establishment" anti-Semitism, at least in English-speaking countries, and due to secularization and a marked decline in levels of Christian belief and practice throughout most of Western Europe (Wilson 1982). It is no longer much of a disadvantage in Britain to be Jewish or of much advantage to be a practicing Christian when seeking high office. Perhaps for this reason, Britain's Jews have moved to the right, and Jews have held many of the most powerful and prestigious positions in successive Conservative administrations.[1] The former British Chief Rabbi now sits in the House of Lords as Lord Jakobovitz, having been ennobled by the Queen at the request of Mrs. Thatcher. In Britain as in America, it is no longer necessary for Jews to renounce their faith or their identity to enter the Establishment. Should they choose to do so anyway, they will find that their Christian neighbors have come out to meet them in a common agnostic and secular spiritual wilderness.

In the latter half of the twentieth century, a new and very different threat to Jewish identity has emerged—the NRMs, the New Religious Movements. Jews no longer convert to Protestantism, Roman Catholicism, or Eastern Orthodoxy for social advantage, but instead have been joining new cults existing on the margins of society, membership in which offers no benefits or kudos and makes heavy demands on the members' time, resources and commitment. Charles Selengut has noted that:

> Studies of new religious movements report a disproportionate number of Jewish converts. Although Jews comprise only 2.5 percent of the total American population, various studies show that between fifteen to eighteen percent of Hare Krishna devotees, 6 to 8 percent of Unification Church members and 9 percent of Church of Scientology members come from a Jewish background. Disproportionately high levels of Jewish membership are also reported in some lesser-known cult movements. (Selengut 1988: 95)

We may also add that the cult "Jews for Jesus" has by definition a highly Jewish membership, and that according to Rabbi Joseph Telushkin, Jews are disproportionately represented among Americans attracted to Eastern religions and mysticism. He quotes an estimate that "one-third or more of those who journey to India to study with spiritual masters are Jews" (1992: 129). There is no question of status-seeking here. You don't get into a elite gentile country club by handing out Jews for Jesus leaflets; nor does it help your professional career to parade down Oxford Street in London in a saffron robe chanting "Hare Krishna."

Perhaps for this reason there are few Jewish jokes about the conversion of Jews to New Religious Movements, though the assiduous Rabbi Telushkin has one:

> An elderly Jewish woman sets out from her home in Brooklyn for India. She travels by foot over hilltops and mountains. She crosses valleys and streams, and finally she arrives in a small rural village alongside a steep mountain. At the top of the mountain is an ashram, housing a great spiritual leader, the guru Baba Ganesh.
>
> It takes all the woman's determination and many long hours to reach the mountain top. There she announces that she has come to see the guru.
>
> "Oh, that is impossible," the guru's assistant tells her. "Nobody is allowed to see the great guru for the next six months."
>
> "I must see him," the old woman cries. And she sits at the doorstep of the ashram without food and water for three days.
>
> The keeper of the gate is desperate and finally makes her an offer. "Okay, you can go in to see our leader, but you must promise to say no more than three words."
>
> The woman promises, and the man leads her down a long marble walkway. Tapestries and flowing fabrics cover the walls. They turn into a room at the end of the hall and enter through the archway. A young man is sitting on a bamboo mat in a yoga position, chanting, "*Om chanti*."
>
> The woman steps in front of him and pleads: "Come home, Sheldon." (1992: 129–30)

This is more a joke about Jewish mothers than it is about conversion. It is also noteworthy that the Jewish mother's son Sheldon has been upwardly mobile as befits a good son and has made it to leader and great guru of the ashram with the appellation Baba Ganesh, after the elephant-headed Hindu god of wealth. The entire tableau is absurd and the joke says nothing about his original conversion.

However, many serious Jewish (and non-Jewish) commentators on conversions to New Religious Movements have also failed to understand the nature of the problem. It has been alleged for instance both that the converts are psychologically disturbed and that the religious cults have brainwashed them. However, evidence on cults supports neither of these suggestions (Barker 1984; Selengut 1988)—and in any case, can it really be argued with conviction that (American) Jews have more psychological problems and are more easily brainwashed than gentiles? The views of the new cults are no further removed from the mainstream Western views, and certainly smack of no anti-Semitism, when compared with various extreme Marxist political

groups, such as Trotskyites and Maoists, which have had a disproportionately high Jewish membership in the past (Cohen 1980). Yet the
latter were not referred to as having psychological problems or having
been brainwashed, despite some evidence to that effect; so why should
we unjustly stigmatize cult converts in this way? Perhaps significantly,
several of Selengut's sample of Jewish converts to the cults had tried
Trotskyism first before entering their present organization, and a very
high proportion had been involved in idiosyncratic activities such as
vegetarianism, yoga, and the antinuclear movement.

No external explanation of these new-style conversions away from
Judaism is available to feature in Jewish jokes; such conversions cannot be reduced to some other social phenomenon that can be ridiculed
as mere self-interest. Rather they indicate a problem within American
Judaism, which, in the long run, could constitute a threat to the preservation of Jewish identity. It is not the numbers of converts that is the
problem—for in absolute terms the numbers converting to these cults
is trivial—but rather the fact that proportionately far more young adults
from a Jewish than from a Protestant or Roman Catholic background
choose to desert their original faiths in this dramatic way. For this
reason it is worth studying the disturbing testimony by the converts as
to why they left, as reported by Jewish sociologists like Selengut.
They perceived their Jewish parents as having a secular rationalist
outlook in which Judaism had become a combination of a folk religion
of brief Chanukah candles that required little effort or commitment,
and the humanistic values of upper-middle class white liberals (Selengut
1988). From other American sociological surveys it is clear that this
description fits a substantial proportion of the American Jewish population (Glazer 1990: 34–35; Herberg 1960: 192, 196; Telushkin 1992:
130). How stable or transmittable is a "transformationist" religion without a spiritual dimension?

The great strength of Judaism that has enabled the Jewish people to
survive in exile is that it is both a religion and a national tradition. If
either of these dimensions is weakened, then the other will also fail.
The problem may be stated like this: if a religion becomes purely
instrumental so that its sole purpose becomes the survival of the group,
then the group will not survive. The transformationist Durkheimian
Judaism propounded by American liberals is not viable as a means of
conserving Jewish identity (Durkheim 1965; Herberg 1960: 198, 210).

Intermarriage

A second major threat to Jewish identity in the West is the high incidence of inter-marriage in modern Britain and America. Until the early 1960s, American Jews were very largely endogamous (in the 1930s the intermarriage rate was only 3 percent) but by 1985–90 more than half of all Jews who married, married non-Jews (Norden 1991: 36–43; Waxman 1990: 75). The trend can be seen in table below.

The falling incidence of gentile partners who convert to Judaism is somewhat misleading, since there is now less pressure on a non-Jewish woman marrying a Jewish man to convert, following the ruling by the Central Conference of American Rabbis (Reform) that any child with one Jewish parent, who had been raised with a Jewish identity, would be regarded as Jewish (Telushkin 1992: 210). Nonetheless the National Jewish Population Survey (of America) indicates that only 28 percent of the children of mixed households are reported as being brought up to be Jewish (Norden 1991: 42). There are in the United States 700,000 half-Jewish children being brought up in another religion; they are mostly the children of intermarriages where the non-Jewish parent has not converted. We find a further 415,000 (mainly) adult offspring of intermarriages who are practising another religion and 210,000 Jews who have converted to another religion, presumably as a result of marrying a spouse of that religion (Ibid.: 41).

The problem arises because American Jews live in a country where the dominant milieu is Christian and where citizens are expected to worship at the church of their *choice,* which is not necessarily that of their parents or the one they were born into. If Methodists become Presbyterians or vice versa, it doesn't much matter for either denomination since their new recruits compensate for their losses. Judaism is not a proselytizing religion, but the religion of a people, and cannot

Table 8.1

Date	% of Intermarriages in United States	% of Gentile Partners going over to Judaism
Before 1965	10%	20%
1965–74	25%	18%
1974–84	42%	15%
Since 1985	over 50%	10%

From Norden (1991:41), based on the National Jewish Population Survey use this strategy. Likewise for the Christians it doesn't matter if ethnic identity is lost through intermarriage or denominational shift. A person of Polish-Irish-Italian-Cuban descent is still a Roman Catholic. Welsh Baptists or Danish Lutherans who crown their upward mobility by becoming Episcopalians are still Protestants. A large proportion of the children of intermarriages between a Jew and a gentile are probably agnostics, but they will tend to have a Christian social identity because the majority has, and because a strident rejection of religion is not socially acceptable in America; in Britain they would probably call themselves Church of England because it is the established church. Only in Israel is the situation different. Anybody married to a Jew, or who is a child or grandchild of a Jew has the right to enter Israel and obtain Israeli citizenship under the Law of Return. A high proportion of recent immigrants from the former Soviet Union are not actually Jewish, but have family members who are. As Norden puts it, "Many new Israelis have been registered as Jews who were not Jews before and would not be Jews anywhere else" (1991: 39). However, their descendants will be ordinary Jewish Israelis because that is the norm in Israel; they will be absorbed into the majority culture. They may not be devout or observant—but then it is doubtful whether the Christian offspring of mixed marriages in Britain or America are devout or observant Christians.

There are two interesting Jewish jokes that comment on these situations:

> A Jewish wife is not just a luxury, she's a means of transportation. [Russia, 1980s; Jews and spouses of Jews could leave the Soviet Union to go to Israel. Other Soviet citizens were trapped in that prison-house state.]

> What do you call the grandchildren of intermarried Jews? Christians. (Attributed to Milton Himmelfarb in Norden 1991: 42).

In the past, Jewish families were shocked and horrified if one of their members married out, and some Orthodox Jews even observed the laws of mourning for a son or daughter who intermarried. Rabbi Telushkin has "one story [that] tells of a man who married a non-Jew, whereupon his brother sat seven days of *shiva*, mourning him as dead. On one of the days, his intermarried brother paid him a condolence visit! (1992: 138)

There seems to have been relatively little joking about intermarriage among the observant Jews of Eastern Europe. Most jokes about marrying centered around the traditional marriage broker, the *shadchen* (i.e., it was assumed that marriages would be arranged within the community). Later, when jokes about intermarriage did emerge in America they tended at first to reflect the antipathy with which it was regarded.

> David came from an Orthodox family. One day he announced, "Mama, I'm going to marry an Irish girl named Maggie Coyle!"
> The woman froze in shock.
> "That's nice, David," she said, "but don't tell your papa. You know he's got a weak heart.
> "And I wouldn't tell your sister, Ida. Remember how strongly she feels about religious questions.
> "And don't mention it to your brother, Louis. He might give you a bust in the mouth.
> "Me, it's all right you told. I'm gonna commit suicide anyway." (Wilde 1978: 143; see also Telushkin 1992: 137–38)

Columnist David Schwartz told this one in the *California Jewish Voice*:

> A Jewish boy was in love with a girl of another faith. The boy's father was against the marriage, but the son married her anyway.
> The son was employed in his father's store and on the Sabbath following the honeymoon, the bridegroom failed to show up at the place of business. He explained to his father that his wife would not allow him to work on *Shabbes*.
> "Aha!" exclaimed the father, "Didn't I warn you not to marry her?" (Spalding 197: 390–91)[2]

JAP Jokes

However, following the rise in the incidence of intermarriage noted earlier, a new Jewish joke-cycle appeared in America in the late 1970s, and rapidly spread to Jews in other countries: the JAP jokes about the Jewish American Princess. The JAP of the jokes is vain, pampered, spoiled, sexually manipulative, materialistic, bossy, uncultured, loud, overdressed and bedecked with jewels, a bubble-head, a younger version of the Jewish wife and spoiled by a doting father (Alperin 1988: 4):

> How many Jewish American Princesses does it take to replace the light bulb?
> Two—one to pour out the Tab, the other to call daddy. (Novak and Waldoks 1981: 126)

> A female skull was accidentally uncovered during an oil exploration in Beverley Hills, California on October 7th 1958. Archaeologists from UCLA have estimated the skull at more than 22,000 years. Through carbon measuring techniques they have also ascertained that the skull belonged to a 5–foot 5–inch girl in her late

teens weighing approximately 140 pounds. Predicated on the discovery of a primitive nose job, wooden orthodontic braces on the teeth, and transparent fish-scale contact lenses, the consensus is that this was the first Jewish American Princess. (Burns and Weinstein 1978: 55)

What do JAPs most often make for dinner?
Reservations. (Rosten 1970: 168; see also Sequoia 1982)

How do you tickle a JAP?
Gucci, gucci, goo. (Dundes 1987: 70)

What's a JAP's idea of perfect sex?
Simultaneous headaches. (Ibid.: 71)

What is Jewish foreplay?
Thirty minutes of groveling. (American Jewish 1970s; also Dundes 1987: 71)

These jokes have been attacked by some American commentators as anti-Semitic and as an expression of misogyny (Alperin 1988; Fuchs 1986). This is nonsense. The jokes are entirely of Jewish origin and must at times be puzzling to gentiles because they do not have access to the appropriate comic scripts. Some gentiles will not understand the jokes for the same reason they did not understand the earlier generation of Jewish mother jokes, when they failed to realize that for the purposes of the joke mothers are assumed to be demanding, nagging, over-possessive women who dote on their sons and expect "an equally all-devouring devotion on his part while pretending to be self-effacing" (Raskin 1985: 217). Without the necessary esoteric knowledge, anti-Semites can hardly be expected to master, let alone invent and exploit, these jokes. No doubt from time to time a JAP joke will be taken over and used in an anti-Semitic way but such a fate can overtake almost any ethnic joke (Davies 1990). It doesn't make these jokes anti-Semitic. Likewise the term JAP can be used as a hostile term of abuse by gentiles but, then, they have plenty of other negative epithets to choose from.

The anti-Semitism thesis is nonsense; but the misogyny thesis is nonsense on stilts. There are no corresponding jokes about Irish American Princesses, Puerto Rican American Princesses, Costa Rican American Princesses, Japanese American Princesses or WASP American Princesses.[3] The jokes are told by American Jews about a section of their own women-folk, *not* about women in general. As usual it is the jokes that could be invented and told but are not that explain the true significance of those that are in circulation (Davies 1990: 84–101).

The jokes have come about because of a clash between duty and temptation that did not arise in the past in America. In the past it was taken for granted that it was the duty of every male Jew to seek a Jewish spouse and to ensure the continuity of Jewish life from one generation to the next. Today there is a conflict between this duty and the temptations to intermarriage offered by the increasingly open and secular societies of present-day Britain and America. It may well be that individual Jewish men are more likely to end up happily married by following the path of duty than by sampling the variety of temptations offered by the female gentile world, but that is beside the point. The point rather is that Jewish duty is a community-generated and imposed constraint on a choice that society at large suggests should be made in an irrationally individualistic and romantic way. As increasing numbers of Jewish men give in to the temptations of intermarriage, so there has been a wave of jokes making fun of the women they ought to marry or have married. Some critics of the jokes have even claimed that the jokes will cause an increased rate of intermarriage and assimilation (Alperin 1988: 9–10), but this is simply a Jewish twist on political correctness. Jokes are not thermostats controlling human behavior, but thermometers that give us information about what is going on (Davies 1990: 307–324).

Jewish women may well object that they are caught in the same dilemma but that they do not tell distinctive jokes about male Jewish American Princes. However, far more Jewish men than Jewish women marry out, presumably leaving a residuum of Jewish spinsters (Telushkin 1992: 210, n. 11). Also, women have a stronger internalized sense of family and community duty and are less likely to experiment and to initiate relationships with outsiders, and less inclined to rebel. Jewish men are thus both more tempted to intermarry and more likely to rail against what they perceive as an externally imposed constraint on their choice; hence we have Jewish Princess jokes not Jewish Prince jokes.

Shikse Jokes

My thesis is further reinforced by two further humor phenomena: the changing humorous significance of the *shikse* and the rise of the Blonde Girl joke. The word *shikse* which literally means "female abomination" (Telushkin 1992: 139) has long been used routinely to refer to gentile women, often with a connotation of sexual availability. *Shikses* were for casual enjoyment, not for marriage. Yet in 1978 Marsha Richman, a Jewish divorcee, and Katie O'Donnell, a left-footer who described herself as a *shikse*, published a book entitled *The Shikse's Guide to Jewish Men,* in which they ask, "Can a girl from another world meet and fall in love with and marry him?" The answer is, "absolutely maybe" (Richman and O'Donnell 1978: -1). And we are told that,

> To a Jewish man, the *shikse* is:
> desirable because she is non-Jewish
> inferior because she is non-Jewish
> wonderful because she is non-Jewish
> forbidden because she is wonderful
> wonderful because she is forbidden. (Ibid.)

When the comedy takes this form, when humor about *shikses* ceases to result in coarse sniggers but becomes an enjoyable and public form of playing with the forbidden, then intermarriage has clearly become a much greater threat. This kind of humor reflects an American society in which intermarriage is common and the allure of temptation has overcome community duty.

Perhaps Richman and O'Donnell's *shikse* is the origin of the American Blonde Girl jokes (ibid.: 81). The Blonde Girl is wildly promiscuous and very stupid, the *shikse* fantasy pushed to its ultimate extreme. These two types of jokes (JAP and Blonde Girl) taken together form an antithesis that is symptomatic of a world that has gone out of control.

Kashrut

A study of the two main threats to Jewish identity—conversion and intermarriage—and the Jewish humor associated with them has proved somewhat disturbing. It is perhaps appropriate to look next at one of the institutions that has helped to sustain Jewish identity in the past: the dietary laws. Waxman notes this point when he quotes one of the sages of the past to the effect that "our nation of the children of Israel is a nation only by virtue of its laws" (Waxman 1990: 81).

Jewish jokes about food and the dietary rules seem to have gone through three (overlapping) stages. During the first stage the dietary rules are taken for granted and over-applied in a ludicrous way in the jokes. In the second stage the jokes have as their key theme individuals evading the dietary rules while still admitting their validity. In the final stage there are merely irreverent one-liners that make the dietary rules appear bizarre.

It is noteworthy that Rabbi Telushkin has a special section on Orthodox Jewish humor set apart from the rest; much of it "attacks the extreme ritual punctiliousness of some observant Jews" (1992: 163). A joke retold by Spalding has presumably been imported to America as part of an older East European tradition of joking; curiously he classifies the joke below under *schnorrers*:

> A beggar who was not averse to petty thievery when he thought he could steal without detection knocked on a door and pleaded for something to eat. The compassionate housewife set the table for him and served him a hearty meal.
> The scoundrel, however, instead of feeling gratitude, pocketed a silver spoon and left. The housewife missed the spoon almost at once. She ran down the street shouting, "Mister, wait a minute. I want to talk to you."
> A police officer was on the corner just ahead of the beggar, so the beggar thought it prudent to halt.
> "What is it?" he asked fearfully, one eye on the curious policeman.
> "That spoon you took," the woman gasped, "remember, it's *milchik*." (Spalding 1973: 28)

The later American jokes refer to intended or actual rule-breaking.

> A man with pronounced Jewish features stood before the display case and pointed to a tray.
> "I'll have a pound of that salmon," he ordered.
> "That isn't salmon, it's ham," corrected the clerk.
> "Mister," snapped the customer, "in case nobody ever told you, you got a big mouth." (Ibid.: 246–47)

> Late one rainy afternoon, when he saw no other customers inside, Mr. Finkelstein walked into an elegant but not kosher delicatessen. He bought some tomatoes and with elaborate insouciance, asked, for the first time in his life, "By the way, how much costs that—bacon?" Came a terrific flash of lightning and clap of thunder. Finkelstein looked up to the heavens, protesting, "I was only asking!" (Rosten 1970; also in Ford, Hershfeld and Laurie, Jr. 1947)

It is interesting to note how this joke changes slightly over time by comparing the joke about Finkelstein above with the slightly later version below:

> One morning, Weintraub went to a restaurant and ordered bacon with his eggs. He was an Orthodox Jew and his wife kept a strictly kosher home. But Weintraub felt

the need just this once. As Weintraub was about to leave the restaurant, he stopped in the door frozen with terror. The sky was filled with black clouds, there was lightning and the ground shook with the rumble of thunder.
"Can you imagine!" he exclaimed, "All that fuss over a little piece of bacon!" (Wilde 1979: 81)

Weintraub, unlike Finkelstein, had managed to complete his purchase and was in the process of taking it home when the heavens turned wrathful. Unlike Finkelstein, who accepted that he was at fault and backed off from his attempt at rule breaking, Weintraub regarded his transgression as a trivial matter and was annoyed that it produced a disproportionate response. Finally, whereas Finkelstein is just any Jew, Weintraub is specifically described as being Orthodox with a wife who keeps kosher. The implication is that other Jews and their wives do not bother with such matters.

Since 80 percent of American Jews today do not observe the dietary laws (Glazer 1990: 35), it is not surprising that jokes about the eating of *traife* by curious, careless or non-observing Jews have gone into decline. In his collection *American Jewish Humor*, Spalding comments, "The dearth of such stories—at least of those comparable in excellence with the older jokes—is reflected in the collection presented in this chapter, which contains only one funny story about the eating of forbidden food" (Spalding 1969: 196).

These changes in behavior and outlook have themselves been mocked in Jewish humor, notably by Hochstein and Hoffman in their satire *Up from Seltzer: A Handy Guide to Four Generations of Jews in the United States*. According to them, the sequence in dietary rules has been:

First Generation: Anything that isn't kosher.
Second Generation: Anything that isn't kosher except Chinese food.
Third Generation: Anything with cholesterol.
Fourth Generation: Anything with meat in it and anything that wasn't organically grown. (1981; see also Telushkin 1992: 131)

The change in the jokes about the dietary restrictions is one more indication of the precarious state of Jewish identity.

Concluding Thoughts and Recommendations for the Future

Humor reflects reality, but it can also be consciously used to shape that reality. I stress "consciously" because the functional and conflict theories of humor are completely invalid in any macro context. The only way to employ humor in the achieving of any particular goal is to first design a policy which you think will be effective for other reasons and then incidentally to reinforce the policy by an appropriate and pragmatic use of humor.

The demographic and sociological data from the United States (the country with the world's largest Jewish community), as well as from Britain and Canada, tend to show that severe problems exist for the maintenance of Jewish identity in the twenty-first century in those countries due to secularization, intermarriage and a neglect of boundary markers such as the dietary laws. However, analysis of this data has divided Jewish sociologists into optimists and pessimists. A study of modern Jewish humor tends on the whole to support the views of the pessimists, or at least to indicate that the Jews who invent and tell jokes about Jewish identity seem more likely to perceive things in this way. The jokes thus reflect a crisis of identity. The survival of the Jewish people as an entity is not in immediate danger but we can expect a continued steady dilution of Jewish identity, a merging at the edges with a variety of host communities, and the creation of a large category of people who have some Jewish ancestry but little or no sense of Jewish identity; this will be true even if patrilineal as well as matrilineal descent is recognized. Some of these quasi-Jews may be eligible to enter Israel under the Law of Return and will become Jewish if they do so, but if they stay in their countries of origin they will tend to take on the ethnic and religious identities of the surrounding majority.

What this demonstrates is the continuing importance of the movement to Israel. The penumbral secularized intermarried Jews of the countries of the former Soviet Union have been rescued from assimilation by coming to Israel. Is it possible to entice their counterparts to leave the fleshpots of North America and Western Europe and come to Israel in greater numbers? It will be difficult to achieve this, since the gentile world in these countries today is not in general hostile, anti-Semitic and/or coercively assimilationist as it was in the time of Herzl and for many decades after; it is largely indifferent towards, and enticing to, its Jewish citizens. Nonetheless the effort is necessary. It is vital to go beyond the joke that "A Zionist is a Jew who collects money from another Jew to send a third Jew to Israel." The Anglo-Saxon and Francophone Jews themselves should be the preferred targets of Zionist persuasion; they are the ones in danger of being lost to the Jewish community. Israel can and should provide the sense of communal commitment that too many children from liberal secular Jewish homes are finding in Hare Krishna and Jews for Jesus.

It is also vital that Israel be a haven where Jews are not pestered to convert to another religion. It is inappropriate that American evangelists should be allowed to target Israel in search of converts. Such evangelists have done immense good in countries such as Guatemala, Mexico, or Brazil where they have introduced the Judeo-Christian moral tradition to previously irreligious syncretist Roman Catholic pagans. They should concentrate their resources in these countries, where the rate of return on their efforts has been very high rather than pestering Israelis because of the historic significance of the Holy Land. The easiest way to stop them is to forbid them to import personnel, foreign currency and other resources for the purposes of proselytism. This would not in any way infringe the rights of Israel's Christian minorities; and many churches (such as the Mormons) that have set up study centers in Israel have already tacitly agreed not to seek converts locally. It seems to me that American evangelists would make a wonderful target for Jewish humor because of the techniques they use. Members of the established Christian denominations poke fun at them all the time; why shouldn't the Jews?

Also there is a very large population of former Israelis in the United States who are subject to the same pressures of assimilation as other Western Jews; it may well be that their children or grandchildren can be persuaded to return. They should not be made to feel embarrassed about their parents' defection; rather there should be great rejoicing over the return of the lost sheep to the flock. Even those who are agnostic or atheist Jews with gentile spouses should be encouraged to take advantage of Israel's remarkably generous Law of Return. Even if Israel is "diluted" in this way, this would be far less of a threat to Jewish identity than if these people merge into the gentile wilderness of America and Britain and disappear. They may not be good Jews but they would make good Israelis and good citizens of the Jewish state.

There is a second strategy that should be adopted in North America and Western Europe, which is for Jews in general to withdraw their children from the state-run school system, to take them out of the system of comprehensive public schooling (in the American sense) that processes most children in those countries. The education system in those countries is anyway in decline, and characterized by falling educational standards and rising delinquency, teenage pregnancy, drugs, and classroom violence. Instead Jews should create more (and more separate) schools with a distinctive religious ethos that will even attract Jewish parents who are indifferent to religion because the education in science, languages and the liberal arts is superior to that provided in the gentile schools. It will be an act of *positive* segregation, along the lines of that achieved by the Roman Catholics, but with higher educational standards driven by a Jewish zeal for learning and for social mobility. Although this may be a controversial issue for some Jews, such schools should be coeducational to help minimize the rate of intermarriage with gentiles. Most pupils will be relatively irreligious, just as they are in the Christian schools; but for those suddenly struck by devotion these feelings can be channeled in a Jewish direction rather than being exploited by outside cults. In Britain the running of religious community schools can be largely paid for from state funding, and this may become even easier in the future if vouchers are introduced. In the United States it is time for Jews to renounce their "liberal" interpretation of the U.S. Constitution and to denounce any over-rigid separation of church and state. Let the Christians of Alabama have their school prayers and crosses—provided this also means exclusively Jewish schools in Los Angeles and New York and in any small town where there are enough Jews to fill a one-room schoolhouse.

Such institutionally segregated schools will provide far greater protection for Jewish identity than those state schools which are "Jewish" merely by virtue of being located in a Jewish neighborhood, and whose ambiance is gentile/ agnostic. This totality of Jewish educational experience will be far more effective than the attempt to tag on Hebrew school or Jewish history classes at the end of an unprofitable week of American-style classical education. Extramural activities should be limited to other Jewish schools, since in any case it would be impossible to hold joint activities with gentile schools because of differences in timetable (particularly in relation to the Sabbath) and in eating arrangements. The new Jewish schools would be strictly kosher regardless of the parents' behavior at home. Every meal would be a reminder of the barriers between the Jewish and gentile worlds.

Some Jews might at first be unwilling to support such schools because of fears of gentile criticism. Such fears are unfounded for two reasons. First, the gentiles are coming to see the creation of strict denominational schools as an answer to their own moral problems. Working-class parents in Gateshead (the tough post-industrial town in the northeast of England that also houses a yeshiva) compete to send their children to the Emmanuel school run by evangelical Protestants, not for reasons of religion or identity but because it is an oasis of order and learning in a crumbling world. Why should the Jews not have their own schools of this kind? Second, most Anglophone societies have collapsed into obsessive postmodernist multiculturalism. Whatever the minority wants the minority must have, even if it is a difficult, troublesome, uncooperative minority. Consider the appeasement of the Hispanics in the United States or of the Muslims and the Welsh-speaking minorities in Britain, where both local and central governments are permitting the destruction of their own social order in the name of political correctness. Are they going to have the gall to deny the same rights to the Jews who are demonstrably productive, patriotic, and participating members of the countries whose citizenship they hold? Unless there is an upsurge of political anti-Semitism, which is far less likely in the English-speaking countries than in Continental Europe or the Middle East, it should be possible to use the magnitude of the Jewish contribution to society as an argument for convincing gentiles that they, as well as the Jewish people themselves, have a major interest in the survival of Jewish identity. Without a strong Jewish community, the intellectual and entrepreneurial life of Britain, France, and the United States would be greatly impoverished. Self-interest as well as altruism demands that the gentiles provide any support that the Jews may request or require in their task of ensuring Jewish survival and maintaining Jewish identity.

Humor will follow such policies in a spontaneous way. If more Anglophones go to Israel, they will become the butt of Israeli ethnic jokes much as German, Romanian, Georgian, Moroccan, and Kurdish Jews have been in the past. It would be pointless and destructive to try to "plan" such humor. However, where humor already exists it can be *used*. Within the highly bounded Jewish schools that I have advocated for North America and Western Europe, Jewish humor could be a subject on the curriculum, an enjoyable vehicle for conveying the nature and necessity of Jewish identity and the foolishness of *goyische nachus* or a valuable tool for and adjunct to other subjects on the curriculum. You cannot invent a humorous tradition for community

purposes—but you can exploit one that already exists as a spontaneous expression of popular humor. However, it should always be remembered that humor, Jewish humor included, has a life of its own
and may well evolve in directions that are not suited to these purposes.
Should it do so, it is neither possible nor desirable to try to hem it in.
Censorship is futile; the important thing is to choose and use.

Notes

I wish to acknowledge the invaluable help I have received in writing this essay
from Rabbi Barry Schechter and Roy Wolfe.

1. For example, Sir Keith, later Lord Joseph, Nigel Lawson, later Lord Lawson, Mrs.
   Edwina Currie, Sir Leon Brittan, Michael Howard, Malcolm Rifkind; but see
   Clark (1994: 185).
2. Unless the bride was a Seventh-Day Adventist or Seventh-Day Baptist, Spalding's
   joke doesn't work properly in the form in which he has worded it. See Telushkin
   (1992: 140) for a more consistent version.
3. Gentiles now know about the JAP jokes. If the jokes were an expression of
   misogyny, they would transfer them to their own womenfolk in the way that the
   Irish transfer British jokes about the Irish to the Kerrymen.

References

Alperin, Mimi. 1988. *JAP Jokes, Hateful Humor.* New York: American Jewish Com-
    mittee.
Barker, Eileen. 1984. *The Making of a Moonie: Choice or Brainwashing.* Oxford:
    Blackwell.
Burns, Stan and Mel Weinstein. 1978. *The Book of Jewish World Records.* Los
    Angeles: Pinnacle.
Clark, Alan. 1994. *Diaries.* London: Phoenix.
Cohen, Percy. 1980. *Jewish Radicals and Radical Jews.* London: Academic.
Davies, Christie. 1990. *Ethnic Humor around the World: A Comparative Analysis.*
    Bloomington: Indiana University Press.
———. 1983. "Religious Boundaries and Sexual Morality." *Annual Review of the
    Social Sciences of Religion* 6 (Fall): 45–77.
———. 1982. "Sexual Taboos and Social Boundaries." *American Journal of Sociol-
    ogy* 87 (5): 1032–63.
Dines, Michael. 1986. *The Jewish Joke Book.* London: Futura.
Dundes, Alan. 1987. *Cracking Jokes.* Berkeley: Ten Speed.
Durkheim, Émile. 1965. *The Elementary Forms of the Religious Life.* New York: Free
    Press.
Ford, "Senator" Ed, Harry Hershfield, and Joe Laurie, Jr. 1947. *Cream of the Crop.*
    New York: Grosset and Dunlap.
Fuchs, Esther. 1986. "Humor and Sexism the Case of the Jewish Joke," pp. 111–122
    in Avner Ziv (ed.) *Jewish Humo.* Tel Aviv: Papyrus/Tel Aviv University.

Glazer, Nathan. 1990. "American Jewry or American Judaism," pp. 31–41 in Seymour Martin Lipset (ed.) *American Pluralism and the Jewish Community*. New Brunswick, NJ: Transaction Publishers.

Herberg, Will. 1960. *Protestant, Catholic, Jew*. Garden City, NY: Doubleday.

Hochstein, Peter and Sandy Hoffman. 1981. *Up from Seltzer: A Handy Guide to Four Jewish Generations*. New York: Workman.

Kumove, Shirley. 1986. *Words Like Arrows: A Treasury of Yiddish Folk Sayings*. New York: Warner.

Novak, William and Moshe Waldoks. 1981. *The Big Book of Jewish Humor*. New York: Harper and Row.

Oring, Elliott. 1984. *The Jokes of Sigmund Freud: A Study in Humor and Jewish Identity*. Philadelphia: University of Pennsylvania Press.

Raskin, Richard. 1993. *Life is Like a Glass of Tea: Studies of Classic Jewish Jokes*. Aarhus: Aarhus University Press .

Raskin, Victor. 1985. *Semantic Mechanisms of Humor*. Dordrecht: Reidel.

Richman, Marsha and Kate O'Donnell. 1978. *The Shikse's Guide to Jewish Men*. New York: Bantam.

Rosten, Leo. 1970. *The Joys of Yiddish*. London: W. H. Allen.

Selengut, Charles. 1988. "American Jewish Converts to New Religious Movements." *Jewish Journal of Sociology* 30(2): 95–109.

Sequoia, Anna. 1982. *The Official JAP Handbook*. New York: New American Library.

Spalding, Henry D. 1973. *A Treasure Trove of American Jewish Humor*. Middle Village, NY: Jonathan David.

———. 1969. *Encyclopaedia of Jewish Humor*. New York: Jonathan David.

Telushkin, Rabbi Joseph. 1992. *Jewish Humor: What the Best Jewish Jokes Say about the Jews*. New York: William Morrow.

Waxman, Chaim I. 1990. "Is the Cup Half-Full or Half-Empty? Perspectives on the Future of the American Jewish Community," pp. 71–85 in Seymour Martin Lipset (ed.) *American Pluralism and the Jewish Community*. New Brunswick, NJ: Transaction Publishers.

Wilde, Larry. 1986. *The Ultimate Jewish Joke Book*. New York: Bantam.

———. 1979. *More The Official Jewish/Irish Joke Book*. Los Angeles: Pinnacle.

———. 1978. *The Complete Book of Ethnic Humor*. Los Angeles: Corwin.

Wilson, Bryan R. 1982. *Religion in Sociological Perspective*. Oxford: Oxford University Press.

Bibliography

Abraham, Samuel. 1993. *Les toutes derniéres Histoires Juives*. Paris: Zélie.

Cohen, Steven. 1988. *American Assimilation or Jewish Revival?* Bloomington: Indiana University Press.

Douglas, Mary. 1975. *Implicit Meanings: Essays in Anthropology*. London: Routledge and Kegan Paul.

———. 1966. *Purity and Danger*. London: Routledge and Kegan Paul.

Draitser, Emil Abramovitch. 1994. "Sociological Aspects of the Russian Jewish Jokes of the Exodus." *Humor: The International Journal of Humor Research* 7 (3): 245–267.

Fieldhouse, Paul. 1986. *Food and Nutrition, Customs and Culture*. London: Croom Helm.

Finestein, Israel. 1988. "The Future of American Jewry." *Jewish Journal of Sociology* 30(2): 121–6.

———. 1977. "The Secular Jew: Does He Exist and Why?" *The Jewish Journal of Sociology* 29(2): 185–95.

Glazer, Nathan. 1957. *American Judaism*. Chicago: University of Chicago Press.

Gould, Julius. 1984. *Jewish Commitment: A Study in London*. London: Institute of Jewish Affairs.

Katz, Molly. 1991. *Jewish as a Second Language: How to Worry, How to Interrupt, How to Say the Opposite of What You Mean*. New York: Workman.

Kosmin, Barry A. and Stanley Waterman. 1986. "Recent Trends in Anglo-Jewish Marriages." *Jewish Journal of Sociology* 28(1): 49–57.

Kosmin, Barry A. and Caren Levy. 1985. "Jewish Circumcisions and the Demography of British Jewry 1965–82." *Jewish Journal of Sociology* 27(1): 5–12.

Lipset, Seymour Martin. 1990. "A Unique People in an Exceptional Country," pp. 3–29 in Seymour Martin Lipset (ed.) *American Pluralism and the Jewish Community*. New Brunswick, NJ: Transaction Publishers.

Marks, Alfred. 1985. *I've Taken a Page in the Bible: A Medley of Jewish Humour*. London: Arrow.

Meyer, Michael A. 1967. *The Origins of the Modern Jew*. Detroit: Wayne State University Press.

Négre, Hervé. 1973. *Dictionnaire des histoires drôles*. Paris: Arthème Fayard.

Norden, E. 1991. "Counting the Jews." *Commentary* 92 (4): 36–43.

Oring, Elliott. 1992. *Jokes and their Relations*. Lexington: University of Kentucky Press.

Porter, Joshua Roy. 1976. *Leviticus, Commentary*. Cambridge: Cambridge University Press.

Rinder, I. R. 1973. "Mental Health of American Jewish Urbanites: A Review of Literature and Predictions." In *Ethnic Groups of America: Their Morbidity, Mortality and Behavior Disorders*, vol. 1: *The Jews*, edited by A. Shiloh and I. C. Selavon. Springfield, IL: Charles C. Thomas.

Rosenburg, B. and G. Shapiro. 1958. "Marginality in Jewish Humor." *Midstream* 4: 70–80.

Rosten, Leo. 1983. *Hurray for Yiddish: A Book about English*. London: Elm Tree.

Saper, Bernard. 1993. "Since when is Jewish Humor not Anti-Semitic?" In Avner Ziv and Anat Zajdman (eds.) *Semites and Stereotypes: Characteristics of Jewish Humor*. Westwood, CT: Greenwood.

Schmool, Marlena. 1991. "Synagogue Marriages in Britain in the 1980s." *Jewish Journal of Sociology* 33(2): 107–115.

Soler, Jean. 1973. "Sémiotique de la nourriture dans la Bible." *Annales* 28 (4): 943–955.

Sowell, Thomas. 1981. *Ethnic America: A History*. New York: Basic.

Toker, Eliahu, Patricia Finzi, Moacyr Scliar 1991. *Del Eden al Divan, Humor Judio*. Tucuman, Argentina: Shalom.

Weinfield, Morton 1990. "Canadian Jews and Canadian Pluralism," pp. 87–106 in Seymour Martin Lipset (ed.) *American Pluralism and the Jewish Community*. New Brunswick, NJ: Transaction Publishers.

Wilde, Larry. 1980. *The Official Jewish Joke Book*. London: Futura.

Williams, Janice. 1987. *Conceptual Change and Religious Practice*. Aldershot: Avebury/Gower.

9

Jewish Identity in the Twenty-first Century

Solomon Poll

Introduction

The first year in Israel we lived in Givatayim. On the Sabbath we prayed in a small synagogue. One Sabbath there was a Bar Mitzvah celebration. An elderly gentleman sat down next to me; he turned out to be the grandfather of the Bar Mitzvah boy. The *gabbai* of the synagogue approached the gentleman and offered him a *talit* (prayer shawl). He refused to take it, and turned to me with a smile, saying in Yiddish, "For fifty years I have not worn this."

As his grandchild was called to the Torah and beautifully recited the *Haftorah*, tears came to the gentleman's eyes. I said to him, "For fifty years you have not worn a *talit*, but you still have a Jewish heart?"

He replied, "I always had a Jewish heart."

It was my naive impression that this was a typical nonreligious Jew—one who may not observe the Jewish laws and the commandments, but who has a Jewish heart. But is this Jewish heart still ablaze in every Jew? Is it the basis of identity today? And is this Jewish heart strong enough to maintain Jewishness into the twenty-first century?

Historical Background

Since its beginnings, the main function of the Jewish religion has been to retain its identity. Intermarriage and close relationships with non-Jews were prohibited. Jews were commanded, "Do not walk in the customs of the non-Jew . . . I [the Lord] have set you apart from other nations" (Numbers 20: 23, 26). Dressing like gentiles was not allowed, for assimilation in dress was believed to be the first step toward assimilation in ideas (Marcus 1977: 193). Jews were prohibited from drinking the wine or eating the food of non-Jews. Social relationships were prohibited to safeguard against possible diversification and assimilation. Association even with lapsed Jews was not permitted:

> Those who alienated themselves from the community and threw off the yoke of the commandments and are excluded from the community of Jews, in the observance of the holidays or attendance of the synagogue, shall not be mourned; upon their death the family shall dress in white and shall eat, drink, and be merry. (*Yoreh Deah* 345:5)

It is argued that these Jewish laws, together with society's anti-Semitic practices against Jews, such as restricting their activities in commerce, designating the location of their residence,[1] excluding them from social interactions, and depriving them of formal social positions, minimized the assimilation of Jews throughout the ages. Jews speaking the Jewish language, associating with other Jews and living with them in the same neighborhoods, and having minimal contact with the outside world, retained a homogeneous community. A great deal of control was also exercised by the leaders of the Jewish community. Rabbis had a free hand to invoke the *herem* (authority of excommunication).

Jewish identity was simple. Jews identified themselves as Jews. In the eyes of the non-Jewish community they were considered Jews regardless of their personal beliefs, the extent of their religious practices, the degree of their observance of the religious laws, personal character, ability, knowledge, and status in the community. A Jew was a Jew.

The Eighteenth and Nineteenth Centuries

In the middle of the eighteenth century a new way of thinking emerged. Rationalism became the new philosophy: the Age of Reason had arrived. The principles of the Enlightenment challenged religion as the absolute truth. This era was the beginning of basic human rights. It was not known by this name, but it was the movement that eventually led to the French Revolution in 1789, to the Declaration of the Rights of Man, the abolition of feudalism in 1791, the freeing of serfs in Russia with the Emancipation Act of 1861, and the freeing of slaves in the United States with the Emancipation Proclamation in 1863. During this global atmosphere of freedom and human rights came the emancipation of the Jews, namely, the abolition of restrictions, the recognition of Jews as equal citizens, and the granting of formal citizenship.

In Europe

In 1782 Emperor Joseph II of Austria issued a Toleration Edict that lifted some of the restrictions on Jewish occupation and mobility. It also demanded "reforms" of some of the Jewish educational practices. New schools were established in German and Austrian cities. Jewish education in Germany and the Austrian Empire, which included Bohemia, Moravia, Hungary, Galicia, and part of the Slavic Balkans took on a new structure. Jewish schools were modernized, the educational methods for teaching traditional Jewish subjects were improved, and secular courses like the country's language, arithmetic, geography, history, and good manners, were introduced. The various governments helped to strengthen these new schools and programs (*Encyclopedia Judaica* 6: 416). In Berlin, in 1778, the *Freischule* and youth education programs replaced the *heder*.

Beginning in Prussia in 1763, attendance at primary schools was compulsory for all children, and eventually compulsory education reached all Western societies. Jewish children became knowledgeable in gentile languages, secular discipline, and cultural values. Gradually Jews were allowed (by quota) into universities, and to participate in the cultural and intellectual life of society.[2] Jews became integrated into the larger social systems in which they lived. They identified themselves as Jews by religion, and French, German, Galician, Austrian, Hungarian, Polish, Lithuanian, Russian, or Dutch by nationality.

Hence Jews faced two cultures, the Jewish religion, on one hand, and the secular culture of the larger society, on the other. This dual culture created the so-called "marginal Jews"—a term introduced by Park in 1928—who by reason of their participation in two cultures, were not fully committed either to Jewish values, or to the standards of secular society. Consequently they were not fully accepted in either of the two groups. Many of them faced these conflicting values and norms with great difficulty. In addition, the Jewish community itself had to reduce its own authority. Jewish leaders no longer commanded the control they once had. Rabbis were prohibited from using the coercive authority of the *herem* (excommunication).[3]

How did Jews deal with this cultural duality? I suggest that Jews gradually emerged into three categories of cultural variation:

The religious resolute. Jews with strong religious values opposed the dual culture. They rejected the liberal viewpoint of the secular society. They did not seek any acceptance in, nor participation with, the secular society. This group remained loyal to the traditional Jewish religious values. They removed themselves from all possible secular cultural exposure. They isolated themselves, as much as possible, to create an insular society, with minimum contact with the outside world. There were even parents who did not allow their children to receive the minimal secular education of reading and writing, as was required by law.

The secular resolute. Jews educated in secular discipline, with no strong religious convictions, moved easily into the new secular society. This group did not remain faithful to traditional values. They did not accept both cultures. They found fundamental contradictions in the opposing cultures. They chose to abandon religion and their traditional culture. They opted for the secular culture of the larger society. They no longer associated with Jews and Jewish activities. They gradually assimilated into the non-Jewish secular society.

In small communities Jews assimilated because of the lack of Jewish education and limited social contacts with other Jews. At first they neglected and gradually abandoned their Jewishness. In large cities Jews assimilated because of their involvement in secular education, exposure to the secular society, and relative ease of mobility into the larger non-Jewish community.

Jewish/secular duality. In this category there are diverse patterns. There were those Jews who tried to remain loyal to both cultures. They observed the Jewish laws and rituals and at the same time participated, to some extent, in the secular social system. An example of this approach is Rabbi Samson Raphael Hirsch's (1808–1888) *Torah im Derech Eretz* principle, which advocated the study and the observance of the Torah together with worldly occupation and secular education. There were also Jews who no longer observed all the religious rituals, but remained loyal to Jews and Judaism. They did not fully participate in religious activities, but associated with other Jews and were cognizant of their obligation to Jewish continuity and national identity.

This category, consisting of the great majority of Jews, kept up the struggle throughout the centuries, right up to today. These Jews still make all efforts to maintain a balance between the secular culture and Jewishness. This group continuously formulates a variety of programs and activities that allows them to participate in the secular culture and retains their Jewishness.

While many of the Jews in this category maintained their Jewishness through religious belief, religious activity, observance of Jewish laws, community customs and norms, many of them did not. They considered traditional practices old-fashioned, obsolete, outdated, and backward. They wanted to modify the Jewish laws and practices. They introduced into the Jewish religious observances practices that were borrowed from the dominant culture, which were considered relevant, modern, and up-to-date. But they simultaneously affiliated themselves with other Jews in a great variety of activities. The circumstances allowed these Jews to identify concurrently with Jewishness and with the secular culture.

In the United States

In the United States, most Jews (75 percent) identified themselves with religious congregations, temples, and synagogues. Those who did not join religious congregations, held membership in organizations in which the focus of interest was not religion or religious observance, but a variety of secular programs and activities. Jews became active in some of the following organizations, clubs, brotherhoods, societies and fellowships:

- Landsmanschaften—associations based on ethnic backgrounds and country of origin;
- Charity projects—benevolent societies, mutual assistance groups, and loan establishments;
- Politics—such as the Socialist party, local clubs of the Democratic party, the Bund, known for their anti-religious activities;

- Yiddish language—Yiddish speaking groups, literary groups, subscribers to Yiddish newspapers, Yiddish writers and readers, Yiddish advertisers, Yiddish-language radio programs.
- Health organizations—clinics, hospitals, and homes for the aged;
- Labor-related organizations—the Jewish Labor Committee, the Jewish Workman Circle, the American Federation of Labor, the Garment Workers Union;
- Rescue activities—saving and aiding immigrants from Europe and refugees from Nazi Germany, Children's rescue programs, Hebrew Immigrant Aid Society;
- The Arts—Yiddish theater;
- Organizations against discrimination—American Jewish Congress, American Jewish Committee, B'nei Brit.

Jews in the United States thus identified with a great variety of activities that were Jewish in essence and spirit, although not necessarily religious. While secular Jewish activities may not necessarily promote religious Judaism, they do not necessarily diminish it either. Minimal involvement may lead to no involvement, but it could also lead to further participation. Inclusion is preferable, by far, than excluding Jews from any Jewish membership.

The Post-Holocaust Era

In the 1930s, anti-Semitism took on a new dimension. What Daniel Jonah Goldhagen, in his book, *Hitler's Willing Executioners*, calls "eliminationist anti-Semitism," caused the Holocaust. This most tragic episode in Jewish history, resulted in the eradication of six million Jews. During the Nazi terror some Jews went underground and lived like Christians in order to save themselves from the Nazi concentration camps. After the war, survivors and their children, who thought they were Christians all their lives, had to face the decision of their parents to hide their Jewishness. Despite the grief, affliction, and agony of Jewish communities worldwide, and the personal sufferings of individual Jews, the Holocaust became a basis for Jewish unity. The great majority of the Jewish survivors, with a renewed spirit, vigor, and energy revitalized Jewish life.

As the Holocaust was one of the greatest tragedies in Jewish life, the establishment of the Jewish State in 1948 was the Jews' most glorious achievement. The establishment of Israel gave rise and legitimacy to secular Jews. One did not need religious affiliation, or the observance of rituals; Jews identified themselves with Zionism and Israel. The State of Israel provided options for American Jews to consider themselves Jewish, particularly after the Yom Kippur War of 1973 when Israel was threatened with annihilation. The Jews of America responded as they themselves would be driven into the sea. Israel became a secular religion for the Jews in America.

The affectionate tenderness of Jews toward Israel did not require them to settle in Israel. It demanded that they do whatever they could to ensure the security and the survival of the Jewish state. They gave money. They helped to elect American politicians friendly toward Israel. They held public discussions and debates about Israeli political and ideological issues. They invited Israeli diplomats, representatives, and academicians to lecture about Israel, the United Nations, economics, territories, political parties, Arabs, oil, immigration, and *aliya*.

Jews connected with Israel emotionally. This emotional connection gave Jews a basis for Jewish identity. Even for those who considered Israel as a modern secular state, it did not alter their feelings of love and commitment. For a vast number of Jews, Israel sustained their Jewishness. Consequently, any Jew who was compassionate towards the State of Israel, was considered a "good Jew." A non-Jew who was sympathetic towards Israel was considered a "good gentile"; if he spoke against Israel, he was considered an anti-Semite.

Contemporary Problems of Jewish Identity

In recent times, there has been a grave concern about the continuity of Jewishness. *The Jewish Advocate* (Abramowitz: 1996: 1) states, "Fast approaching is Kaddish time for the American Jewish community . . . Nearly every dimension of organized Jewish life is in decline." Brenda Lipitz, national chair of the Women's Division of the Council of Jewish Federations, predicts: "In fifty years all we will have left is a small *Hasidic* enclave" (ibid.: 32–33). The three major Jewish religious groups compete as to which type of Judaism holds the key to future Jewish survival. Reform Judaism, (including Progressive Judaism) advocates modification in traditional observances that complement contemporary life and thought. It is reaching out to intermarried couples, gays, and lesbians. In March 1996, the Central Conference of American Rabbis resolved "to support the right of gay and lesbian couples, to share fully and equally in the rights of civil marriage . . . "

(*Forward* 1997b). Conservative Judaism (including Reconstructionist), while opposing extreme changes in traditional observances, promotes modifications in response to the changing life of Jews. It argues that it is the only Jewish religious movement that has its roots in America. It claims that its middle-of-the road approach may have a greater appeal among secular Jews. Orthodox Judaism (including *Hasidim*) places excessive restrictions upon behavior, additional constraints on interactions, limitations upon free access to information, prohibitions on food products, and great emphasis on external appearance, in order to safeguard any possible infraction of traditional observances.

The concern of Jewish identity reaches beyond the competition of the three major religious groups. Jewish leaders and organizations are alarmed about the continuity of Jewish life. The main distress is not only about the future of religion and the degree of religious observances; it is about the future of the Jews, as a people. According to some, the issue in America is no longer how, but *why* should Jews survive? (*Forward* 1997a)

In the United States

While the question of Jewish survival in the United States and in Israel may be the same, the causes for concern are different. The following are the central issues in Jewish survival in the United States:

Intermarriage. A 1990 National Jewish Population Survey based on interviews with 2,441 "qualified respondents" reports, "In recent years over half of born Jews, at any age, whether for the first time or not, chose a spouse who was born a gentile and has remained so, while less than five percent of these marriages include a non-Jewish partner who became a Jew by choice" (*NJPS* 1990). The New York Jewish Population Survey of 1991 as well as an independent study by Gordon and Horowitz (1994), subdivide Jews in America into five categories: Secular; Reform; Conservative; Centrist Orthodox; and *Hasidic* and Yeshiva Orthodox. Mixed marriages among secular Jews are alarmingly high. The data show that intermarriage among secular Jews is 72 percent, among Reform Jews 53 percent, among Conservative Jews 37 percent, among Centrist Orthodox 3 percent, and among *Hasidic* and Yeshiva Orthodox 3 percent. Only 28 percent of the offspring of mixed marriages were being raised as Jews, the rest gradually become non-Jews.

Decline in the Jewish birth rate. The aforementioned study further shows a declining birthrate among Jews—so low, in fact, that Jews are not even maintaining a stable level within the population. The average number of children per family, among the secular is 1.52, among the Reform 1.72, among the Conservative 1.82, among Centrist Orthodox 3.23, among *Hasidic* and Yeshiva Orthodox 6.4. On average, Jewish couples have around 1.8 children—well below the replacement level of 2.1. Even the high number of children, among Orthodox and *Hasidic* Jews does not counterbalance this deficit (Gordon and Horowitz 1994).

Decline of Jews in the U.S. population. The rate of growth of the Jewish population is low (and declining) compared with the United States population generally; not only is the absolute number of American Jews in decline, the proportion of Jews to the total population is decreasing as well. The total population in the United States as of 1994 was 265 million. The Jewish population of the same year was 5,840,000 (*American Jewish Yearbook* 1994). Thus, whereas in 1937 the Jewish population in America was 3.6 percent, today the percentage of Jews is about 2 percent. Jewish leaders lament that in fifty years the Jewish population will not be able to sustain Jewish life and its institutions in any meaningful way.[4]

Not affiliated. There are about 1.54 million Jews that are not affiliated with any religious congregation. Out of the 5,840,000 Jews in America, the Union of American Hebrew Congregations (Reform Judaism) with 818 temples, claims 1.3 million members (22 percent). United Synagogue of America (Conservative Judaism), with 800 synagogues, claims 2 million members (34 percent). The Union of Orthodox Jewish Congregations of America (Orthodox Judaism), with 1,200 synagogues, claims 1 million members (17 percent) (*Yearbook of American and Canadian Churches* 1994). Even according to these probably inflated figures, the total number of Jews affiliated with a synagogue is 4.3 million; thus there are 1.54 million Jews (26 percent) who do not hold any membership in a religious congregation.

The Holocaust. There is a fear that the Holocaust will no longer stir the conscience of the young. As the memories are fading and the survivors are gradually dying, the remembrance of the Holocaust may not summon conscious identification for Jews, especially for those who are not associated with Jewish organizations.

Decline in Jewish involvement. All of the items mentioned in the context of past participation in Jewish activities have declined in the

post-Holocaust decades. Fewer and fewer Jews attend Yiddish theaters, join Jewish men's clubs or ladies' groups, or read Yiddish newspapers. For example, in America in 1901 a daily newspaper, *Der
Morgen*, was established; in 1916 its circulation reached 111,000, in
1970, circulation dropped to 50,000, and in 1971 *Der Morgen* ceased
publication altogether. Today there is not a single daily Yiddish newspaper in the United States.

Non-theistic options. There is a decline in Jewish ideology. Some
Jews desire to be ideologically neutral. The Society for Secular Judaism offers a non-theistic option for non-religious Jews. The society's
leader claims, "Our members don't believe that there is an intervening
force that responds to prayers" (*New York Times*, 7 December 1996).
The Society is a group that did not only remove religion and religious
observance from its congregation, it also removed God. Removing
God from a Jewish Congregation places in danger Jewish continuity.

Decline of Zionism. Once, Zionism provided an important basis for
Jewish identity; today, intellectuals talk about the post-Zionist age.
When Zionism is considered an ideology of the past, and Jewish historical continuity is repudiated, this may not have an attraction for
young secular Jews.

In Israel

In the United States, there is a concern that Jews will gradually
assimilate, and become non-Jews. In Israel, the problem of assimilation assumes a different dimension. Jews living in a Jewish state,
serving in the armed forces, paying taxes, participating in the Jewish
community, and associating with other Jews, are instinctively Jewish.[5]
They do not need to practice any traditional religious ritual in order to
be considered Jewish. By definition, in Israel a Jew cannot become a
non-Jew, but one may become an Israeli without the traditional meaning of Jewishness.

In Israel, Jews are divided into two basic ideological groups: religious and secular.[6] The religious demand the establishment of Jewish
traditional theocracy, and the secular group insists on complete adherence to democratic and liberal values. The ideology of religious Jews
ranges from extreme vigilantes, who insist upon the retention of all the
ancient culture under Jewish religious authority, to religious zealots
who refuse to recognize the Jewish state altogether. The ideology of

the secular Jews, also, ranges from those who are moderately respectful of Jewish tradition, to those who are aggressively hostile to traditional religious sentiments.

The following issues are the basic concern in Israel relating to Jewish identity:

Zionism. Although some facets of the identity issue are different in the United States and in Israel, there are also many similarities. One problem common to both societies is the decline of Zionism. Today writers and intellectuals talk not only about post-Zionism, but they even repudiate Jewish historical continuity. There is an alarming anti-Zionist attitude in Israel, as secular Jews tend to abandon the Zionist ideology.

Hillel Halkin, in an article entitled, "Israel against Itself," quotes Aharon Megged thus: "Hundreds of [Israeli] leading writers, intellectuals, academics, and journalists . . . have been unceasingly and diligently preaching that [Israel's] case is not just . . . They attack Zionist legitimacy [by] the denial of the historic link of our people with the land of our fathers" (Halkin 1994). Megged further states that with the aid of newly-opened Israeli government and Zionist archives, intellectuals have reexamined the Israeli account of the Jewish-Palestinian conflict. They have revealed a "conclusion that is almost uniform: [namely] that in practice Zionism amounts to an evil, colonialist conspiracy to exploit the people dwelling in Palestine, enslave them and steal their land" (ibid.).

The attachment of the Jews to the Land of Israel did not begin with the Zionist movement. The Land of Israel was always held as one of the most sacred symbols of Jewish life, an integral part of Jewish destiny. Jews always believed that the very first Jew, Abraham, was told that his descendants would inherit the land. "The Lord made a covenant with Abraham, saying: 'Unto thy seed have I given this land . . . '" (Genesis 15:18). Thus, Jews always believed that the Land of Israel was part of the Jewish faith. It was this faith that gave vigor and energy to the movement of political Zionism, calling for "the return to Zion."

At the time of the establishment of the State of Israel, secularist leaders believed strongly in, and declared unequivocally, the right of the Jewish nation in all its generations to the Land of Israel. This buttressed their and their followers' Jewish identity. However, in more recent years some secularist leaders have relinquished the exclusive right of Jews to their land and have coupled this with visions of a new type of Israeli citizen, with a new personal identity shaped by the idea of a "citizen of the world". Thus, particularist nationalism is fading, and both the Jewish and the Israeli identities are being diluted and weakened.

Israel without the sacred. Closely related to the decline of Zionism is the attempt to transform Israel into a secular state. "Life in Israel today makes one long for a naked public square: politics without God, without myth and fantasy, without eternal enemies, without sacred causes or holy ground" (Hazony 1996). I would ask, then, if there is no God, no religion, and now, no Zionism, what is there in the contemporary world that will nourish Jewish existence? In other words, if God, religion, and traditional observance were replaced by the State of Israel, and now there is no allegiance to the state either, then to what is there Jewish allegiance? And if there is no Jewish allegiance, then what will be the meaning of Jewish identity in the future?

Population issues. Almost one-third, 32.4 percent, of Israel's population is under the age of fifteen (in the United States, 21.7 percent fall into this category). Moreover, Israeli citizens over the age of sixty constitute 13.3 percent of the population (compared with 16.9 percent in the United States). Thus, older people for whom tradition and the Zionist ideology are meaningful are relatively few. Who, then, will serve as a role model for young Israelis today—and who tomorrow?

Aggressive hostility. The current ideological controversy between the religious and the secular revolves around the demand of religious groups that all the ancient Land of Israel be under Jewish religious authority, whereas secular Jews would like to transform Israel into a nonreligious, liberal democracy, under elected pragmatic political leadership. Ideological discourse in Israel has entered into a phase that has seldom occurred in Jewish history: two belligerent factions aggressively hostile toward each other.

In addition, there is a vocal secular group that provokes and agitates against religion and the religious. An example is, this comment by Ze'ev Chafetz: "To survive, democratic Israel must knock the fundamentalist rabbis off their pedestals and lock up their violent disciples. This means cutting off public funds to schools and youth organizations that indoctrinate children in anti-democratic ideals . . . " (Hazony 1996).

These sentiments are not empty words. A public opinion poll in

Israel showed that Orthodox Jews are less popular than Arabs. It further showed that 20 percent of Israelis refuse to be married by the official rabbinate. The majority of people who marry are the young and if they refuse to be married by rabbis, what are the future prospects of Israeli Jewish identity?

The Future of Jewish Identity

I would like to believe that the situation is not as bad as it sounds. Firstly, there has always been a nonreligious element alongside the mainstream Jewish community. These two communities composed *klal Yisroel*—the totality of the Jewish people. Secondly, conflicting ideologies may actually help clarify the issues: a group that feels threatened by another will make a greater effort to strengthen and reinforce the valued perceptions. Furthermore, conflicting ideologies may even demonstrate that no single group can have a monopoly on Jewishness. Conflicting ideologies demonstrate that citizens are involved and care about their destiny. But society must deal with its differences with respect and dignity.

In every society throughout the ages, people have needed a transcendental meaning for their lives, a mystical force that reaches beyond ordinary experience, and relates to the society's social heritage. It promotes and advances the culture that gives significance to the group's social existence. It extends itself into the future and gives purpose to the present. Out of the psychic vision, a group spirit emerges, providing a reason for existence that surpasses individual membership. In this sense, Jews as a group, will identify with Judaism for ever.

There will, of course, be those who profit from doom and gloom, inciting Jews against one another. But there will also be Jews whose faith in the absolute persistence of the future generation will be strong, secure, and powerful. There will be the loyal and devoted supporters of faith, religion, and hope. There will be Jews who will forcefully defend their right to exist as Jews, in a Jewish land and elsewhere, against predicaments, obstacles, and adversity.

Jewish life and identity will be sustained through two basic factors:

Internal Renewal. This is a collective reaction to the threat of assimilation, intermarriage, and the general neglect of Jewishness. Today there is a desperate move by Jewish organizations, rabbis, lay leaders, educators, publishers, and businessmen to mend and to renew the impaired Jewish tendencies. They organize and support various programs and projects aimed at revitalizing Jewish identity. Some of these programs will restore confidence in Jewishness. In recent years, some success has been achieved through:

- Jewish Day Schools—An increased number of Jewish day schools, and growing enrollment in these schools, reflect good results in providing Jewish children with an adequate background for facing the disturbing influences of secular culture.
- Charity Foundations—Jewish Foundations are the driving force behind programs to promote and cultivate Jewish identity. For example, the Charles R. Bronfman Foundation of Montreal sponsors programs for Jewish children to visit Israel. Mr. Bronfman says. "One's Jewish identity cannot be fulfilled unless one is identified with Israel on a personal basis" (*Forward* 1996). The Avi Chai Foundation of New York, with $60 million in assets, is funding a preparatory program "that will allow students who did not go to Jewish day schools to catch up Judaically" (ibid.). Other foundations which are devoting financial assets and energy to the retention of Jewish identity are the Jim Joseph Foundation (aid to Jewish day schools) and the Nathan Cummings Foundation (making synagogues more appealing) (ibid.)
- Study groups—Telephone access to lectures on the Talmud, the weekly Bible portion, and other subjects; distribution of tapes about Jewish ethics, etc.
- Conferences—Recently a meeting was held in California consisting of 125 Conservative and Reform synagogue leaders in order to revitalize American Jewish life (*Forward* 1997).
- Publications—Books on religion and Judaism, as well as Jewish classics, translated into readable English.
- Outreach, Ba'al Tshuvah and community organizations—Many organizations and *Hasidic* groups are active in disseminating Judaism in colleges, universities, business centers, and even on the streets.
- Cyberworship—The Internet is providing ways for Jews to connect with Judaism. It is called Cyberworship. Proponents say, "it is an ideal way to inspire and recruit inactive Jews and feed the faith of practicing Jews, when they are too busy to go to synagogue" (*Miami Herald* 1996).

External pressure. Another means by which Judaism and Jewish identity was maintained in the past was the insistence of the outside world that Jews remain Jewish. The Jews of Russia provide a case in point. From 1950 onward, every individual who was born to Jewish parents had to register as "Jewish nationality." Even when these individuals declared that they were atheists, or even when they converted to Christianity and erased all traces of Jewish heritage, they were obligated to register. This Jewish identity remained in force even after the collapse of Communism. The obligatory registration of each individual born to Jewish parents, as being of "Jewish nationality," was considered anti-Semitic. In fact, the registration induced younger Jews to study Hebrew and Jewish history and to congregate in and around the synagogues in the larger cities. And it was these Jews who ultimately emigrated, to Israel and elsewhere.

There are still other ways that external pressure helps retain Jewish identity. The principle of Western Civilization is based on Athens and Jerusalem—the democracy and freedom of Athens and the reverence for God and man of Jerusalem. The non-Jewish world wants the Jew to remain Jewish. Jews are the forerunners of the worlds' three major religions. Religions need a true index by which to ascertain the extent of the good and the bad in the world. The existence of the Jews seems to provide the standard for comparison of global morality. As long as Jews will be held accountable for morality and justice, Jews will be the focal point of the world.

Judaism's rich faith and long tradition, advanced decency, and morality will continue to shape the conscience of man. Even the harsh criticism and self-flagellation of Jewish intellectuals about the occupation of Arab lands, are based on deep Jewish concern for fairness, mercy, and morality. The world will continue to see to it that these ills and pains and guilt shall continue to be rooted deep into the Jewish heart.

Perhaps this is the meaning of what the old man told me in the synagogue, "I did not wear the prayer shawl for fifty years, but I always had a Jewish heart."

Notes

1. Jews tended to isolate themselves in Jewish neighborhoods. Most communities in which Jews lived had Jewish quarters with designated names: Latin: *platea judaeorum*, Spanish: *juderia*, French: *juiverie*, Italian: *guidecca*, English: *Jewry*, Hungary: *zsido negyed*, German: *Judengasse*, Polish: *ulica zydowska*, In Moslem countries: *harat al-yahud*, Jewish: *shekhunat ha-yehudim*.

2. To illustrate the extent of Jewish participation in the larger German society for which higher educational training was necessary, one must consider the Nazi policy of excluding Jewish people from German life. In the 1930s the Nazis dismissed thousands of Jews from their jobs and positions. 10,000 public health and social workers were stripped of their positions; 4,000 lawyers were deprived of their license to practice law; 2,000 doctors were expelled from hospitals and clinics; 800 university professors and 800 elementary and secondary teachers were discharged from their positions.

Another illustration concerns Hungary. Jonathan Kaufman (1979) notes that in 1920, "half of Hungary's lawyers were Jewish, along with two-thirds of its doctors, 35 percent of its journalists, 27 percent of its professors and 24 percent of its actors."

3. In the Netherlands, in 1809, the use of Yiddish in official documents was prohibited. Even sermons in the synagogue were to be delivered only in Dutch.

4. The world Jewish population: in 1918, 14 million; in 1937, 16 million; at the end of World War II, 11 million; in 1970, 14 million; in 1993, 17 million.
   Current Jewish population by continent: Africa, 337,000; Asia, 5,587,0000; Europe, 1,469,000; Latin America 1,092,000; North America 7,003,000; Oceania 58,000; Former USSR 2,236,000; total, 17,822,000 (Gordon and Horowitz 1996: 14).

5. The official definition of a "Jew" was laid down in the Basel Program of 1897 in Article 6 of the 1922 mandate. In the Declaration of Independence 14 May 1948 (and formally enacted in the Law of Return of 1950, Section B), "Jew" is defined as "a person who was born to a Jewish mother or has become converted to Judaism and who is not a member of another religion."

6. As a somewhat imprecise definition, religious Jews are those who accept the concept that God, the Torah and the Jewish people are one unit; believe that the Torah (written and oral law) was given in Heaven and that there is divine reward and punishment; and heed the obligation to observe the traditional laws and commandments.

   As a somewhat imprecise definition, secular Jews are those who identify with Jewish culture, history, society and Israel; do not accept the concept that the Torah (written and oral law) originates in Heaven, do not believe in divine reward and punishment; do not consider it an obligation to observe traditional laws and commandments; and view festivals and other observances as national celebrations and social customs instituted by society.

References

Abramowitz, Yosef I. 1996. "Kaddish Time for American Jews?" *The Jewish Advocate* (September).
American Jewish Yearbook 1994.
Encyclopedia Judaica. 1972. Jerusalem: Keter Publishing House.
Forward 1997a. 31 January 1997.
———. 1997b. 17 January 1997.
———. 1997c. 10 January 1997.
———. 1996. 15 November 1996.
Goldhagen, Daniel Jonah. 1996. *Hitler's Willing Executioners.* New York: Alfred Knopf.
Gordon, Anthony and Richard M. Horowitz. 1996. In *The Jewish Observer:* 14.
———. 1994. "Independent Survey."
Halkin, Hillel. 1994. "Israel against Itself." *Commentary* (Nov.): 33–39.
Hazony, Yoram. 1996. "The Zionist Idea and Its Enemies." *Commentary* (May).
———. 1995. "The End of Zionism and the Last Israeli." *Viewpoint* (Winter).
Kaufman, Jonathan. 1979. *The Hole in the Heart of the World in Eastern Europe.* New York: Viking Press.
Keysar, Ariela. 1996. *New York Jewish Population Survey of 1991.* Cited in *The Jewish Observer* (December): 14.

Marcus, Jacob R. 1977. *The Jew in the Medieval World.* New York: Athenaeum.
Miami Herald, The. 1996. (5 December).
National Jewish Population Survey. 1990. Cited in *The Jewish Observer* (December): 14.
New York Times, The. 1996. (7 December).
Park, Robert E. 1926. "1950, The Race Relation Cycle," pp. 149–151 in *Robert E. Park Collected Papers* (vol. 1: *Race and Culture*). Glencoe, IL: The Free Press.
Yearbook of American and Canadian Churches. 1993. *The World Almanac and Book of Facts* 1994: Mahwah, NY: Funk and Wagnalls.

10

Jews in Israel and the United States: Diverging Identities

Naftali Rothenberg

Introduction

Cultural development and the consolidation of one's individual and social identity (in the broad sense) are processes that take place over a span of many years and are influenced by a long series of elements. To profile these elements requires an analytical capacity that extends over at least two or three generations and which takes into consideration the full gamut of earlier and parallel processes (Eisenstadt 1992: 5–42).

During the last hundred years, two parallel but essentially different processes have been taking place in the Jewish people: the development of a Jewish society in Israel, in a sovereign framework, and, at the same time, of a Jewish society in the United States, in voluntary community frameworks and other settings. Not only have the contexts been different; with no less impact, the cultural elements that influenced them and from which they sprang, the different ethnic components of the two societies, political events, and the economic situation—all these, and other factors, have contributed to the emergence of two different Jewish groups with quite different identities.

The two processes, in Israel and the United States, have demanded a massive effort from all who took part in them.[1] The consolidation of identities is, consequently, also an outcome of individual, organizational, and community efforts. We are looking at two simultaneous investments of phenomenal energy. It is only natural that this created a schism: efforts were focused on different goals, usually parallel but sometimes conflicting.

The schism between the two societies is not total. On the contrary, various forms of contacts and ties exist between different components of the two communities. Bonds of cultural and social identity weld some sectors into shared circles (Eisenstadt 1992: 225–33; see Liebman and Cohen 1990). Yet even the totality of the phenomena that unite them does not obscure the fact that we are speaking here of two different societies with respect to their identity and culture. In this context I would like to point to factors that I believe are contributing to the divergence of identities.

Factors of Divergence

The divergence of identities may be attributable to:

Frameworks and Affiliation

Sovereignty versus voluntary community affiliation or non-affiliation. I am not referring merely to a simplistic distinction that notes the fact that organized and affiliated Jews in the United States have aligned themselves with a voluntary association—a community or synagogue; whereas run-of-the-mill Israelis satisfy their need for belonging simply by being citizens of their town and country: although this factor is of great significance, of course.

Beyond it, however, we must examine the phenomena of local communities in America against the background of Jewish communities in general and their development from a public and political institution that served the most basic day-to-day needs of local residents. How has the community evolved from the traditional *kehila,* an institution in which the religious component has always been only one of many elements—and generally not even the most important (see Elazar and Cohen 1997: 113–14, 161–76)[2]—into the modern synagogue congregation, which today constitutes the most significant circle of affiliation? (Kosmin et al. 1990). The prophets of "civil religion" who predicted the "Jewish Federations Movement" have become strangely silent (see Bellah 1970: 168–193; Woocher 1986). Today, Jewish Federations are evincing more and more religiosity, more and more spirituality, and have no public or civic gospel to disseminate. The UJA and the Federations have concluded a "holy alliance" with the flourishing Jewish "churches" and their representatives, the *pulpit* rabbis. Witness the fact that rabbis of all streams are the honored guests and keynote speakers of the campaign to rescue the vocation of fundraising.

The public and governmental frameworks of Western society have inherited the principal tasks of the traditional *kehila:* managing public spaces, the water supply, law and law enforcement, medical, educational, and welfare services, public security, and so on. This has left the individual a large degree of cultural and religious freedom.

By contrast, the sovereign jurisdictions of local and central government in Israel have assumed all the functions of the classic Jewish *kehila* (Liebman 1983: 53–66). This state, which was born as a political community, like most of its predecessors in the annals of Jewish communities, has split up into a confederation of communities that satisfy all needs, including cultural and religious ones. Thus the difference between sovereignty and voluntary communities is not merely one of structure, but also an authentic gulf that hastens the divergence of the identities of the two societies.

The individual and the state: political cultures from different galaxies. This subject should be self-evident, and I see no reason to deal with it at length. There is simply a vast gulf of political culture that impedes any communication and understanding between the carriers of the two political cultures (Lipset 1990; Liebman and don-Yehiya 1984; Showstack 1995). Any attempt at political discourse is a dialogue of the deaf, and doomed to failure.

Culture

Religion, secularism, traditionalism. The religious renaissance in the United States has not omitted the Jews, who occupy an honored place in every development, as part of the American majority culture (Eisenstadt 199: 118–139). There is unprecedented creativity in the domain of Jewish theology, sometimes of an extremely high caliber. American Jewry is experiencing a religious process of theological debate as a manifestation of high culture. Religion is not a refuge from distress or some kind of popular glue. It is a high stage in the cultural development of an intellectual society that is endeavoring to preserve its identity and continuity; as such, it is an expression of a major effort by many persons, in all streams and settings. This religiosity has garnered serious recognition and great esteem as an authentic part of the majority culture: American culture, which loves to love God and asserts that a good American is one who is affiliated and believes in God.

All of this is quite alien to Israeli culture, which has developed an "areligious" and nontheological religion, a traditional mass culture that can do without spirituality, and an elitist secularism for intellectuals.

Language. Language is a decisive component of culture. In my opinion, the Hebrew language is the best guarantor of Jewish continuity, and vice versa (Rothenberg 1993). It constitutes the most significant, powerful, and distinguishing cultural force that shapes the identity of Israeli society. With regard to language, two opposing cultural processes are in motion in Israel and the United States: the complete translation of every facet of Jewish experience into English, over there; and the focusing of Israeli culture in Hebrew, over here. These processes have a decisive impact on the divergence of identities.

Ethnic Differences and their Influence on the Shaping of Identity

A comparison of ethnic maps and their influence on the divergence of identities. It is clear that the ethnic differences in Israel constitute a veritable abyss. Jews in America do not understand that twenty percent of us—one-fifth of all Israelis—are not Jews. For them, the Arabs simply do not exist. Another 40 percent of us are Jews of Asian or North African ancestry—Sepharadim. The minority of Sepharadim in American communities have already become more "Ashkenazi" than the grandchildren of Polish Jews here in Israel.

The different influence of identical ethnic groups on each culture. The different ways in which Jews from the same country of origin have been culturally integrated in Israel and the United States accelerate the divergence of identities. It resembles the generation gap between immigrants and their children, but is much more severe.

All these factors have a major influence on the divergence of identities. Nevertheless, it seems that differences in religious identity, more than others, are at the center of the divergence. "Divergence of identities" does not mean that key concepts and elements of identity are not at work in both societies: *Land of Israel, Hanukkah, Passover,* and the holidays in general, the *Jewish people,* and even the *State of Israel* and the *Israel Defense Forces.* However, the *meaning* attributed to these concepts on either side of the Atlantic is different. In many cases it is precisely the different meanings given to "shared" concepts that catalyze the divergence of identities, for they constitute an extremely divisive cultural factor.

For example, I mentioned the Israel Defense Forces (IDF). On the face of it, we in Israel should be more militaristic than American Jews, especially because the IDF is a unifying experience for many Israelis. But this is not the case: for many American Jews who never served and never will serve in the IDF, and perhaps may never even visit our "perilous" country, the IDF is a component of identity and a motif of Jewish normative reference—a sort of remote-control Jewish militarism.

All the cultural components, on both sides of the Atlantic, indicate a widening divergence between the two identities. Hence the faltering dialogue between the two societies will become even more difficult.

Is this a cause for pessimism? Not necessarily. There is a reasonable chance that new factors—some of them not connected to cultural identity—will modify the picture in the future. For example, economic development in Israel could enhance the ties between the two societies. A continued rise in the trickle of *aliyah* from the United States would create a group of Israelis who can bridge the communication gap. Finally, to a small extent, the tremendous effort being invested in Jewish education in the United States today may bear some fruit.

Until that future arrives, we shall continue to live and misunderstand each other, and the gulf between the two major centers of world Jewry will gape even wider.

Notes

1. S. N. Eisenstadt has well described these parallel processes (1992: chapter 5, "The Incorporation of the Jews in the United States" and chapter 7, "The Formation and Transformation of Israeli Society"; idem. 1986). About the process in America, see for instance Sarna 1990; Howe 1976; Liebman 1973.
2. My analysis of Biblical and Talmudic texts has led me to different conclusions.

References

Bellah, R. N. 1970. "Civil Religion in America," pp. 168–193 in *Beyond Belief.* New York: Harper and Rowe.

Elazar, D.J. and Stuart A. Cohen. 1997. *The Jewish Polity.* Jerusalem: Rubin Maas Publishers and Jerusalem Center for Public Affairs.

Eisenstadt, S.N. 1992. *Jewish Civilization.* Albany: State University of New York Press.

———. 1986. *The Transformation of Israeli Society.* London: Weidenfeld and Nicolson.

Howe, Irving. 1976. *World of Our Fathers: The Journey of East Europeans to America and the Life they Found and Made.* New York: Simon and Schuster.

Kosmin, Barry A., Sydney Goldstein, Joseph Waksberg, Nava Lerner, Ariella Keysar, and Jeffrey Scheckner. 1991. *The Highlights of the CJF 1990 National Population Survey.* New York: Council of Jewish Federations and CUNY.

Liebman, Charles S. 1983. "The Dilemma of Reconciling Traditional Culture and Political Needs: Civil Religion in Israel." *Comparative Politics* 16: 53–66.

———. 1973. *The Ambivalent American Jew.* Philadelphia: Jewish Publication Society of America.

Liebman, Charles S. and Steven M. Cohen. 1990. *Two Modes of Judaism: The Israeli and American Experiences.* New Haven, CT: Yale University Press.

Liebman, Charles S. and E. Don-Yehiya. 1984. *Religion and Politics in Israel.* Bloomington: Indiana University Press.

Lipset, S. M., ed. 1990. *American Pluralism and the Jewish Community.* New Brunswick, NJ: Transaction Books.

Rothenberg, Naftali. 1993. "Hebrew as a Guarantee for Jewish Continuity." *Hado'ar* (1993). New York (Hebrew).

Sarna, Jonathan D., ed. 1990. *The American Jewish Experience.* New York: Holms and Meier.

Showstack, Gerald L. 1995. "The Quest for Religious Freedom and Pluralism in Israel." *Journal of Jewish Communal Service.*

Woocher, J.S. 1986. *Sacred Survival: The Civil Religion of American Jews.* Bloomington: Indiana University Press.

11

Hasidic Jews: Social Boundaries and Institutional Development as Mechanisms of Identity Control

William Shaffir

Introduction

Benchmarking has become an intellectually fashionable term over the past few years, as organizations attempt to grow and introduce effective change. The common dictionary definition regards benchmarking as a standard against which something can be measured, or as a mark of previously determined position used as a reference point. Benchmarking's essential principle is to tap into a tremendous pool of knowledge—the collective learning and experience of others—that can be used by those wishing to improve their own organization. Business managers are pushed to look outside their organizations at their competitors or other best-in-class companies and use the collective knowledge of these other organizations to make their own organization stronger.

Though it may be possible to designate objective standards both to measure and compare productivity and performance, it is more difficult to meaningfully measure concepts like identity transformation, ethnic identity change, and assimilation. While social scientists attempt to signify the parameters of identity, and to identify the consequences of assimilation, it is questionable whether there exist consensual benchmarks against which useful measurements are undertaken. Research on the sociology of Jews illustrates this point.

As considerable research on Jews has shown, Jewish identity is difficult to define in a pluralistic society where new avenues have emerged for Jews to connect Jewishly (Gordis and Ben-Horin 1991). Measuring Jewish identity poses a significant problem, since the issue of what is being measured lacks clear definition. In an analysis of Jewish identity, Phillips (1991) summarizes several empirical studies in which identity has been conceptualized and measured. What has been learned about Jewish identity? While the findings reveal considerable overlap and consistency over the scope and direction of generational change, social scientists have reached divergent conclusions about the meaning of that change. Along this line, Cohen (1983) differentiates between "assimilationists," who tend to be pessimistic about the chances for Jewish survival (see, for example, Liebman 1995; Sklare 1967; Ritterband 1991) and the "transformationists," who challenge the assimilationist thesis (Cohen 1983, 1988; Goldscheider 1986; Goldstein and Goldscheider 1968; Mayer 1995; Sandberg 1986).

Were scholars of Jews and Jewish communities charged with the task of identifying a Jewish group in North America that has resisted the assimilationist tide and managed to preserve a distinctive identity, they would clearly be hard-pressed to overlook the Hasidim. Though some might decry the selection of Hasidim as a benchmark against which to assess mechanisms of social control and identity maintenance, a case can be marshalled that Hasidim *have* organized their respective communities to safeguard a distinctive way of life to be transmitted to successive generations. Can one identify features of community organization that have contributed along these lines? And can the tactics employed by the Hasidim be adapted, either selectively or in their entirety, by the larger Jewish community, struggling to preserve Jewish identity?

This chapter focuses on selective elements which have enabled Hasidic Jews to preserve a distinctive identity. I analyze some institutional arrangements that are common to Hasidic communities and whose distinctive organization enables Hasidim to shape and control the social identity of their members. I draw particular attention to one Hasidic community—the Tasher—which I have studied intensively and which has enjoyed striking success over the past decade. I conclude that the Hasidim's homogeneous commitments towards identity maintenance and social control, which characterize their communities, are absent among Jews in the larger Jewish community. As such any model set in place by the Hasidim may, at best, be relevant for only a minor segment of North American Jewry. Nonetheless, the model suggests a blueprint or benchmark for strategies of identity shaping and identity reinforcement.[1]

Boundaries and Identity Preservation

Hasidic sects attach primary importance to preventing assimilation by insulating their members from the secular influences of the host culture. An essential question concerns how the various sects are organized to ensure that their boundaries remain secure. As Kanter (1972) observes, boundaries not only define a group, setting it off from its environment but, in giving it a sharp focus, also facilitate commitment. Frederik Barth's formulation of "ethnic group boundaries" is especially insightful in this regard. "If a group maintains its identity when its members interact with others," he writes, "this entails criteria for determining membership and ways of signaling membership and exclusion" (1969:51). Thus there may be social contact between persons of different cultures, such as Hasidim and outsiders; however, as long as all members of the group consider themselves to be members and frequently interact with other group members on a primary level, while keeping the rest of society at arm's length, the ethnic boundary is maintained. Barth's concept remains innovative because it suggests that it may actually be boundaries, rather than the structures enclosed by them, that both primarily define ethnic groups and account for much of the dynamics of ethnic persistence. In his discussion, Barth identifies two interacting sets of influences affecting boundaries: one facilitating integration of the group, and another differentiating the group from other groups. Applying Barth's formulation to the Hasidic communities, we note that the persistence of boundaries requires not only criteria and signals for identification, but also a structuring of interaction that allows for the perpetuation of cultural/religious differences. Along a similar line, Breton refers to "enclosure" which he defines as "the existence of social boundaries between groups and . . . the mechanisms for the maintenance of the boundaries" (1978: 149).

Insulation from outsiders remains the strategy most commonly adopted by the Hasidim both to cultivate and maintain a distinctive identity. In some specific instances, the adopted strategy has even included physical isolation, as in the case of the Satmar in Monroe,

New York, and the Tasher in Boisbriand, Quebec. As Mintz (1968: 138) has observed, their exotic customs serve as a protective fence around their respective communities.

Secular Education

In this section, I focus on the organization of one institution over which the Hasidim exercise close supervision: secular education. Efforts along this line are to insure that the boundary separating inside from outside influences remains secure.[2]

A feature common to the Hasidic sects is the organization of institutions to minimize the potentially harmful impact of surrounding cultural influences. Chief among these are the schools which, while emphasizing religious studies, also include a secular curriculum.

The manner in which the Hasidic schools coordinate their secular offerings represents a form of boundary maintenance. The secular principal of a Hasidic school explains the philosophy to me:

> One day, in a discussion with the Chief Rabbi, I told him, "Three hundred years and you haven't changed. You still wear the same clothes and everything. It boggles my mind. . . . "
>
> He told me, "Listen, if you have a nice piece of furniture that has been there three hundred years, you're not just going to sand it and make it into any old piece that you can buy in the store. . . . "
>
> See, you get his idea here. These are things we cherish, not suffer through. You have to be proud of your parents and grandparents and what they left you. You have to nourish it and keep it alive. So I understand this philosophy, build on it and try to teach these kids as much as possible without breaking down any of their values.

The Hasidim maintain that secular education threatens their traditional values. In order to shield their children against its potentially harmful influences, several of Montreal's Hasidic sects—Lubavitch, Satmar, Belz, Tash, and Square—run their own schools in which secular classes are closely supervised to ensure that the pupils will not see any conflict with the contents of their religious studies. In each case, separate schools are maintained for boys and girls in accordance with the principle of separating the sexes.

Of the Hasidic schools, those of Lubavitch, Square, and Belz are subsidized by the Quebec provincial government and meet its minimal standards. The Satmar and Tasher schools, however, have long refused any government subsidies, as a Satmar school official explains:

> Were it [the school] subsidized, then there'd be a minimum of three hours per day of secular studies. . . . They don't want to be obliged to be exposed to things they don't want their children exposed to.

The program, particularly for the boys, who end their secular studies at the Grade 6 level, is oriented around practicality. A school principal explains:

> All they want is to know how to read, how to write, mathematics, a bit of geography, a bit of French to communicate. . . . They want the basic language to communicate, to get along in society. . . . And they need it for business because most of them become businessmen.

The schools must look to the outside to staff their secular departments as their own graduates lack the qualifications to provide such instruction. When the ideal secular teacher—a practicing Orthodox Jew with a teacher's certificate—is difficult to find, gentiles may be hired in preference to nonreligious Jews, since some Hasidic authorities believe that the former is less likely to sway students, intentionally or otherwise, from their religious beliefs.

To help ensure that students' religious beliefs are not challenged by secular materials, teachers are specifically instructed about the constraints within which they must conduct their work. Typically, they receive oral instruction from the principal concerning proscribed topics. As one administrator remarks:

> Teachers are told that we don't expect them to talk about boys and girls. Girls have their activities and boys have activities, but not together. You shouldn't talk about sex or anything that has to do with reproduction. Or boyfriends, girlfriends. . . . Then there's the great theories—evolution and the creation of the world millions of years ago. We don't get into these conflicts. A secular teacher does not talk about religion. It's out of his field. That's the way we lessen the friction.

Written instructions may be circulated to make matters more formal. Secular teachers in the Satmar school are informed in writing that:

1. Every book, workbook, reading book, which is used in the classroom by the teacher or the students has to be checked and approved by the religious committee appointed by the school; the teacher is not allowed to bring or advise the students to use any book which is not given in the school.
2. No stencil or photocopy of any book except school books which are stamped approved are allowed.

3. Sending students to libraries or reading to students from library books is strictly forbidden.
4. No reading of newspapers is allowed in class. The teacher should not encourage the students to read newspapers; only publications approved by the school are permitted in the classroom.
5. No tapes or recors [sic] are allowed in the classroom.
6. All books are strictly edited from harmful influences according to our religion. If you notice anything which might have been overlooked, please notify us promptly.
7. No subjects, books, magazine supplements, information which have not been given to you by the school are to be taught or brought to school.
8. When setting up school projects, all ordering of materials is to be done by our staff office.
9. Avoid discussing any subject involving Zionism or the State of Israel.
10. Do not speak Hebrew.
11. Do not talk about boyfriend-girlfriend-parties and so on.
12. Do not discuss adult subjects which are not for children.
13. Do not discuss radio, television, movies, theaters, which you might have heard or seen on these with the students.
14. Do not discuss your private life with the students.
15. Do not discuss any religious subject, including the Jewish faith.
16. No homework should be given before a Jewish holiday.
17. Any discussion or story regarding boy-girl relationship, romance, sexual problems, sexual organs, etc . . . is strictly forbidden.
18. Please behave in school in a way befitting for a religious school such as dressing and talking in a modest way.
19. Certain subjects should never be discussed when in the classroom: the theory of evolution; the creation of the world. . . .

These instructions demonstrate the stringent measures taken to ensure that children are not exposed to ways deviating from a strict Hasidic lifestyle. Complementing these limits is a censorship applied both to the selection of books for classroom use and to the specific material that such books may include.

Textbooks go through a detailed screening. To paraphrase one school administrator, stories told the children must not include "ultramodern" views. An example of what he considered harmful, he offered a tale about a Jewish boy who was a pupil in a non-Jewish school and was accepted by the baseball team. One Saturday, the group came to pick him up to play, but his father refused to let him go. The administrator comments:

> Now that's a game we think a boy shouldn't have on his mind, that he could go and play baseball on *Shabbess* [the Sabbath] afternoon. . . . I'm not saying that

that's the worst example of a story that might be passed [over]. But there are stories that have sex in them, and things like that which are totally out.

The process of book selection is typically initiated by the principal, who is charged with the responsibility of reviewing the appropriate material for a particular grade. For those schools accredited by the Ministry of Education, such a review includes examination of the multitude of books and material it recommends. If the program does not conform to the Ministry's guidelines, the principal can look for any material in making his selection. In either case, however, the principal simply recommends; the final decision rests with the sect's religious authorities. The process was described by one of the principals as follows:

I don't order the books. I make recommendations. I say, for example, for the first grade I'd like this and this book. So I receive complimentary copies of the book from the publisher. . . . Now the books that are selected are evaluated by the rabbis. There's someone in the community specifically charged with this task, and he might conclude that a particular book is inappropriate because of the material. So the rabbis might say: "Page 84, you can't use the material on that page." Now if there are too many deletions, then I just don't order the book. And I take the texts they have selected and try to adapt them. So we don't use books *per se*. We make photostats. We create our own texts and we distribute the material to the students. Students receive the texts that we have assembled.

Only the Lubavitcher and Belzer schools distribute actual textbooks to the students. The other schools provide photocopied materials, allowing the authorities to exercise even greater scrutiny over what their students see.

The techniques for censoring materials range from actually removing pages to substituting more appropriate words, phrases or sentences in a text. With the help of modern computer technology Hasidim can now print their own texts with specifically selected materials, and the practice of excising any written or pictorial content deemed offensive with black marker has virtually ended. To a large extent, censorship varies according to the predilection of the individual. For instance, in one school, an individual was charged with screening for photographs that showed women and even young girls dressed immodestly. By contrast, another Hasidic administrator considered it unnecessary to ink out a picture of a little girl not wearing socks, especially when it was clear from the context that the child was a gentile. As he explains:

Our kids are aware that the goyim [gentiles] do not dress the way we dress. . . . I mean, if you're reading a story about goyim, then you know that goyim don't wear socks. As long as it's not a mini skirt or anything like that, it's O.K. It's no use blacking out everything.

All the Hasidic schools except those of Lubavitch limit the secular educational experience to the classroom. Only occasionally are students expected to complete assignments at home; and extracurricular activities are seen as offering too many temptations to secular involvement and are simply discouraged and even forbidden.

In the end, however, the Hasidim are aware of the impossibility of shielding their students completely. However, as an intentionally organized mechanism of social control, the coordination of secular studies helps the Hasidim to maintain the boundaries separating their youth from the surrounding culture.

The Geographic Isolation of Tash

In his analysis of the confrontation between haredi Jews and the modern city, M. Friedman argues that the urban center has been largely responsible for the renaissance of such groups. He claims that the urban environment " . . . enables the Haredim to maintain an independent culture, which can borrow selectively elements from the surrounding culture, and to maintain a large measure of internal social control" (1986: 95). As mentioned, the process by which such social control is organized distinguishes the Hasidim from many other groups that have assimilated into the mainstream.

Although Hasidim have been very successful at making use of conditions in large urban centers, some Hasidic sects have chosen to literally distance themselves further by moving to a more rural-like setting (Gutwirth 1996). The two most well-known cases of such relocation include New Square and Kiryat Yoel, the communities established by the Squarer and Satmar Hasidim respectively. The Tasher Hasidim, who have established the town of Tash—Kiryat Tash—in Boisbriand, Quebec, provide an additional example. A popular magazine article about them reports that they are " . . . cloistered in their self-imposed ghetto in Boisbriand, lead a life of strict devotion totally dedicated to carrying out the will of *Ha-Shem* on Earth and to raising children to do the same" (Kezwer 1994).

A pamphlet published by the Tasher in English—*The Story of Tash*—makes the following statement:

While Tash seeks to imbue its members with a set of specific religious attitudes and values, it also generates a moral climate that ensures its members will comply with the social and ethical standards the community believes ought to be cherished and upheld by the larger society. It is precisely in this area that Tash is proud to deviate from some of the major trends in contemporary society such as delinquency, divorce, drug and alcohol abuse. These social ills are unheard of because the society is strong. Quite simply, no one in Tash need turn to these things. Each *Hassid* is basically content with who he is; he knows his life holds meaning and purpose.

The realization of such meaning and purpose is more readily achieved in a secluded setting, where the members of the community, and especially the younger generation, can be carefully shielded from exposure to undesirable influences. For the Tasher, it is difficult enough to bring up children as devout and law-abiding Jews without having the additional burden of constantly ensuring that they are not influenced by the behavior of modern city dwellers. A Tasher remarks that even in Williamsburg, Brooklyn, where Hasidic Jews are concentrated, his children would be exposed to many things which he would not want them to see—things "which don't exist" in the Boisbriand enclave.

Another Tasher tells of the problems encountered when he went with his son into a department store for the first time:

And my son said, "Look at this."
And I said, "You're not allowed to look. She's not modest dressed. Don't look."
We went by a television.
"*Tattee* [Dad] look. Look, look, he's jumping."
"Don't look, the television is not for you to look." He doesn't have so much to fight with [at Tash] because he doesn't see it. . . . So it's not so hard for him to fight. A boy [in Montreal] who's going every day to *cheder* [religious school] and is going by a Radio Shack and the television is out there with the big screen, every day he has to turn around.

Moreover, the secluded location of the Tasher ensures not only the moral but also the physical welfare of children. They can play without risk of danger in the streets and at meal times all a mother has to do is go out and call them home. She can attend to her household duties without having to check constantly that her children have not strayed too far. Tash parents, furthermore, do not have to be concerned about their children's playmates, as urban dwellers must in order to guard against harmful influences. In the Tash enclave, the role models for the young are provided by the resident adults and it is claimed that the physical security which prevails makes it possible to achieve the spiritual richness of life in the community. A Tasher explains:

I don't have to be concerned if my kid leaves school at 5 o'clock or 6 o'clock to know exactly where he was 'till 7 o'clock. I'll assume he was playing in the snow because there's no place to go. Had I lived in town, I'd have a real problem. And there are people in town who would pick up their kids from school and they would take them home and they would be locked indoors. . . . Someone can succeed with the same objectives as we do but their social life is the one that suffers. We have more *gashmeeus* [social life] even though we don't have to lose on our *ruchneeus* [spiritual life].

The name "Tash" is derived from a little town in Hungary near the Czech border where the great-grandfather of the present Tasher Rebbe began gathering Hasidim around him about a century ago. The Tasher moved from Montreal, where they had lived in close proximity to other Hasidic groups since 1951, upon the receipt of a loan from the Federal Government's Central Mortgage and Housing Corporation and the purchase of 130 acres of land. In 1963 the community promptly built a yeshiva, a synagogue with accommodation for 1,000 persons, a ritual bath, classroom space for boys and girls, offices, eighteen bungalows for the Rebbe and senior staff members, dormitories, and a kitchen and cafeteria.

The community has experienced dramatic growth over the years, both demographically and institutionally (for a detailed discussion of the Tasher community, see Shaffir 1997). In 1987, the Tasher settlement had about 115 households and some 70 yeshiva students; the total population numbered about a thousand souls (Shaffir 1987). Several new structures have been erected since 1987 to cater to population growth: from 115 households then to 180 in 1997, with approximately 1,500 residents. A girls' school, Bays Tzirl, which was under construction in 1987, was completed and has a spacious auditorium which serves as a center for wedding celebrations. The school's enrollment, drawn exclusively from the community's pupils, stands at roughly 300, a significant increase from the 160 total in 1987. Classes extend from kindergarten till grade 12, by which time the girls are expected to become engaged and married.

At the end of the main road extending through the enclave, opposite the yeshiva, stands a new imposing two-story structure. It was completed in 1993, named Talmud Torah Bays Yehuda D'Tash, and serves as the elementary school for boys. It, too, has an enrollment of some 300 boys ranging in age from three to thirteen years. The student population there has also increased, from 160 in 1987. A new school is under construction in 1997; it will be reserved for boys age thirteen to sixteen; there are about 120 pupils in that age group, seventy of them from Tash, and the remainder from Hasidic families in the New York area.

The administrative offices, originally centered in the yeshiva, and then for several years in a converted house, now have a new building which was completed in 1992. There are twelve offices and an elegantly furnished modern boardroom for meetings with political and other dignitaries. Two further buildings were added recently. One, completed in 1992, serves as a home for the elderly. The other building is a synagogue; it was completed in 1995, and includes four large rooms, three of which are used for daily prayer while the other is reserved exclusively for study.

The occupational breakdown for males has changed as the community has grown. The majority of the men are still engaged in religious-oriented types of work (as teachers, ritual slaughterers, and *kashruth* supervisors) and in religious study in the *kollel* (advanced Talmudic academy) for which they receive a financial subsidy. But there are also now, more than before, small-scale independent businesses which people operate from their homes; these include stores selling hardware or sewing necessities, a shop for altering clothes, and a bookstore. Others sell supplies for photography, vitamins, toys, dry goods, jewelry, and computer hardware and software. According to one source, about 10 percent of the men work outside the community: an electrician, a real estate agent, and employees in two business concerns owned by Tasher Hasidim. As the community has grown, more men have been given administrative positions; there are several bookkeepers and other salaried personnel.

The community's high degree of self-sufficiency has been maintained. The variety store is stocked with produce, canned goods, and household articles and was recently expanded with more kosher products imported from New York. The Tasher's paramedic team, established some ten years ago, remains fully prepared for emergencies and in 1996 included some ten men who had acquired various levels of training. A new model defibrilator is a very recent addition, and the ambulance, already present for several years, contains state-of-the-art medical equipment.

A set of bylaws, established by the community's *Rebbe* [spiritual leader and teacher], governs the behavior of the residents; and each adult, whether male or female, must agree to abide by these bylaws before taking up residence in the settlement. Anyone who transgresses may be liable to eviction. What follows is a translation of these bylaws from a document in French prepared by the Tasher in 1979 for Quebec's Provincial court in connection with their bid for autonomy:

- No book, newspaper, or magazine is permitted in the buildings of the community, unless their content is in conformity to Orthodox Judaism.
- All members of the community must attend religious services, three times per day, at the synagogue.
- No radio, television, record, or cassette is allowed in the buildings of the community.
- No member of the community may attend the cinema or be present at any theatrical performance under the penalty of immediate expulsion.
- All women residing in the community must dress in accordance with the Orthodox laws of modesty, as follows:
  - All dresses must be at least four inches below the knee, no trousers or pantyhose may be worn by young girls 3 years of age and older.
  - [Married women's] Hair must be completely covered 24 hours a day, by a kerchief or by a wig which is no longer than the nape of the neck.
- It is forbidden for men and women to walk together in the street.
- Men and women must be separated by a wall, at least 7 feet high, when attending any gathering of a social or religious nature.
- All food consumed in the buildings of the community must conform to the dietary laws of the Code of Laws and be approved by the Chief Rabbi [Rebbe] or his second-in-command.
- No car may be driven by a woman or by an unmarried man.
- The members must submit any interpersonal conflict to the arbitration of the court established by the Chief Rabbi.
- The Sabbath day must be observed in strict conformity to Jewish law.
- Members must study the Bible and other religious texts for at least two hours daily.

The above bylaws are permanent and cannot be amended by a democratic vote of the residents. As a Tasher explains, they are imposed and not proposed:

> You don't have no choice. He [the individual] had a choice. When he came here he knew that this is what he will eat. This is what we're cooking and this is what we will eat. . . . Therefore, it's not like we're making votes and we voted this and this and a minority is not happy. Everybody who comes here knows what he will get.

It is unnecessary to paint an idyllic portrait of the Tash community that distorts or masks some of the practical problems confronting it. In fact, there is the challenge posed by a steadily increasing birth rate coupled with the necessity to provide gainful employment for the residents. The institution of the *kollel* where married men receive a financial subsidy to pursue religious studies fails to provide an adequate occupational option for all males, especially for those who are not inclined to intensive and advanced religious learning. Along the lines of adding employment opportunities for the residents, the community will be the beneficiary of a diamond cutting center which it, along with substantial investment by the Quebec government, will establish in the municipality of Boisbriand.

Over the past decade the citizens of Montreal and Quebec have become increasingly familiar with the Tasher through articles and reports in the French and English media. The degree of the Tasher's openness to the outside world is carefully limited through a series of meticulously engineered social boundaries; and, as I have argued elsewhere, pragmatic considerations govern the nature of their involvement in the political affairs in the province whose current government is committed to separating from Canada and to achieving sovereignty (Shaffir, forthcoming).

In sum, the Tasher pride themselves on the success with which they have preserved their distinctive lifestyle, and their geographic isolation is seen as an integral part of the success. "What can be better than here?" asks a Tasher, and adds: "It's safe, it's not polluted and, most of all, the children are not exposed to bad things that you cannot help but see in the streets of the city."

Boundaries, Hasidim, and Jewish Identity

Everett C. Hughes, writing about the many small societies not yet swept out by the broom of our industrial and urban civilization, reflected: "How long will it take to mop them up, no one knows. The process seems to be going on rapidly now, but it will probably last longer than any of us would predict" (1952: 25–26). Social scientists have been perplexed by the success which Hasidic communities have shown in resisting and countering the surrounding asismilative influences. Some have pointed to the strains and stresses which affected that lifestyle and threatened it. Kranzler, for instance, believed that the external symbols of Hasidic tradition—including the men's long jackets, their fur-trimmed hats, and their side-curls—would not endure, adding: "Only a small minority will cling to the extreme pattern of their parents" (1961: 240). In his study of the Williamsburg Hasidim, Poll commented: "As more members of the community move into a greater variety of occupations and as the types of occupations increase, there may be more extensive involvements in external systems of social relations" (1962:253); occupational mobility would enhance the possibilities for members to assimilate and lose their identity as Hasidic Jews. Rubin's (1972) study of the Satmar cited several strains affecting the community, including economic pressures and rapid natural increase of the population. While Hasidic Jews and their communities have not managed to eliminate all social problems that beset persons and groups in the larger society, the facts are that Hasidic communities are increasing in numbers, they experience relatively few defections, and, perhaps most surprisingly, they are skillfully transmitting their values and traditions to successive generations.

Although I have focused on two boundary-maintaining mechanisms in this chapter—the control over secular education, and the isolation of the Tash Hasidic sect—several others can be identified. In fact, I have written about two others in an earlier publication (Shaffir 1995), specifically, the proselytizing activities of the Lubavitcher Hasidim and the negotiation of public controversies involving Hasidic Jews and their gentile neighbors in Quebec. I regard these as boundary-maintaining devices in that their outcome, both intended as well as unanticipated, draws members of the Hasidic community together, thereby separating them from outsiders.

One aspect of boundary maintenance that I have not investigated in detail, and which requires careful scrutiny, is the institution of the *Rebbe*, or charismatic leader of the Hasidic sect. Numerous accounts, both of a literary and scientific nature, testify to the *Rebbe*'s extraordinary powers. So central is the role of the *Rebbe* that his position defines, interprets, and reinforces reality for the members of the sect. The institutional arrangements around which the Hasidic community is organized—for instance, the schools, prayer houses (*shteeblech*), charity funds, occupational training—are but a reflection of the Rebbe's vision and influence. As any researcher of Hasidim can attest, members of the community regard the Rebbe as the central axis from which all in the community extends. Indeed, the boundaries fashioned by the Hasidim to organize their personal lives closely mirror the intensity of their relationship with their Rebbe. His hopes, desires, and aspirations are incorporated into the community's organization but, more immediately, into the Hasid's sense of self. How this is accomplished, and the implications of this phenomenon for channeling socialization and exercising social control in the Hasidic community, are interesting topics for investigation in the future.

While boundaries, like fences, are designed to separate and to keep out untoward influences, it is at the interstices, where insiders and outsiders inevitably meet, that they are most fruitfully studied. At these junctures we examine the phenomenon as it affects the individual in day-to-day life—trips to hospitals and to health care professionals, shopping in supermarkets and department stores, and visits to government offices readily come to mind—enabling us to comprehend how individuals construct and impose boundaries around themselves. In addition, we are obliged to carefully chart the institutional structure of Hasidic communities as these provide for the needs of their members, thereby obviating the necessity of contact with outsiders. In short, the dynamics of boundary maintenance intimately connect with the preservation of a distinctive lifestyle.

I now turn to the larger issue of Jewish identity. It is not unusual for researchers to conclude their argument by stressing the need for additional research, and students of Jewish identity are no exception. Two directions for future study seem particularly relevant (I am certainly not the first to point them out). The first is a call for more qualitative research. As Cohen observes: "The debate over the Jewish future is essentially a debate over the quality and durability of middle Jews' group identity. Only qualitative research can probe this issue with the subtlety and nuance it demands" (1991:29). We must understand how persons construct their Jewish identity and this requires an appreciation of how they define their situation and organize their behavior. The second is to cast the net more narrowly in examining Jewish identity, and to focus closer attention on those institutions and persons that have proven influential and instrumental in channelling and transmitting Jewish identity. To quote David Rosenhan, "We should concentrate upon the values, beliefs, allegiances, moral commitments, community supports, and ideologies that we think are important and especially useful" (1991:280). Here again, I emphasize the gains to be derived from qualitative research. Arguably, qualitative research is time-consuming, but I believe that it will yield a deeper understanding of the problem.

As we know, identity is fashioned through social interaction. As Prus (1997) emphasizes, identity work reflects ongoing assessments and negotiations as the parties involved develop definitions of "self" and "other," in view of the social context in which they find themselves. It is best to regard these definitions in terms of processes, since identity shifts typically occur as people move from one set of relational others to the next.

Why not study people in the contexts where they are situated and observe how their sense of themselves as Jews is strengthened, challenged, weakened, or enhanced? We ought to study synagogues and synagogue groups, schools, summer camps and summer trips to Israel, singles and encounter groups, and so on. The key to such research is to examine social interaction *in situ* and to better understand how peoples' activities and daily lives shape and influence the meanings they attribute to Jewishness and Jewish identity.

Despite the Hasidic sects' cultural and ideological differences, their goal—the cultivation of a lifestyle grounded in Torah observance—is highly uniform. Though they may pursue various, and seemingly incompatible, routes to achieve this goal—witness the proselytizing of Lubavitch in contrast to the deep insularity of the Satmar—there is neither confusion nor disagreement over the importance of the Commandments and their relevance to daily life. To this extent, at least, Hasidic institutions are complementary in that each is organized to achieve a common goal, and the larger Hasidic community is highly homogeneous. By contrast, the non-Hasidic Jewish community has acculturated and even assimilated, and is comprised of a heterogeneous complement of institutions and lifestyles. As a consequence, it is less accurate to speak of Jewish identity than of Jewish identities.

Jewish diversity has implications for identity organization and identity maintenance. Jewish identity assumes different meanings for the different publics within the Jewish community. Moreover, meanings shift and even change over time. In the absence of a common set of objectives, the organized Jewish community is characterized by a plethora of institutions, all of which may, and do, claim to be in the business of manufacturing, solidifying, and reinforcing Jewish identity. Under such circumstances, it is hardly possible to anticipate a uniform set of strategies for preserving Jewish identity: a strategy deemed enlightening and progressive by one segment of the Jewish community may be contested by another as regressive and even destructive. The debate over intermarriage, for instance, offers a relevant case in point. As different Jewish publics organize their daily lives around different norms, values, and expectations, they identify with their Jewishness in myriad ways.

Conclusion

In his study of work, Everett C. Hughes observed that " . . . progress is apt to be commensurate with our ability to draw a wide range of pertinent cases into view. The wider the range, the more we need a fundamental frame of reference" (1958: 88–89). Similarly, the student of identity seeks to label underlying processes by which identity is constructed and organized. Hughes also emphasizes the importance of the comparative dimension in social research: "The comparative study of man's work learns about doctors by studying plumbers; and about prostitutes by studying psychiatrists" (1958: 88). In the attempt to designate features commonly shared by occupations, however seemingly different they may appear, one may serve as a yardstick—or the benchmark concept that began this chapter—against which others may be compared. It is in this respect that researching the Hasidim may shed light on the processes and dynamics of identity preservation in general and among Jews in particular.

Notes

1. Boldt suggests a similar point in his discussion of the Hutterites. He is interested in understanding how the pace of assimilation proceeds; he claims that the Hutterites represent a group that has resisted the process of assimilation most successfully. He then adds the following:

   To the extent that the Hutterite experience can shed light on issues such as these, it would be a mistake to regard them as an ethnic anomaly. Although their cultural heritage and record as ethnic survivors make them somewhat exceptional, in many respects they also represent what other ethnic groups once were and perhaps what some would wish to regain. This is not to suggest that other groups who are not content with the prospect of a merely symbolic ethnic identification should (or could) adopt the Hutterite model in toto, but some broad principles might be derived which can be generalized beyond the Hutterite experience (1985: 90).

2. Data on the schools are derived from my research in Montreal.

References

Barth, F. 1969. *Ethnic Groups and Boundaries*. Boston: Little, Brown and Company.

Boldt, E. 1985. "Maintaining Ethnic Boundaries: The Case of the Hutterites," pp. 87–103 in R.M. Bienvenue and J.E. Goldstein (eds.), *Ethnicity and Ethnic Relations in Canada: A Book of Readings*. Toronto: Butterworths.

Breton, R. 1978. "Stratification and Conflict between Ethnolinguistic Communities with Different Structures." *Canadian Review of Sociology and Anthropology* 15: 148–157.

Cohen, S.M. 1991. "Response to Bruce Phillips," pp. 27–29 in D.M. Gordis and Y. Ben-Horin (eds.) *Jewish Identity in America*. Los Angeles, CA: University of Judaism.

————. 1988. *American Assimilation or Jewish Revival?*. Bloomington: Indiana University Press.

————. 1983. *American Modernity and Jewish Identity*. New York: Tavistock.

Friedman, M. 1986. "Haredim Confront the Modern City," pp. 74–96 in Peter Y. Medding (ed.) *Studies in Contemporary Judaism*. Bloomington: Indiana University Press.

Goldscheider, C. 1986. *Jewish Continuity and Change*. Bloomington: Indiana University Press.

Goldstein, S. and C. Goldscheider. 1968. *Jewish Americans: Three Generations in a Jewish Community*. Englewood Cliffs, NJ: Prentice-Hall.

Gordis, D.M. and Y. Ben-Horin, eds. 1991. *Jewish Identity in America*. Berkeley and Los Angeles, CA: University of Judaism.

Gutwirth, J. 1996. "Hassidism and Urban Life." *The Jewish Journal of Sociology* 38 (2): 105–113.

Hughes, E.C. 1958. *Men and Their Work*. New York: The Free Press.

————. 1952. *Where People Meet*. New York: The Free Press.

Kanter, R. M. 1972. *Commitment and Community: Communes and Utopias in Sociological Perspective*. Cambridge, MA: Harvard University Press.

Kezwer, G. 1994. "Shalom, bonjour." *Canadian Geographic* July/August.

Kranzler, G. 1961. *Williamsburg: A Jewish Community in Transition*. New York: Phillip Feldheim.

Liebman, C. 1995. "Jewish Survival, Anti-Semitism, and Negotiation with the Tradition," pp. 436–450 in R.M. Seltzer and N.J. Cohen (eds.)*The Americanization of the Jews*. New York: New York University Press.

Mayer, E. 1995. "From an External to an Internal Agenda," pp. 417–435 in R.M. Seltzer and N.J. Cohen (eds.) *The Americanization of the Jews*. New York: New York University Press.

Mintz, J. 1968. *Legends of the Hasidim*. Chicago: University of Chicago Press.

Phillips, B.A. 1991. "Sociological Analysis of Jewish Identity," pp. 3–25 in D.M. Gordis and Y. Ben-Horin (eds.) *Jewish Identity in America*. Los Angeles, CA: University of Judaism.

Poll, S. 1962. *The Hasidic Community of Williamsburg*. New York: The Free Press.

Prus, R. 1997. *Subcultural Mosaics and Intersubjective Realities*. Albany: SUNY Press.

Ritterband, P. 1991. "ModernTimes and Jewish Assimilation," pp. 377–394 in R. M. Seltzer and N.J. Cohen (eds.) *The Americanization of the Jews*. New York: New York University Press.

Rosenhan, D. 1991. "Jewish Identity and Policy Research," pp. 279–281in D.M.

Gordis and Y. Ben-Horin (eds.) *Jewish Identity in America.* Los Angeles, CA: University of Judaism.

Rubin, I. 1972. *Satmar: An Island in the City.* Chicago: Quadrangle Books.

Sandberg, N. 1986. *Jewish Life in Los Angeles: A Window to Tomorrow.* New York: University Press of America.

Shaffir, William. 1997. "Still Separated from the Mainstream: A Hassidic Community Revisited." *The Jewish Journal of Sociology* (June 1998).

———. 1995. "Boundaries and Self-Presentation among the Hasidim," pp. 31–68 in J.S. Belcove-Shalin (ed.)*New World Hasidim: Ethnographic Studies Of Hasidic Jews in America.* Albany: SUNY Press.

———. 1987. "Separation from the Mainstream: The Hassidic Community of Tash." *The Jewish Journal of Sociology* 29 (1): 19–35.

Sklare, M. 1967. *Jewish Identity on the Suburban Frontier.* New York: Basic Books.

Part Three

Factual Accounts from the Diaspora and Israel

12

Naming Norms and
Identity Choices in Israel

Benjamin Beit-Hallahmi

Introduction

What we mean by identity is a conscious (but also unconscious) meeting point between the individual personality and society. On the individual level, it is a collection of perceptions and feelings tied to our different and many social roles: being a man or a woman, young or old, parent, child, brother, sister. Beyond these—which represent our primordial roles and subidentities—there are subidentities—based on social class, occupation, religion, and nationality. On a collective level, identity may exist as the self-definition of a group of men, women, young, old, psychologists, or Italians. Both collective and individual identity may have an objective basis. Common experiences, language, ritual, customs, and traditions. Beyond the lived and shared experiences, there is the subjective element of an assumed common history, sometimes claimed to go back thousands of years.

Zionism and Jewish Identity

What we see in Israel, and in the Zionist movement which created it, is a deliberate attempt to create a secular nationalism and a secular identity out of a collective history which is totally marked by religion. Since Jews and Judaism became separate in the nineteenth century, the need arose for a new definition of Jewish identity (see Beit-Hallahmi 1992). Zionism is one response to the process of secularization among Jews, which has been more radical than in any similar group. The Zionist definition of world Jewry stated that Jews were members of a national group, deserving its own nation-state. Israel is that nation-state, intended to provide a home for all Jews.

The greatest achievement of Zionism is the creation of an Israeli identity, reflecting the fact that the dream of a new nation, a new human reality, has been realized. An Israeli culture has been created, expressing Israeli experience through language, music, literature, poetry, and art. Those in Israel who are officially defined as Jews do have a choice in defining themselves consciously as more Jewish or more Israeli.

In a systematic survey conducted in 1987, such individuals were asked whether they see themselves as more Jewish or more Israeli. The responses were:

- Jewish only—3 percent
- Israeli only—4 percent
- Equal degree—27 percent
- More Israeli—28 percent
- More Jewish—34 percent
- No opinion—4 percent

In this survey the "Jewish" side was stronger among observant, older people and the less educated. The Israeli side was stronger among the young, the secular, the better educated and second-generation natives (Hassin 1987). This seems to support the notion of a developing Israeli identity.

What does being an Israeli mean? It means sharing a certain cultural reality, and being ready to adopt a personal label. Not all Israeli citizens will adopt it. Those who do not share the trait of being Jewish as defined by law in Israel, are obvious outsiders. Those who follow Orthodox Judaism do not need any new labels. Those who adopt the new label willingly have adopted the Zionist message of the need for newness. Their conscious individual identity is the product of Zionist efforts to create a new culture. The content of the Israeli identity proves that.

Israeliness comes out of the experience of growing up in Palestine or Israel under the Mediterranean sky, under a set of cultural conditions—especially the Hebrew language—and historical conditions. Defining Israeli identity is done by separating it from Diaspora Jewish identity and from all non-Israelis. Israeli identity and culture today are the products of Zionist history and deliberate Zionist efforts to create a new, secular Jewish nationalism, based on a new mythology, unlike anything in Jewish tradition. The cultural heritage includes both Judaism and European elements, together with the will to innovate, to reject the past, and to assert novelty, all characteristics of other settler societies. Most Israelis will say that they are also Jewish, thus confirming the Zionist notion of a worldwide Jewish nationality, of which Israelis are only a subgroup. They are still aware of the boundary separating Jews and gentiles. At the same time, "Jewish" in Israel signifies another boundary—between Israelis and the native Arabs— which has figured prominently in the Israeli consciousness. Israeli/ Palestinian as a pair of opposites both duplicates and supersedes the Jew/gentile opposition.

Creating a New National Identity

In a way, the appearance of a new Israeli identity is a failure of Zionism, which proclaimed that all Jews in the world make up one people with one identity. But this development is still a direct consequence of Zionism, in its rejection of what it has traditionally meant to be a Jew or have a Jewish identity. A separate identity was formed because Zionism proclaimed a contradiction: a nation which must be preserved through being transformed; a national culture which must be rejected.

The sources of this new identity include the rejection of the past, the positive ideology of a new nationalism and the objective experience of the new reality in the Middle East. The creation of Israeli identity started with two acts of total rejection. The first was a rejection of the Jewish past and present, its culture and experience, as it was known to Zionists in the nineteenth century, who equated Diaspora existence with passivity, cowardice, and subservience. The second was a rejection of the image of the Jew, which represented the despised Jewish culture. This almost total rejection of Diaspora traditions is the cornerstone and capstone of the new Israeli identity, the most tangible product of Zionist ideology. Jewish identity is preserved only on condition that it be redefined and actually negated.

Rejecting Jewish History

Defining Judaism as a nationality has created the novel possibility of a new Jewish nationalism, modeled after the European kind. Judaism has claimed religious superiority for the "nation of priests," and outsiders were considered unclean and unworthy of respect.

The Zionist conception of Jewish history offers a division into distinct periods. Jewish history is divided into periods of activity and heroism. Ancient history is joined with modern Zionism; that is, the period before A.D. 135, when the last rebellion against the Romans ended, is viewed as belonging in the same class with the period after 1880, when Zionist settlement in Palestine began. Contrasting dramatically with these two eras of heroism and positive movement is the long period of submission and passivity between A.D. 135 and A.D. 1880, 1745 years which should be erased from the collective memory. The ancient Jewish past in Palestine was seen as marked by activism, pride, and a readiness to fight and die for national independence. A nationalist mythology was developed by selectively recreating past glories.

Zionism, by rejecting rabbinical Judaism, began a Biblicalization of Jewish history and identity. Biblical Hebrew and Biblical mythology became the cornerstones of the new nationalism. The leap over 2000 years of rabbinical tradition and Diaspora experience was aimed at landing in a past of glory of power, overshadowed only by future grandeur.

The reinterpretation of the Hebrew Bible started with nineteenth century Hebrew literature and the Haskalah movement, with new heroes and new ideas being discovered in the ancient text. Those who wanted to revive Hebrew found in the Bible a source of classical Hebrew style, and a repository of great literature. It is certainly both, and plays a central role in literate Israeli culture. Today's interpretation of the Bible, as it is studied in the majority of Israeli schools, is a direct continuation of the nineteenth-century approach.

Rejecting Yiddish: The New Identity

In the nineteenth century, revival of a national literature written in the national language was a part of every national movement, and dividing lines among national groups coincided with linguistic boundaries. The various ethnic groups of Eastern Europe intermingled to create a heated cauldron of cultures and movements separated by language. For speakers of German, Lithuanian, Ukrainian, Polish, Russian, etc., language defined both identity and social differences. In this melange, Jews spoke Yiddish and were defined by it. Some Jews did speak Polish or Russian, and considered Yiddish only a dialect. But Yiddish was unique to Jews. It served to unify them and mark the boundaries of the community. Today, when this language has been disappearing from the world scene, a few words in Yiddish are all that many Jews have to show of their cultural heritage.

For Jews, the spoken language was Yiddish, but Zionism offered it neither a new home nor renewed respect. Yiddish was rejected by Zionism as the language of Diaspora and suffering, part of the Diaspora identity. It had to be eliminated because it was a creation of the Diaspora and any Diaspora attachment had to be extinguished. Yiddish also quickly became identified with movements which opposed Zionism and were based on either socialism or Jewish cultural autonomy in the Diaspora. Moreover, it was, and it remains, the language of the Orthodox, the majority of whom opposed Zionism and preserved historical Jewish culture as it was known in the Diaspora. The end of Yiddish and the revival of Hebrew was another triumph of Zionism, and became a key element in Israeli identity.

Rejecting Jewish Names

Individuals do not choose their own names, but are able to select names for their children. In most societies, surnames and first names reflect the strength of cultural traditions and the continuity of identity across generations. Names are a cultural code, a discourse, a text. In every culture they convey important messages. The story of Israeli names is crucial to our understanding of how a new and different identity was formed.

Surnames. Traditional Jewish last names, such as Landau, Sachs, or Kovner, reflect Jewish history in the Diaspora. Jewish surnames teach a history and geography of exile and wanderings. In the new Israeli nations, Diaspora names, evidence of exile and alienation, of weakness and oppression, of Jewishness and otherness, had to be erased, just like the foreign geography. Foreign names reflect past realities, and do not mean anything to speakers of Hebrew, whereas real Israeli surnames carry clear meanings, reflect new realities and ideals. Popular Israeli last names were fashioned to replace familiar Jewish names. Names connected with geography of exile—Rosenthal, Rosenberg, Goldberg, Goldstein, Schwartz, Greenberg, Silverberg, Hirschfeld, Finkelstein—were transformed to reflect local geography, the return to nature, and the ideal of strength and forcefulness. The new names include Golan and Galili (of the Galilee), Sella (rock), Even (stone), Gazit (rock), Shaham (granite), Samir (rock), Tamir (tall), Peled (steel), Regev (earth clod), Telem (furrow) and Nir (furrow).

Ben-Gurion, Israel's first Prime Minister, was born in 1886 in Plonsk, Poland, as David Green—quite a common name. When he went to Palestine in 1906, he found a new last name in Talmudic writings about the Great Rebellion against the Romans in A.D. 66. In Israel, just as in the Diaspora, last names have been dropped because "they sounded too Jewish." In some cases, this included such classical Hebrew names as Cohen and Levy, which still sounded too Jewish. Thus, someone named Cohen (priest) changed his name to Keidan (spear) and somebody named Levy (Levite—member of the priesthood) changed his named to Lavi (lion). The popularity of certain adopted Hebrew names has created new anonymity. If those who were previously Rabinowitz, Zimmerman, Kovalsky, Rabinov, and Rabelsky are now (all of them) Amir or Tamir or Golan, the new name does not carry with it any common identification.

First names. One's first name is psychologically close to the sense of self, or the sense of personal identity (Erikson 1958). Personal identity develops in relation to the given name before he uses the word "I," and throughout life the name remains one of the most stable attributes of self. Choosing a name for a new baby, an intensely private matter, is determined by strong historical and cultural forces. Every name is a cultural product. Every individual carries with him, through the name, a message from those who gave him that name. Names like any cultural product and any cultural production, are a text to be read and interpreted. The audience, or the addressee, upon hearing or reading a name, engaged in a decoding process, through which cultural codes are utilized, when known, to determine certain attributes of the bearer of the name. Knowing the culture better means knowing more cultural codes, enabling the recipient to decode more effectively surplus meanings, a cultural tradition of naming, or a culturally innovative fashion in naming children constitute a system of signs, a special cultural language.

The choice of a first name for a child places that child, and his parents, in the flow of history, be it the history of the family, the tribe or the whole of humanity. Traditions of naming within human groups are quite persistent over generations.

Jewish first names. What are Jewish names? The answer can be given exactly and empirically. Jewish names are the names used by Jews over the ages, and they are well recorded and easily found. Naming norms can best be defined as rules restricting the domain from which names could be selected. Such norms exist in most societies. Diaspora Jews had very clear rules, which are kept for hundreds of years. The ancient Jewish naming tradition, limited the Jewish name pool to Old Testament names other than those which "preceded" the patriarch Abraham in Jewish mythology. This rule was stated explicitly in Talmudic literature. There were only three exceptions to the rule forbidding names which in the mythological chronology of the Bible are antecedent to Abraham: Hava, Noah, and Hanoch. In fact, the names of the mythological patriarchs and their children were not commonly used in Talmudic times, and became traditional only in the Middle Ages, in the Diaspora.

The Jewish naming tradition in the European Diaspora included two elements. One was keeping the limited, traditional pool of names. The second was that of keeping names in the family by naming newborn babies after deceased relatives. Despite the fact that the Old Testament contains 1400 male first names, fewer than 100 were used by Jews in the Diaspora. These included the Patriarchs, Abraham, Isaac and Jacob, Jacob's children, some of the prophets, and some of the kings. The judges were mostly excluded. To the traditional, limited onomasticon were added genuine Diaspora names.

Thus, for 1500 years, Jews used a fairly limited number of names. The Jewish rabbinical tradition has used a relatively limited onomasticon (list of names), with clear rules, reflecting a commitment to Judaism. First names were selected from among Biblical and Talmudic figures who deserved to be remembered. Biblical figures involved in any misdeeds, or simply lacking in religious distinction, were never the namesakes of Jewish children.

The Zionist Rebellion and Naming Traditions

The cultural rebellion of Zionism was aimed against all facets of Diaspora existence, including the Diaspora naming tradition. Changing one's first or last name was regarded as an expression of the true national spirit and the creation of a new national identity, and a rejection of the Jewish past in the Diaspora. The first norm in the creation of the Zionist onomasticon was that of the rejection of the Diaspora names, which included traditional Old Testament and Yiddish names. These were rejected in favor of Old Testament Talmudic names connected to periods of national sovereignty and success. This trend can be seen in the nineteenth-century Haskala literature.

The tradition of Zionist names began in the first Jewish settlements in Palestine. The children of Eastern European Zionist settlers, born in the ancient homeland, were given names connected with the glorious Jewish past. These names were symbolic of either Jewish sovereignty (Absalom, Amaziah, Shaul) or nationalist leadership during periods when Jews lacked sovereignty (Giora, Bar- Kochba). Bar-Kochba (nickname of Shimon Bar-Koziba) was the leader of the last Jewish revolt against the Romans, A.D. 132–135. He was denounced by Talmudic sages, and Diaspora Jews never used his name and rarely mentioned him. Zionism returned Bar-Kochba to the national pantheon. Another dominant motive in Zionist name giving is that of identification with the Biblical past through the selection of the name of a Biblical figure. Choosing, for example, the name of the prophet Ben-Amotz betrays a certain grandiose pretense. The choice of pre-Diaspora, Old Testament names symbolized the desire to get around 2000 years of exile and back to the golden age of Jewish sovereignty and productive life.

Some Diaspora names were corruptions of Yiddish versions of Hebrew names—Salman for Solomon, Sanvil for Shmuel (Samuel), Mendel for Menachem, Hirschel for Zvi. These, and names created and used exclusively in the Eastern European Diaspora (Issar, Sender, Fishel, Bonem, Getzel, Feivel, Faivush, Zelig) became stigmatized to such an extent that they have disappeared completely from the scene; some may properly be called "ethnic epithets" (Allen 1983). However, among the very Orthodox, these names are still used.

In many of the new Zionist names, an explicit element is rebellion against Jewish traditions, and an identification with rebellious individuals in general. Thus, names figures described in the Old Testament as defying the will of God are consistently selected. The name of Absalom, the rebellious son, which never appeared among Jews for 2000 years, reappeared in the new Jewish settlements in Palestine at the end of the nineteenth century. Another trend starting in the early settlements after 1882 is the use of Old Testament non-Jewish names, such as Na'aman, who is described in II Kings 5:1 as "captain of the host of the kings of [Syria]", and a leper later miraculously cured by Elisha.

Using Old Testament names that have been for countless generations outside the repertoire of acceptable names may stem either from sincere ignorance of Jewish culture and traditions, or from a deliberate defiance towards them. In either case, it is an act that marks a break with the past, and a distance from what was once a common structure of beliefs. A good example is the name Ben-Ami, which appears in Palestine around 1900 as a Zionist name, meaning "son of my people" (there is also a feminine version, Bat-Ami). The name happens to be identical with the Ben-Ami described in Genesis 19: 38 as the son of an incestuous union between Lot and his younger daughter. Ben-Ami became "the father of the children of Ammon unto this day." It is quite clear why this name was never used by Jews, but the Zionists who used this name simply ignored the reasons for not using the name, thereby rejecting Diaspora naming practices.

The rejection of Diaspora Jewish history became a rejection of all things Jewish, and accompanied the development of a nativist ideology devoted to the development of a new identity referred to as "Hebrew," which emphasized the language and ties to the Middle East and ancient Middle Eastern, pre-Israelite traditions. The rejection of Diaspora names, and the search for a new system of naming, began with the mainstream of Zionism, but reached its culmination with the Young Hebrews movement of the 1940s. This movement was a radical expression of nativist ideology among Jews in Palestine. This ideology and search for a nativist identity symbol led to the adoption of names which belong to the ancient pre-Israelite Middle East. Members of the movement thus became known by the derogatory name of "Canaanites." The Canaanites based their ideology on the following assumptions:

1. Jews in the Diaspora are a religious group, bearers of a religious culture.
2. Jews in Palestine, living a more normal existence and speaking Hebrew, are a separate group, with a separate identity.
3. Language and language culture are the basic components of identity.
4. Therefore, Jews in Palestine should be known as Hebrews.
5. Hebrew culture in the Middle East should find its inspiration in the ancient cultures of the Middle East.

The victory of the Canaanites started with a small group of writers who adopted Canaanite- sounding names, led by Uriel Shelah (Yonatan Ratosh), followed by Aharon Amir and Binyamin Tammuz. By now, most Israelis have become Canaanites without realizing it. Amir has become one of the most common family names in Israel. Some of the popular names in Israel, which are recognized by all as Hebrew-sounding, are in fact names of Canaanite gods, such as Anat or Nevo. These and other Old Testament names attached to non-Jewish, pagan traditions—names like Osnat, Hagar, Nimrod, and Canaan—thus came into fashion in Israel in the 1950s, after having been dormant for all of Jewish history.

In summary, the changes in naming traditions since the beginnings of Zionism have included two elements: the rejection of traditional Jewish given names, which had come to symbolize Diaspora culture; and the use of ancient Hebrew or non-Hebrew names from the Bible, or totally new Hebrew terms. With the revival of Hebrew, Biblical names never used in the Diaspora suddenly came into vogue. The Land of Israel was once again peopled by names like Gideon (a Biblical judge), Yoav (a Biblical hero), Boaz (Biblical ancestor of David) and Bar-Kochva. For 2000 years there was no Jewish Amos or Yoram (both Biblical kings who "did evil in the sight of the Lord"). But, with the Zionist rejection of Diaspora tradition came the rejection of the rules which forbade the use of such names. Even more dramatic than the naming of Jewish babies according to such precepts is the adoption by immigrants of Hebrew names, who thereby situate themselves very consciously in the renewal of Jewish history.

It is among Orthodox Jews in Israel that historical Jewish first names can be found, together with a historical Jewish identity. They never had any qualms about naming their children Avraham (Abraham), Yitzhak (Isaac), Ya'akov (Jacob), or Moshe (Moses), because they never had any problem with being just Jewish (see Sobel and Beit-Hallahmi 1991). It is among secular Israelis, who do not want any part of being Jewish, that we may today find such names as Tom, Guy, Dean, or Shirley. All these names have the advantage of sounding both American and Israeli, and of not sounding Jewish.

Changing fads in the choice of first names, and trends in the choice of last names are viewed as reflecting instability in one's identity, and a consequent attempt to create "identity anchors" both individually and collectively. The general historical trend in any social onomasticon is that of continuity. Extreme and sudden changes should be rare. When we look at cultural variations in naming patterns over time we are engaging in an archaeology of cultural symbols.

Israeli Names Today

Looking at typical Israeli names one hundred years after this process began, we find such combinations as Ayelet Sella (Gazelle Rock), Orly Oren (My Light Pine Tree), Aviv Orani (Spring of The/My Pine Tree), Yoram Eshet (Y. Strong as Steel), Yael Segev (Ibex Lofty), Idan Agmon (Epoch Bullrush), Shahar Ram (Dawn Thunder/Tall), Amnon Meydan, Netta Moran (Seedling Snowball Bush), Yael Sagi (Ibex Exalted), Ran Ziv (Happy Radiance), Anat Admati (A. of My Land). When first heard, these names sound Turkish, Indian, or Arabic. If we look at them as text to be read and interpreted, one clear message encoded in all of these names is, "We are not Jewish." And indeed no one will suspect at first sight that these names have anything to do with being Jewish. They represent the new Israeli identity, developed over the past one hundred years through a series of rejections and choices. Orna Amir (Pine Treetop), Eyal Arad (Ram Bronze), Oren Aviv (Pine Tree Spring), and Amir Peled (Treetop Steel) are names that have nothing in common with Diaspora Jewish culture. They represent Israeli culture and Israeli identity; they have been created in a deliberate attempt to erase any Diaspora connections. These names express an admiration for power and for nature. Oren Aviv, Amir Peled, and Orna Amir are authentic Israelis.

Israeli names (as opposed to Jewish ones) can be classified into the following groups, which can also be arranged chronologically, or, to use the archaeological analogy, by strata:

1. Zionist names (since 1882, reaching their peak between 1910 and 1949): Absalom, Bar-Kochba, Na'aman, Ben-Ami, Yigal.
2. "Classical" Sabra names (since 1920, reaching their peak between 1930 and 1950): Uri, Danny, Yoram.
3. Foreign ("Canaanite") Old Testament names (since 1940, reaching their peak during the 1970s): Nimrod, Anat, Hagar.
4. Nature names—plants, flowers (since 1960): Oren, Alon, Sigalit, Sigal, Moran, Nophar, Rotem.
5. Bilingual names, used in both Hebrew and English (since 1960). Tom, Shirley, Karen.

TABLE 12.1
Frequency Ranks of First Names of Females—
Individuals Born in 1900, 1978, 1991

Rank	1900	1978	1991
1	Esther	Karen	Sapir
2	Sarah	Michal	Nophar
3	Rachel	Meital	Adi
4	Miriam	Rachel	Mor
5	Hanna	Liat	Shani
6	Rivka	Yael	Danielle
7	Leah	Adi	Tal
8	Rosa	Sharon	Hen
9	Shoshana	Esther	Gal
10	Regina	Galit	Or

What do all Israeli names have in common? What they all share is the simple fact that they have not been in use until recently, and that in no case have they been part of the Jewish Diaspora tradition. Most of the names are mentioned in Jewish sources, but were never used as first names. What Israeli parents are looking for, apparently, is newness and non-Jewishness.

The major quantitative change in the creation of the Israeli onomasticon has been its growth. In other words, as Weitman (1981) shows, the Jewish onomasticon has traditionally been quite limited. There was a prescribed list of Old Testament, Talmudic and Diaspora names. When the Jewish naming tradition was rejected, the number of acceptable alternatives increased. The development of a new repertoire stems from two opposing trends. One is the rejection of old names included in the traditional repertoire, and the other is innovation and the creation of new names.

The appearance of bilingual first names (Hebrew/English) was initially accidental, as happens in many cultures, but in recent years (since 1970) there has been a real trend favoring names such as Guy, Shirley, Karen, Roy, and Sharon.

Evidence from analysis of population data. Let us now turn to an analysis of historical trends in name-giving, as reflected in population statistics. Tables 12.1 and 12.2 show the ten most popular names given in 1900, 1978, and 1991 to individuals who at some point have been Israeli citizens.

It should be remembered that over 99 percent of those individuals

TABLE 12.2
Frequency Ranks of First Names of Males—
Individuals Born in 1900, 1978 , 1991

Rank	1900	1978	1991
1	Yossef	David	Daniel
2	Moshe	Moshe	Bar
3	Avraham	Yossef	Or
4	Ya'akov	Yaniv	Yossef
5	Yitzhak	Yitzhak	David
6	David	Ya'akov	Amir
7	Haim	Shai	Moshe
8	Shmuel	Roy	Guy
9	Simha	Avraham	Gal
10	Shlomo	Assaf	Tal

born in 1900 were born outside Israel, and thus their names represent traditional Jewish naming practices in the Diaspora. Those born in 1978 and 1991 bear the marks of modern Israeli, as opposed to Jewish, naming traditions. Table 12.1 demonstrates, in addition, that naming traditions for girls change faster than for boys. Weitman (1982) confirms that the onomasticon for females is always larger than the one for males. Here only one name (Esther) that numbered among the top ten in 1900 appears among the top ten in 1978. The list of the ten most popular female names in 1900 is made up of seven Old Testament names, two Diaspora names, (Rosa, Regina) and one innovative Hebrew name (Shoshana).

Among the ten most popular female names in 1978, four come from the Old Testament: Esther and Rachel, which were traditionally used in the Diaspora, find themselves side by side in popularity with Michal and Yael, which were never used by Diaspora Jews, but were adopted by the Zionist revival. Meital, Liat, Adi, and Galit are Israeli creations, never used before 1948, and rarely used before 1960. The most popular name in 1978, and number eight on the list are obvious American imports, eagerly picked up by Israeli parents. The 1991 list for females shows not a single traditional name.

As expected, table 12.2 reveals greater traditionalism regarding given names for boys. Six of the top names in 1900 are still among the top ten in 1978 (Yossef, Moshe, Avraham, Ya'acov, Yitzhak and David). The 1900 list is made up of eight Old Testament names, and two Diaspora names (Haim, Simha). The 1978 list includes six traditional

Old Testament names. The four remaining names include one Old Testament name used only recently (Assaf), and three new Israeli names, representing trends in the creation of new names since 1940. The 1991 list for males shows three traditional Old Testament names, with all the rest coming into fashion quite recently.

Conclusion: Names and Identity Crises in Israel

When traditions of name giving in a society show rapid or drastic changes, we should expect either a serious disruption of cultural traditions, or a deliberate attempt to create new individual and collective identities. Two interesting phenomena in the choice of names can be observed in Israel. One is the adoption of new names by adults, which has been an accepted part of Zionist practice and an act of commitment to Zionism. Another is the changes in the choice of first names for children, which correspond to some extent to the first, but has shown more instability over time.

The rejection of Diaspora culture is expressed through many rituals of discontinuity, and two such rituals in Israel have been the rejection of the Yiddish language and the rejection of traditional Jewish names. Emphasis is placed not only on the act of name change (and identity change), but on the choice of names for both the self and one's children, and the psychohistorical meaning of different names and naming fashions. Changing fads in the choice of first names, and trends in the choices of last names are viewed as reflecting identity instability and the attempt to create "identity anchors," both individually and collectively.

For some Jews, the creation of political Zionism—and, later, the creation of the State of Israel—did not present any problems as far as identity was concerned. For religious Jews, and especially non-Zionist religious Jews, nothing has changed. Their identity has remained Jewish, and they saw no need to modify their world view because of political development. As Jews have done for millennia, they continue to use the old names of Joseph, Abraham, Jacob, etc., having no problems with their Jewish identity. But even among the Orthodox, there are grades and shades of orthodoxy, which are reflected in names. Thus, it is only among the ultra-Orthodox that no changes can be observed.

Since 1948, we can see the development of Israeli norms, which go beyond the Zionist ones by increasing the range of Old Testament names, and by coining new names that do not reflect the old ideals of Zionism, but new ideals of secularism, and the rejection of both Jewish and Zionist traditions. What has happened in Israel since 1948, and more clearly since 1970, is not just change and cultural innovation, as they can be observed in other societies, but a breakaway from cultural traditions, symbolized so effectively by creating new fashions in naming. In the selection process of names among contemporary Israeli secular parents, two factors are operating: a negative impulse toward names that sound Jewish or are Jewish, and a positive impulse toward names that sound Israeli or are bilingual.

Among secular Israelis, the desire to change and innovate in naming practices cannot be explained on the basis of novelty appeal alone. They are making an important cultural statement in their move away from traditional names. Research on given names and their cultural significance can be categorized as belonging to the realm of social psychohistory, or just social history proper. What has happened in terms of the change in naming traditions among secular Jews in Israel can be regarded as a true cultural break, a true watershed.

References

Allen, I.L.. 1983. "Personal Names that Became Ethnic Epithets." *Names* 31: 307–317.

Beit-Hallahmi, B. 1992. *Original Sins: Reflections on the History of Zionism and Israel*. London: Pluto.

Erikson, E. H. 1958. *Young Man Luther*. New York: Norton.

Hassin, E. 1987. "Face in the Mirror." *Politika*, October. [Hebrew]

Sobel, Z. and Beit-Hallahmi, B. 1991. *Tradition, Innovation, Conflict: Jewishness and Judaism in Contemporary Israel*. Albany : SUNY Press.

Weitman, S. 1982. "Cohort Size and Onomasticon Size." *Onoama* 26: 78–95.

———. 1981. "Some Methodological Issues in Quantitative Onomastics." *Names* 29: 181–196.

13

Tracking Demographic Assimilation: Evidence from Canada's Major Cities

Leo Davids

Introduction

Both scholars and community leaders throughout the Diaspora have long been interested in assessing the demographic as well as educational health of the Jewish community, concerning themselves—in the contemporary phrase—with "Jewish continuity." Jewish continuity has a core of meaning which is very familiar to anyone who worries about the long-term survival of an authentic Jewish community, although the terminology may have shifted. Since it became clear some decades ago that the integration or acceptance of Jews in North American society was no longer the major issue, but that the great challenge had become maintaining a recognizable Jewish collectivity in a free and welcoming society, there has grown a very significant literature on predicting the future size and quality of the Jewish communities in the United States, Canada, and other places (e.g., Bayme and Rosen 1994; Goldscheider 1986; Kosmin et al. 1991; Schmelz and Della Pergola 1995). This chapter will make a contribution to the discussion of these same concerns, based on data made available from the 1991 population census of Canada.

Much demographic information on Jews that may be derived from the 1981 and 1991 Canadian census has already been brought to light through work by Torczyner and associates (e.g., Torczyner et al. 1995, Torczyner and Brotman 1995) as well as in earlier papers by this author (Davids 1985, 1994). These and other studies, however, which provide the reader with background for this chapter, have focused largely on individual characteristics of Jews in Canada (rather than looking at other units, such as families), or have given extensive data without sufficient interpretation and explanation. This chapter will not emphasize information based on individual characteristics, but rather, will focus on understanding something about the Jewish quality of the various cities in Canada (as well as the overall national situation), mainly on the basis of different family types.

The definition of terms such as "family" and "family structure" is something that Statistics Canada has taken pains to address, and we need not repeat these discussions here (See Statistics Canada 1992; Che-Alford 1994: ch.1). What we shall try to do is to sketch the demographic situation (and prospects) for the Jews of Canada by looking at the major urban areas and comparing them to one another. We shall be looking for local or regional patterns, and then the nation-wide picture for Canada, including comparisons of Jewish data with those from the entire population.

Let us also note that our city data, below, does not deal with just the cities in their precise official limits, but with what is called the "Census Metropolitan Area" (CMA). In common parlance, this would correspond to "Greater Montreal" or "Greater Toronto," since each CMA includes the city center plus the close suburbs; the CMA thus gives one a better picture of the entire community rather than only what is contained within specific legal boundaries such as the "City of Ottawa" proper.

We shall not spend much time here in discussing the difference between counting Jews by ethnic origin as compared with Jews by religious denomination. This distinction may be quite important when one wants to do fine analyses of Canadian census data, and it has been discussed elsewhere (See Berkowitz 1994: 3–6; Davids 1994: 2; Torczyner et al. 1995: 10–11, 66–71). Suffice it to say that the "Jewish" community as measured in this chapter refers to anyone who reported their religion as being Jewish, but excludes all those who did not declare themselves of Jewish religion, although they may have some Jewish ancestry (see Schmelz and Della Pergola 1995: 467–8). By contrast, the definition consistently used by Torczyner and his associates, however, includes not only all Jews who are so declared in terms of their religious denomination but also those who reported "no religion" or "atheist" or "agnostic," while having some ethnic ancestry listed as Jewish (Torczyner et al. 1995: 10, 195). This is a broader definition which, I believe, relates more to history than to the present or future, and sometimes leads to questionable overall descriptions of Jewish communities. However, electing, as we did, to address only those who claimed Judaism as their religion, may result in undercounting of Jews or Jewish behavior, particularly in smaller communities and in Canada's West. We ask readers to keep in mind, therefore, that "Jews" in this chapter are all those who declared their religious affiliation to be Jewish, without any regard to their ancestry or ethnic origin. Obviously, we include "Jews by Choice" (converts to Judaism) but exclude Jews who have joined any other faith community.

Recent Trends in Canadian Family Living Arrangements

Before we can describe the situation regarding Canada's Jewish communities, one has to know the larger context—that is, what the family trends are in Canada generally. Statistics Canada has published a number of post-census reports which deal with this, including their book *Families in Canada* (Che-Alford 1994; cf. also Statistics Canada 1992). To summarize that picture very briefly, we know that during the past twenty-five to thirty years, Canada (as is the case with most other Western countries) has seen a very strong movement toward fewer children or smaller families; dual-earner couples; much higher divorce rates, leading to large growth in the number of one-parent families; and a significant increase of unmarried cohabitation, often referred to by the legal term "common-law marriage" (see Statistics Canada 1997: 123–181).

These tendencies became quite pronounced during the 1980s, leading to a family scene in Canada, which contains fewer conventional couples (particularly those with only one "breadwinner" in the labor force) while the other structural possibilities have become more and more common. Although most families in Canada today still involve a legally married couple, we must bear in mind that many more families today are based on a couple who live together without having had any sort of formal wedding, as well as one-parent families (Che-Alford 1994: 1, ch. 2; LaNovara 1993).

Specifically, in 1991 we find that 9.9 percent of all census families in Canada were cohabiting families, rather than those legally married; and a larger number yet (13 percent of all Canadian families) have one parent only. The literature also points out that whereas one-parent families were not uncommon in the earlier part of this century, those one-parent families were usually caused by the death of a spouse. Today, however, the percentage of one-parent families due to bereavement is much smaller, while the majority of such families are attributable to separation and divorce (Che-Alford et al. 1994: 17).

It is also useful to mention briefly that there are important provincial or regional variations with regard to the distribution of these family types within Canada. Indeed, one might expect that the variations among Jewish communities across Canada are to some extent explainable in terms of differences between Canada's provinces, which are far from identical to each other in matters of family demographics (LaNovara 1993: 13).

The Geography of Canadian Jewry

Which are the major Jewish communities in Canada? Obviously, Canada's largest cities—Toronto, Montreal, Vancouver—have substantial Jewish communities, with Toronto being much the largest, Montreal next, and Vancouver third in the country. The fourth-largest Jewish community in Canada (as of 1991), is Winnipeg, which is not that large a city in terms of urban Canada generally, but remains a very important Jewish center. Winnipeg was the number-three Jewish city in previous years, but by 1991 Vancouver had overtaken it as the third-largest Jewish CMA.

When we speak of major communities in this chapter, we use a threshold of 5,000 Jewish souls. Communities smaller than this may be considered less significant in the overall Canadian Jewish picture. Using this criterion, there are only six CMAs which rank as major communities. In descending order, they are: Toronto, Montreal, Vancouver, Winnipeg, Ottawa, and Calgary.

The population counts of these Jewish communities have been dealt with in earlier works. Very briefly, we know that the number of Jews in Toronto exceeds 150,000, while the number in Montreal is a little less than 100,000 (in 1991). In Vancouver, Jews numbered a little over 14,000 (1991 data), while in Winnipeg the number is slightly higher than 13,000; the number in Ottawa fell just below 10,000 souls in the 1991 census, and Calgary counted close to 5,500 Jews (Davids 1994: Table 2; Statistics Canada 1993b: Table 2). Torczyner and his associates argue that this is an undercount of the actual, effective Jewish community in some Canadian cities, which have substantial populations of people who declared some Jewish ancestry in the ethnic origin category, but were of no religion, atheist or agnostic in terms of their current religious denomination (Torczyner and Brotman 1995; but see Schmelz and Della Pergola 1995: 475).[1]

Thus, as we consider specific data on a city-by-city basis, we shall be dealing only with the largest communities. Adding up the number of Jews in these six CMAs gives us over 90 percent of the entire Jewish population of Canada in 1991, leaving fairly insignificant (numerically, that is) pockets of Jews in the smaller communities.

The data that we shall present and interpret in this paper, surveys the distribution of Jewish population in the above-named cities, focusing mostly on the different types of family structure to be found within the Jewish populations there. Although the data were recorded in 1991, we use the present tense in describing the picture emerging from that census.

Concepts and Variables in Jewish Family Demographics

Jewish demographers are obviously interested in phenomena such as mixed marriages or the extent to which Jewish families are one-parent rather than two-parent, because these family structures are a part of the modern scene which—from the standpoint of Jewish survival into the future—presents some major threats. As the studies by Cohen (1982), Goldscheider (1986), Medding (1992) and others have already made clear, when any Jewish community has a significant number of families that involve Jews married to non-Jews, or that fall into the low-fertility category, then the numbers of its Jewish children are very likely to be smaller. Both exogamous (Jews marrying Gentiles) and one-parent families tend to be of lower fertility, and children who are born in these families also have a higher probability (than those having two Jewish parents) of not being raised as Jews who will identify and affiliate with the Jewish community when they become independent. Thus, leaving aside judgments having to do with culture, morality, and other elements, the demographics alone suggest that mixed marriage and one-parent families pose a threat to the Jewish future simply because they tend to mean fewer Jewish children. Of course, this has been stated and explained at length in other work (see Bayme and Rosen 1994; Della Pergola 1995; Kosmin et al. 1991; Rosen 1995: 15, 20–21).

In examining the tables below, it is important to remember some factors that are not shown, but which may be important in interpreting their meaning. For one thing, we should bear in mind the different age structures of the various communities, as we know that the percentage of Jews aged 65 and older in both Montreal and Winnipeg (26 percent there were seniors) is considerable (See table 13.2 below). Moreover, recent arrival in high-attraction cities (such as Vancouver) can also be significant, as migration has an impact on the likelihood of both mixed marriage and single parenthood, which tend to be found among younger rather than older couples (Medding et al. 1992: 8–10). We know as well that the population of Jewish ancestry declaring no religion is much larger in many smaller Canadian cities than it is in Toronto and Montreal (See Torczyner and Brotman 1995: 245, 251). We thus acknowledge the loss of some information, since our method counts only those who claim to be of the Jewish faith (including converts to Judaism). Nevertheless, our tables do provide a substantially valid picture of the Canadian scene.

1991 Statistics: The Facts

Before we present our Jewish data, it is useful to know the overall population size of Canada's largest cities. Particularly for those who are not familiar with the population geography of Canada, the following overview will be useful. In 1991, the census found about 3,900,000 people in the Toronto CMA; somewhat over 3,100,000 inhabitants in greater Montreal; 1,600,000 in the Vancouver CMA. All other cities in Canada had under 1,000,000 inhabitants. Ottawa (without its close neighbor Hull, Quebec) numbers about 700,000 inhabitants; Ottawa and Hull together had over 920,000 inhabitants; there were about 840,000 people in Edmonton, 750,000 in Calgary, and just over 650,000 in Winnipeg. Winnipeg is the seventh-largest city in Canada, descending from Toronto, at the top of the size list. It is no surprise that when we look at numbers of families, and other information, the largest aggregations are found in Toronto, followed by Montreal; for Jews,

TABLE 13.1
Distribution of Jewish Family Types, 1991
6 Census Metropolitan Areas[a]
(Cities by descending size order; nearest 25 cases)

CMA	Total Jewish Individuals	All "Jewish Families"[b]	Legally & In-Married ("Conventional")	Mixed & Cohabitant[c]	Jewish Lone Parents[d]
Toronto	151,125	44,100	32,750 (74%)	7,575 (17%)	3,775 (9%)
Montreal	96,700	28,450	21,400 (75%)	4,275 (15%)	2,750 (10%)
Vancouver	14,350	4,900	2,500 (51%)	1,950 (40%)	475 (10%)
Winnipeg	13,325	4,025	2,950 (73%)	750 (19%)	325 (8%)
Ottawa	9,925	3,275	1,975 (60%)	1,050 (32%)	250 (8%)
Calgary	5,540	1,750	1,025 (59%)	575 (32%)	150 (9%)

a Only those CMAs containing over 5,000 Jewish-by-religion inhabitants.
b That is, all families containing any Jewish-by-religion adult, whether spouse or lone parent.
c Unduplicated count: one enumeration for those individual Jews who are in both a mixed and cohabitant relationship, plus all the Jew-gentile married and the Jew-Jew cohabitant families.
d Lone-parent families are 13% of all Canadian families.

Sources: Statistics Canada, 1991 Census Report 93–319, table 2; custom tabulations for L. Davids.

however, Winnipeg is not the seventh population center but the fourth, as noted earlier.

Table 13.1 provides an overall picture of Jewish family types in six Canadian cities. The table indicates a total of 44,100 families within Greater Toronto that contain one or two Jewish adults. Thus, families containing any Jewish adult as defined by religious category (whether a marital partner or single parent) are included in this total (see note b to the table). We find that 74 percent of all these families are "conventional" Jewish families; a legally married couple in which both partners claim to belong to the Jewish religion.

The remaining 26 percent of Toronto's Jewish families are not "conventional." That is to say, 26 percent consists of 3,775 one-parent families (9 percent of Toronto's total Jewish population); plus 7,575 families which consisted either of a Jewish couple living together without any formal marriage, or "mixed" (one Jewish and one Gentile partner). All these are grouped together in table 13.1 to give us an overview of each community, but table 13.3 will "unpack" this part of each CMA's Jewish population to show more specifically what the situation is.

Thus, three out of four Toronto Jewish families are the sort that community leaders are perfectly content with, in that the couples are formally married and are both Jews. The other one-quarter of all relevant Toronto families raise certain concerns, from a demographic standpoint, and challenge the organized Jewish community to a response (American Jewish Committee 1988; Mayer 1991; Mayer and Avgar 1987).

Moving on to Montreal, we see from table 13.1 that there were 28,450 Jewish families there in 1991, of which 75 percent were conventional (legally married and endogamous) families, with the remaining quarter not falling into this category. Montreal has a fairly high representation of Jewish one-parent families, which constitute just under 10 percent of all Jewish families in that city; on the other hand, Montreal has a very low proportion of mixed and cohabitant Jewish families—only 15 percent of the total Jewish population. This, despite the relatively high level of cohabitation in Montreal's overall population (Statistics Canada 1992: 12; LaNovara 1993: 13).

Vancouver, however, presents a very different picture. We see that Vancouver has 4,900 families involving one or more Jewish adults, but only 51 percent are conventional Jewish families. About 10 percent are one-parent families, while the other 40 percent are composed of mixed-religion and/or cohabiting couples. Thus, the Jewish family demographics of Vancouver immediately stand out in strong contrast to what is seen in Toronto and Montreal.

Continuing to the figures for Winnipeg, there are just over 4,000 Jewish families, with a distribution similar to the picture in Toronto and Montreal. Seventy-three percent of the Winnipeg Jewish families are conventional ones; 8 percent are one-parent units; and 19 percent consist of mixed and cohabiting couples.

The other cities shown in table 13.1 occupy a demographic position between the "traditionalist" central Canada norms (set by Toronto and Montreal) and the exceptionally modernist or assimilated pattern seen in Vancouver. Looking at Ottawa and Calgary, we find that the conventional Jewish families are approximately three out of five in those cities (59 percent to 60 percent). The mixed and cohabiting families in Ottawa and Calgary constitute 32 percent, while the percentage of one-parent Jewish families varies somewhat but is, in all cases, under 10 percent of the Jewish family total for the city.

One would also wish to examine which of these cities had strongly

TABLE 13.2
Age Groups and Marital Status Percentages, Jews,[a] 1991

	Toronto	Montreal	Vancouver	Winnipeg	Ottawa	Calgary
Total Jewish Population[c]	151,125	96,700	14,350	13,325	9,925	5,450
Jewish Child Population[b]	21%	19%	18%	16%	21%	21%
Jewish Seniors Population[b]	16%	23%	17%	26%	16%	11%
All age 15+: (Percentages)						
Never Married	26.1	25.0	26.1	22.7	24.8	26.6
Married & Cohabiting	60.3	59.2	56.2	59.3	61.3	59.8
Divorced & Separated	6.6	6.6	10.8	7.3	7.7	8.0
Widowed	7.0	9.2	6.9	10.7	6.2	5.6
Jewish Pop., 15 yrs.+[c]	119,875	78,750	11,750	11,150	7,825	4,300
Age 30–49: (Percentages)[d]						
Never Married	14.8	15.9	18.6	15.5	16.5	14.5
Married & Cohabiting	75.1	72.8	65.7	73.2	73.1	74.0
Divorced & Separated	9.6	10.6	15.1	10.7	10.4	10.5
Jewish Pop., 30–49 yrs.[c]	48,950	25,700	5,200	3,625	3,600	2,025

a   Jews-by-religion only
b   All those age 0–14, inclusive; "Seniors" are all age 65 and up
c   Rounded to nearest 25 cases
d   For the 30–49 age category, this table does not show "Widowed" _ there are so few
    in that age group, less than 1 percent in all Canadian cities. The percentages shown
    for the 30–49 population do not add up to 100 percent, due to omission of the very
    small "widowed" category.

concentrated Jewish neighborhoods and which did not, but that would be difficult to pursue here. The impact of residential concentration on long-term Jewish continuity has been discussed in the literature, from Louis Wirth onwards (See Rosenberg 1993: 30–34, 43–44).

Before leaving table 13.1, we again point out that the population of Jewish one-parent families does not reach 10 percent in any of the cities that we are studying, whereas across Canada, one-parent families are 13 percent of all families. It might be interesting to study why this disparity exists.[2]

Turning now to table 13.2, which looks at Jewish children and seniors populations, and marital status among Jews in Canada's major CMAs, we take note of large variations between these cities. Calgary has the youngest population, out of these six Jewish communities, while Winnipeg has the oldest.

Data on the marital status of Jews has also been provided by Statistics Canada. Zeroing in on the age group that is normally involved in

TABLE 13.3
Jewish Endogamy vs. Exogamy and Unmarried Cohabitation
in Canada's major cities, 1991
(Slightly rounded, to the nearest 25)

	(a) Married Jewish Couples	(b) Mixed Couples*		(b/a) Percent Ratio**	Jew-Jew Cohabitant Couples
CMA			Thereof Cohabitant		
Toronto, Ontario	32,750	7,050	1,380	22	525
Montreal, Quebec	21,400	3,875	1,020	18	400
Vancouver, B.C.	2,500	1,875	420	75	75
Winnipeg, Manitoba	2,950	700	170	24	45
Ottawa-Hull	1,975	1,025	260	52	25
Calgary, Alberta	1,025	550	110	54	15

* Where husband or wife is reported as being of Jewish religion, the partner is not. This excludes cases where a conversion to Judaism has occurred prior to the 1991 Census. It includes some couples where the partner not declaring their religion as "Jewish" may be, partly or entirely, of Jewish ethnic origin. Many of these should not be counted as intermarriages.

** Not that the religiously mixed are a percentage within the endogamous Jewish counts, but that we divide the mixed total for each city by its endogamous total to get a convenient comparison basis concerning the relative extent of intermarriage per city. This mixed couples count, however, includes both cohabitant and formally married couples, with one Jewish and one non-Jewish partner.

N.B.: For all Canada (including all groups/faiths), cohabiting couples are 9.9 percent of 1991 families. (However, in Quebec they are 16% of all families.) 42% of all Canadian cohabitant couples are parenting in 1991, vs. 58 percent with no children at home. For Jews, however, the figure is 25 percent parenting vs. 75 percent without children at home. (Some are empty nesters, of course.)

Jewish parenting, generation of Jews in their community, let us take a look at the 30–49 age group. Table 13.2 indicates that approximately 15 percent to 16 percent of Jews in this age group are reported as single/never married; between 10 percent and 11 percent are divorced or separated; while the widowed are a very small fraction, under 1 percent of people in this category. Thus, those who are currently married range from 72 percent to 75 percent of the total population of this age in practically all the cities; Toronto has the lowest proportion of unmarried, divorced, or separated, and the highest percentage in a current union.

However, the picture for Vancouver in this regard is markedly different: the population of single/never married among Jews aged 30 to 49 years is close to 19 percent, the divorced and separated are 15 percent, and the currently married (or cohabitant) are just under 66 percent. Thus, one can see that Vancouver Jews in this very important age category are significantly less likely to be in a current union than members of the same category in other cities, where differences in marital status proportions in this age group are slight.

Table 13.3 looks at the extent of intermarriage ("exogamy") and unmarried cohabitation, and provides data on endogamous (both partners Jewish) marriage in the same communities.

The table shows that cohabitation by Canadian Jews is a significant phenomenon, but, in percentage terms, is not that popular in the larger centers. Vancouver and Ottawa do have significant percentages of cohabitants among their Jewish families, but these percentages are smaller in other Canadian communities, with only 4 percent of Jewish families in Toronto involved in cohabitation. Halifax, a smaller city not listed in our tables, has 12 percent of all its "Jewish families" cohabitant, but none of those involve two Jewish adults.[3] For all Canada, as shown in table 13.4a cohabitants are some 5 percent of all Jewish families. This, of course, contrasts with the 9.9 percent of all Canadian families which were cohabiting couples in 1991.

Furthermore, table 13.3 gives us a ratio between the exogamous couples (listed in column b) as compared to the number of conventional couples (shown in column a). This ratio indicates that mixed couples are proportionally least common in Montreal (where the ratio is 18) but rise to a peak in Vancouver, where the ratio is 75. This, of course, dovetails with what we have seen in table 13.1, where Vancouver exhibited the lowest percentage of conventional Jewish families among all the major communities in Canada, with 40 percent of Vancouver's Jewish families involved in cohabitation or exogamy. Looking at table 13.3, we see that the mixed-marriage couples are the largest part of that 40 percent, and that within Vancouver's 1,875 religiously-mixed couples there are 420 cohabiting couples.

Overall, Table 13.3 indicates that the very largest communities (Toronto and Montreal) have quite a low percentage of out-married Jews, although, because these are large communities, the numerical count of mixed couples in the two big cities is considerable. On the other hand, with the exception of Winnipeg (and Hamilton), whose rates or ratios regarding exogamy are quite similar to what we found in the two big cities, out-marriage is a very important phenomenon in most of the intermediate-sized and smaller Canadian communities, with at least a third of the couples which contain any Jew, in these communities, involving one Jewish and one non-Jewish partner.

At the same time, we note that in some communities there is a very large coincidence of religious out-marriage and cohabitation, while in others this connection does not appear.[4]

Before discussing or reflecting on what the statistics teach us, let us pause to see the overall Canadian Jewish "national" family situation. Having observed the major differences between the various cities, and the general contrast between central Canada and the western CMAs, we will not be deceived into thinking that the totals shown in table 13.4a represent a homogeneous, standard reality across the country. Rather, we know that table 13.4a is mainly a reflection of the two numerically predominant communities (of Toronto and Montreal), and the national averages they create do not hold true in Vancouver, Calgary, and smaller cities.

Table 13.4a also examines the fertility of different family types, in a somewhat indirect way. The data here show 18,820 mixed couples, of which 4,070 (22 percent of all the mixed) were cohabiting, while the other 78 percent were formally married. However, 76 percent of the cohabitant mixed couples have no children in the home, versus only 40 percent without children among the legally married exogamous couples. In table 13.4b, we see that a tiny fraction of Jew-Jew couples were cohabiters (under 2 percent of the 68,765), but these also indicated much less child-bearing than among the endogamous legally married: 68 percent of Jew-Jew cohabiters had no child present in their home, versus 43 percent among conventional couples.

Only 21 percent of all Canadian Jews in a union or current couple (married or cohabitant) had a non-Jewish partner, and some of those were nonreligious ethnic Jews (or part-Jews, additionally). Effectively, this suggests about 80 percent in-marriage among Canadian Jews— including some converts to Judaism. (More recent data shows that about 70 percent of Jews marrying during 1995 were marrying other Jews, versus about 30 percent marrying out of the religion. This is consistent with data from the 1980s, and it indicates a future rise in the "stock" of mixed couples.)

Table 13.4a also demonstrates that cohabitation is a low-fertility

TABLE 13.4a
Distribution of Jewish-Gentile* (Mixed) Couples, All Canada, 1991
(Slightly rounded)

	Female Jewish		Male Jewish	Total Mixed Couples	Grand Total
Legally Married	6,550		8,200	14,750 (100%)	
		With children in home:		8,800 (60%)	18,820
		No children:		5,950 (40%)	
Cohabitant	1,700		2,370	4,070 (100%)	
		With children in home:		975 (24%)	
		No children:		3,100 (76%)	

* One partner is of Jewish religion/denomination, the other is not—regardless of their ethnic origins. (Thus, some of these are ethnic Jews, of "No Religion." How many of these are, really, "intermarriages"?)

TABLE 13.4b
Distribution of Endogamous Jewish Couples, All Canada, 1991
(Slightly rounded)

		Grand Total
Legally Married	Total Legally Married, Jew-Jew:	67,625 (100%)
	With children in home:	38,725 (57%)
	No children:	28,900 (43%)
		68,765
Cohabitant	Total Cohabitant, Jew-Jew:	1,140 (100%)
	With children in home:	360 (32%)
	No children:	780 (68%)

		Percentage Mixed/Exogamous
Grand Totals	All Legally Married Couples—Mixed & Endogamous:	82,375 (18%)
(Tables 13.4a	All Cohabitant Couples—Mixed & Jew-Jew:	5,210 (78%)
and 13.4b)	Total Husband-Wife Couples (at least 1 Jewish partner):	87,585 (21.5%)

Source: Statistics Canada, Custom Tabulations for L. Davids

situation, whether religiously mixed or Jew to Jew. On the other hand, marriage is associated with procreation, whether it involves endogamous or exogamous couples. Among the legally married, 60 percent of the exogamous couples have a child at home, versus 57 percent of endogamous couples; that is hardly a significant difference.

Finally, table 13.4a gives a reassuring picture, indicating that Canadian Jewry strongly favors legal marriage over cohabitation, and child-bearing predominantly among the legally married. Our earlier tables help us keep this in proper perspective: from the Jewish demographic viewpoint, Montreal is on "another planet" than Vancouver, and one should never generalize from a national average to particular cities—at least not in contemporary Canada (See Shahar 1996: 12–15).

Discussion and Conclusions

What broad conclusions might one draw from these statistical facts? Yes, Jews in different communities are influenced or affected by the larger social environment, yet the Jewish statistics remain significantly different in a number of respects from the general Canadian pattern. This is most evident in Toronto and Montreal, but still appears even in the smaller communities across the country.

However, we see that Vancouver stands out within the Jewish demographic context of Canada as a city which has much higher proportions of "unconventional" families, i.e., cohabiting and mixed-religion. Why? Can other Census-based information help explain the differences we have found? Community size alone is not the answer, although it does count. It is quite true that the largest communities have stronger Jewish communities, since they are all able to maintain more extensive networks of synagogues, Jewish schools, and other identity-maintaining institutions.

One variable that gives us good clues to understanding the differences between one community and another (aside from proximity to other strong communities, and total size) is marital status, which we examined in table 13.2. That table showed clearly the unfavorable conditions for conventional Jewish family life in Vancouver, where many students and other young adults stay outside a union, or at least a marriage, even at the age bracket of 30–49. However, this is not the case in all the other major communities, where approximately 75 percent of Jews in the 30–49 category are married, and thus, likely to be parents.

Another type of explanatory data would be information from the Jewish school system in each city. One would want to know, for example, what percentage of the Jewish children are in Jewish all-day schools rather than supplementary education (which gives a few hours of Jewish study after normal attendance in a public school). As well,

TABLE 13.5
Yiddish and Ivrit (Hebrew) Home Language in Canada, 1991
(Rounded to nearest 25 cases)

	Jewish Population	YHL Population	YHL per 1,000	IHL Population	IHL per 1,000
Montreal	96,700	4,250	44.0	1,850	19.0
Toronto	151,125	2,025	13.4	4,425	29.3
Vancouver	14,350	25	2.0	200	14.0
Rest of Canada	53,900	300	5.4	475	8.5
All-Canada Totals	318,075	6,600	20.7	6,950	21.8

YHL = Yiddish is their main or usual Home Language
IHL = Ivrit (Hebrew) is their Home Language
N.B.: Remember that Statistics Canada's "random rounding" practice means that small counts (e.g. Vancouver's YHL) are rough approximations, really.

Source: Statistics Canada, 1991 Census Report 93–317 (tables 2 and 3) plus calculations by L. Davids.

what is the proportion of Jewish children who are enrolled in Jewish schools at the secondary level, that is, after the age of Bar Mitzvah? However, the data available to me now on Canadian Jewish schools is fragmentary, and not suitable for presentation in this chapter (on this subject, see Rosen 1995: 15–18).

We do know that the Jewish school systems in Toronto and Montreal are strong, showing a rising proportion of their enrollment in Jewish high schools, rather than the old pattern of almost everyone going to high school in the public system, including those who had gone to Jewish day school at the elementary level. Berkowitz (1994: 8), however, indicates a weak enrollment percentage for Jewish schools in Vancouver, agreeing with Kutnick's (1989:148) assessment on comparing Winnipeg (strong commitment to Jewish education) to Vancouver (1989: 148).

Next we should say a little about the retention of Jewish languages— Hebrew and Yiddish. While we cannot go into language data in any great detail here, it is correct to say that, outside of Toronto and Montreal, neither Yiddish nor Hebrew are today viable spoken languages among Canadian Jews. The Jewish language reality has certainly been transformed, over the past 50–60 years (see Rosenberg 1993: 256–259).

In Montreal, as one can see in table 13.5, 44 per 1,000 Jews use

Yiddish on a regular basis as their language at home; an additional 19 per 1,000 Jews in Montreal use Hebrew as their normal family tongue. In Toronto, the numbers are a bit lower, but we do find that 29 Jews per 1,000 use Hebrew as their normal language of the home, while 13.4 a per 1,000 are using Yiddish.[5] Language retention is a crude measure of ethnic-community cohesion/strength and separateness from the larger society; a fully assimilated group would speak only the dominant society's tongue(s), not that of their own ancestors. (In North American Jewry generally, language is not a "marker" of Jewishness nowadays, and the identity/ continuity literature hardly mentions Yiddish at all.)

All other cities in Canada have home language counts for Yiddish and Hebrew which are much smaller, thus indicating that to all intents and purposes, Yiddish and Hebrew are not actually used at home by any significant population. Here, again, we find a great difference between the Jewish cultural ambience in Toronto and Montreal versus all other Canadian cities (See Davids 1989: 4–5; Shahar 1996: 6–7).

Internal migration to Vancouver is also a part of the demographic problem there (see Torczyner and Brotman 1995: 246–248). That city appears to have more rootless/transient Jews than other Canadian cities do. It is obvious that still other data would be relevant and interesting in this context as well, but one cannot incorporate all such material herein.

It should now be very clear, as we conclude this chapter: It is not valid to simply present "national averages" of Jewish demographic realities in Canada, because such all-Canada demographic data hides too much. That is, the variations between one city and another are too large and significant to allow anyone to simply review national averages and then assume that the variations from one place to another within Canada are insignificant. On the contrary, we have seen that Canadian Jewry is certainly not homogeneous, and therefore it is necessary to study each CMA, or a relatively homogenous stratum of them (e.g. Calgary-Edmonton-Ottawa), and the specific family data which characterize that Jewish community.

We have discovered that there is an enormous difference between Montreal, on the one extreme, and Vancouver, on the other. Some of this has been illuminated, if not necessarily accounted for, by information on marital status, Yiddish and Hebrew use, as well as Jewish population size; the demographic "outputs" in various communities are not totally unpredictable or random, but no doubt the product of cultural, religious, and educational "inputs."

No comparisons to other countries have been presented here, but the literature indicates that the underlying dynamics are quite similar for Jews in other English-speaking societies.

Although individual perceptions and behaviors are shaped and limited by social environment, so that the Jewish identity and family data are typically patterned as stronger or weaker in each particular city, one must not deny each person's choice/freedom. That is, macro-level consistency in the variables we have been reviewing here should not lead to the fallacious fatalism of saying that Vancouver Jews must be this way, or Winnipeg Jews that way. One would also believe that real change cannot be planned and accomplished, because "that's the way things are."

No, let us remember that individuals and groups constantly make choices, yet are influenced by the stream of events and forces around them. The dynamism of identity in modern life means that we should not accept any determinism, but acknowledge the environmental/communal realities as they have been, while trying to improve them. This may involve longer Jewish schooling for adolescents, trips to Israel, family Shabbat programs, and many other strategies. Following success in these actions, we can look forward to better statistics next time around! (Cf. Mayer 1991; Rosen 1995: 10–11, 22–25; Kutnick 1989: 148–150).

Further research on Jewish Canada will have to continue looking both at the overall picture for the entire country and, more importantly, at specific realities in each of the separate communities which are building their Jewish tomorrow in their distinct ways.

Notes

1. The work by Torczyner and associates has dealt with approximately a dozen Jewish cities. For specifics about the smaller Jewish communities, see Torczyner et al. 1995.
2. My research on Jewish lone parents, not reported in this chapter, provides a reasonable answer. Although post-divorce lone parenting is just as prevalent among Jews as for all Canadians, there is less cohabitation and certainly far less non-marital fertility (among the never married) for Jews than in the general population. Thus, overall, fewer Jewish families have only one parent.
3. Although that is what the official census results say, we must remember that even if there are actually three or four cases in the CMA, the report may show "0";

Statistics Canada protects confidentiality by not reporting numbers to such a detailed level.
4. Figures (not shown in this table) for Edmonton and Hamilton indicate that—like Halifax—all Jewish cohabitants there have gentile partners, and the number of known Jew-Jew cohabitant couples there is nil!
5. This is not the place for a substantial discussion of Yiddish and Hebrew demographics, but the census produces rich language data on mother tongue and home language (in reports such as Statistics Canada 1993a). I have reported earlier analyses on this elsewhere (e.g. Davids 1989).

References

American Jewish Committee. 1988. *Spotlight on the Family.* New York: Institute of Human Relations, A.J.C.

Bayme, Steven and G. Rosen, eds. 1994. *The Jewish Family and Jewish Continuity.* Hoboken, NJ: Ktav Publishing.

Berkowitz, Jon. 1994. *The New Demographics: A Review of Past and Current Patterns of Canadian and Greater Vancouver Jewish Demographics.* Vancouver: Jewish Federation.

Che-Alford, Janet et al. 1994. *Families in Canada.* Ottawa: Statistics Canada and Prentice-Hall Canada (cat. no. 96–307E).

Cohen, S.M. 1982. "The American Jewish Family Today." *American Jewish Year Book* 82: 136–154.

Davids, Leo. 1994. "Jewish Age and Family Trends in Contemporary Canada." *Sociological Papers* 3(4): 1–14. Ramat Gan: Bar Ilan University.

———. 1985. "Canadian Jewry: Some Recent Census Findings." *American Jewish Year Book* 85: 191–201.

———. 1989. "Knowledge of Yiddish and Hebrew in Canada: The Current Picture." Paper presented at the Tenth World Congress of Jewish Studies, 20 August, Jerusalem.

Della Pergola, S. 1995. "Changing Cores and Peripheries: 50 Years in Socio-Demographic Perspective" in Robert Wistrich (ed.) *Terms of Survival: The Jewish World since 1945.* London: Routledge.

Goldscheider, Calvin. 1986. *Jewish Continuity and Change: Emerging Patterns in America.* Bloomington: Indiana University Press.

Kosmin, Barry A., Sydney Goldstein, Joseph Waksberg, Nava Lerner, Ariella Keysar and Jeffrey Scheckner. 1991. *Highlights of the CJF 1990 National Jewish Population Survey.* New York: Council of Jewish Federations.

Kutnick, Jerome. 1989. "Jewish Education in Canada," pp. 136–169 in H.S. Himmelfarb and S. Della Pergola (eds.) *Jewish Education Worldwide.* New York: University Press of America.

LaNovara, Pina. 1993. "Changes in Family Living." *Canadian Social Trends* 29 (Summer): 12–14.

Mayer, Egon, ed. 1991. *The Imperatives of Jewish Outreach: Responding to Intermarriage in the 1990s and Beyond.* New York: Jewish Outreach Institute and Center for Jewish Studies, City University of New York.

Mayer, Egon and Amy Avgar. 1987. *Conversion among the Intermarried.* New York: American Jewish Committee.

Medding, Peter et al. 1992. *Jewish Identity in Conversionary and Mixed Marriages.* New York: American Jewish Committee.

Mott, F.L. and J.C. Abma. 1992. "Contemporary Jewish Fertility: Does Religion Make a Difference?" *Contemporary Jewry* 13: 74–94.

Rosen, Sherry. 1995. *Jewish Identity and Identity Development*. New York: American Jewish Committee.

Rosenberg, Louis. 1993. *Canada's Jews*, edited by Morton Weinfeld. Montreal and Kingston, Ontario: McGill-Queen's University Press.

Shahar, Charles. 1996. *A Survey of Jewish Life in Montreal, Part I*. Montreal: Federation/CJA.

Statistics Canada. 1997. *Report on the Demographic Situation in Canada, 1996*. (cat. no. 91–209E), Ottawa.

———. 1993a. *Home Language and Mother Tongue*. 1991 Census Report (no.93–317).

———. 1993b. *Religions in Canada*. 1991 Census Report (no. 93–319).

———. 1992. *Families: Number, Type and Structure*. 1991 Census Report (no.93–312).

Schmelz, U.O. and S. Della Pergola. 1995. "World Jewish Population, 1993" in *American Jewish Year Book* 95: 466–492.

Torczyner, J.S. et al. 1995. *Rapid Growth and Transformation: Demographic Challenges Facing the Jewish Community of Greater Toronto*. Montreal and Toronto: McGill Consortium for Ethnicity and Strategic Social Planning and Jewish Federation of Greater Toronto.

Torczyner, J.S. and S.L. Brotman. 1995. "The Jews of Canada: A Profile from the Census." *American Jewish Year Book* 95: 227–260.

14

The Structure and Determinants of Jewish Identity in the United Kingdom

Stephen H. Miller

Introduction

This chapter reports some of the findings of a large postal survey of British Jews conducted by Marlena Schmool[1] and myself on behalf of the Institute for Jewish Policy Research (JPR). The survey is unique in the breadth of its coverage, incorporating questions on a wide range of social and political issues, measures of religious belief and practice, and indices of ethnic identity and synagogue affiliation (see Miller et al. 1996). The data set will support an in-depth analysis of the Jewish characteristics of the respondents, a separate investigation of their sociopolitical values, and a detailed study of the interrelationship between Jewish beliefs and secular values.

In this chapter, I focus on the Jewish characteristics of the sample viewed, independently of the other measures. The chapter is empirical in orientation. It provides (1) a brief description of the main Jewish religious groupings in the United Kingdom, (2) an analysis of the factorial structure of Jewish identity and a comparison with the American case, and (3) data on some of the determinants of Jewish identity behaviors including marriage choice.

Sampling Strategy

It is virtually impossible to obtain a probability sample of the British Jewish population without investing disproportionate sums. The British Census does not assess the Jewishness of respondents, and the Jewish community does not maintain a comprehensive database. Further, British Jewry is too small (about 0.5 percent of the population) for a random national sample survey or random digit dialing to be a viable option.

Previous studies (e.g., Schmool and Miller 1994) have made use of probability sampling methods, but have applied these to lists of synagogue members or other Jewish membership lists. This introduces systematic bias, excluding those on the periphery of the organized community who are unaffiliated but may nonetheless regard themselves as Jewish. This subgroup is particularly important in the context of the Jewish continuity debate.

In this study we tried to achieve a probability sample of the whole (self-identifying) Jewish community in the following way: First we used computerized screening to determine the percentage of Distinctive Jewish Names (DJNs) on the electoral register in each of the United Kingdom's postcode semi-sectors (effectively a few streets at a time). These figures were used to estimate the percentage of Jews in each area, assuming of course that the proportion of Jews with a DJN is invariant with area.

To convert the percentage of DJNs in a given area to an estimate of the percentage of Jews in that area, one needs the right multiplier. Affiliation lists of synagogues and other Jewish bodies show that about 14 percent (1/7) of Jews have names falling within the set of DJNs. Hence the percentage of Jews in a given semi-sector can be estimated by multiplying the observed percentage of DJNs on the electoral register by 7.

This process yielded a number of areas in which the estimated percentage exceeded 15 percent (called high-density areas); in these areas a random sample of names and addresses (of all kinds) was taken from the electoral register. Questionnaires were distributed by mail to each of the target respondents, with the understanding that the majority would be non-Jews.

In low-density areas, such a strategy would have proved too expensive, and so in these cases we randomly sampled the electoral register for DJNs and used these as our master list. Here we assumed that Jews with distinctive Jewish names would not differ systematically from Jews with more anglicized names, an hypothesis which is at least tenable on the basis of American research.

The problem with the DJN approach in the low density areas is that it excludes Jewish women married to non-Jewish men; such women will generally have acquired their spouses' non-Jewish surnames and cannot enter the master list. (An interesting exception is the case of a Jewish Miss Lewis who had married a non-Jewish Mr. Goldstein and was thus included in our sample!) To overcome this selection bias, we developed a snowball sample of outmarried Jewish women living in low density areas and adjusted the size of this sample to match the estimated proportion of such women in the total population.

The overall effect of this sampling strategy was to generate an achieved sample of 2,194 persons (almost 1 percent of U.K. Jewry). This is certainly the largest and most representative sample yet achieved, though clearly biased in some ways.

A Simple Mapping of Jewish Religious Lifestyle

Any attempt to assess the religious profile of the British Jewish community by looking at the distribution of synagogue affiliation would be doomed to failure. British Jews, unlike their American counterparts, are often found to belong to synagogues that bear very little relation to their personal religious stance. In particular, large numbers of British Jews join Orthodox synagogues because of historical or emotional ties, even though their personal beliefs and practices more closely resemble those of the Progressive or Conservative movements. Indeed the very small number of Conservative synagogues in the United Kingdom probably reflects a nostalgic preference for Orthodox synagogues among the non-Orthodox majority. In any event, synagogue affiliation *per se* is a very poor indicator of religious observance.

Previous research has shown that self-classification of religious lifestyle provides much better discrimination between respondents than classification based on their synagogue affiliation (Schmool and Miller 1994). In this survey we have used the following categories (derived from previous research) to represent religious observance, asking respondents to assign themselves to the appropriate group. The percentages in each group are shown in brackets:

- (26%)   Secular (non-practicing)
- (18%)   Just Jewish
- (15%)   Progressive
- (31%)   Traditional (not strictly Orthodox)
- (10%)   Strictly Orthodox (i.e. would not turn on a light on Sabbath)

Table 14.1 shows the relationship between formal synagogue affiliation and self-classification (where "Just Jewish" and "Progressive" have been combined to simplify the analysis). As can be seen, over 50 percent of the sample claim membership in an Orthodox synagogue, while only one fifth of them (10 percent of the whole sample) report behaviors consistent with such membership. And even within the 10 percent who regard themselves as fully observant, about one-fifth reject certain fundamental beliefs such as the view that "the Torah is the actual word of God," preferring instead a formulation that sees the Torah as "the inspired word of God," and insists that "not everything should be taken literally."

Thus the community is fragmented in a rather bizarre way; the Orthodox bodies claim via their membership statistics to represent the majority of British Jews—52 percent of all Jews, and more than two-thirds of the affiliated community. But those same bodies represent only about 10 percent of the community as far as religious adherence is concerned. The position is more consistent in the case of Reform and Liberal synagogues, but even here a significant proportion of members see themselves as falling to the secular left or Conservative right of their chosen synagogue. All this underscores the need to employ alternative measures.

TABLE 14.1
Synagogue Affiliation by Self-classification of Religious Lifestyle
(N= 2100, row percentages shown)

	Religious Lifestyle			
Synagogue type	Secular %	Progressive or Just Jewish %	Traditional %	Strictly Orthodox %
Orthodox (52% of sample)	4	18	58	20
Reform (14% of sample)	9	85	5	1
Liberal (5% of sample)	13	78	9	0
Non-members (28% of sample)	67	27	6	1

Note: **Members of Masorti (Conservative) synagogues made up just 1 percent of the sample and are not included in this tabulation.**

Belief, Practice, and Ethnic Identity in the four Religious Groups

It is no surprise that respondents who assign themselves to different religious categories differ significantly with respect to levels of ritual observance. Table 14.2 shows the percentage adherence to a set of key measures derived from previous studies (e.g., Miller and Schmool 1992). Ritual observance can be seen to decline steadily across these groups, but with three core rituals (fasting on *Yom Kippur*, attending a Passover *seder* and celebrating *Rosh Hashana*) persisting at a relatively high level in all but the secular group. Following the American pattern, those practices which interfere least with normal social discourse are the most persistent, whilst those that impact most heavily on daily life are prone to extinction. The implication would seem to be that religious rituals have come to serve some purpose other than *halacha,* at least among the non-Orthodox. Those that are retained are unlikely to be seen as religiously prescribed rituals, but rather, are loosely defined, ethnically based ceremonies. It has been argued that such selective practices constitute a constructive adaptation to modernism, since they permit the maintenance of identity without the inconvenience of precise ritual observance (Liebman and Cohen 1990).

Turning now to measures of religious belief and ethnic identity (belonging), Tables 14.3 and 14.4 show how these factors vary across the four religious groupings. The tables show a subset of the indicators used in the full analysis.

Direct comparison of these profiles is, of course, purely speculative. There is no *a priori* reason why different dimensions of Jewishness should be similar in regard to absolute level (i.e., percentage agree-

TABLE 14.2
Ritual Practice by Self-classification of Religious Lifestyle
(N = 2153, Table shows percentage of group who observe)

	Secular %	Progressive Just Jewish %	Traditional %	Strictly Orthodox %
Attends Seder every/most years	19	87	96	100
Refrains from work on New Year	10	86	96	100
Fasts on Yom Kippur (or exempt)	12	79	93	100
Buys Kosher meat	5	17	80	100
Candles lit every Friday evening	2	37	69	100
Refrains from Travel on Sabbath	1	1	18	100

TABLE 14.3a
Religious Belief by Self-classification of Religious Lifestyle
(N = 2147, table shows percentage of group who agree with statements)

	Secular %	Progressive Just Jewish %	Traditional %	Strictly Orthodox %
(Rejects) Universe came about by chance	18	34	36	94
Belief in God is central to being a good Jew	18	35	35	83
Jews have a special relationship with God	17	36	58	96

TABLE 14.3b
Ethnic Identity by Self-classification of Religious Lifestyle
(N = 2078, Table shows percentage of group who agree with statements

	Secular %	Progressive Just Jewish %	Traditional %	Strictly Orthodox %
Unbreakable bond unites Jews throughout world	43	71	90	97
Feels quite/very strongly Jewish	40	80	98	100
At least half friends are Jewish	31	67	94	100

ment) or with regard to their gradients across the four religious groups. Nonetheless, it is worth noting that for a range of rather simple belief statements (not all shown here) levels of adherence seem intuitively to be rather low, lower than those recorded in Israel (Levy et al. 1993) whilst seemingly strong expressions of ethnic identity command high levels of support.

Perhaps more interesting (and somewhat less problematic) is the comparison of gradients. In the case of ritual observance, there is a relatively steady decline across the four religious groups, while the gradient for measures of belief shows a discontinuity between strictly Orthodox and traditional respondents; thereafter it is more-or-less flat. Measures of ethnic identity mimic the ritual observance curve, providing some tentative evidence that ethnic identity may be a more potent determinant of religious observance than strength of belief. I will return to this question in a later section.

TABLE 14.4
Factors Underlying Expressions of Jewish Identity:
JPR and NJPS Compared*

	JPR		NJPS (Wilder 1996)	
	Factor 1	Factor 2	Factor 1	Factor 2
Synagogue member	.91918		.610	
Refrains from work on Rosh Hashana	.86496		.540	
Frequency of attending Seder over a number of years	.85878	.591		
Fasts on Yom Kippur	.75895	.459		
Strictness of Synagogue movement (4–point scale)	.72445	.333		
Supports Jewish charities	.72061	.703		
Proportion of friends who are Jewish (5–point scale)	.71630	.547		
Number of Jewish organizations belonged to	.71263	.540		
Frequency of lighting Shabbat candles in home (3–point scale)	.67741	.362	.451	
Frequency of Synagogue attendance	.59172	.32838	.549	
Reads a Jewish publication regularly	.54320		.557	
Preference for Jewish vs. non-Jewish social ties (3–point scale)	.39958		.399	
Drives (JPR)/handles money (NJPS) on Shabbat		.89988		.495
Separates milk and meat at home		.67245		.834
Strictness in purchase of kosher meat for home	.32129	.60136		.594
Lives in a Jewish neighborhood		.55297	.342	
Participated in Jewish education in past three years		.54080	.365	
% VARIANCE	50.5	7.1	29.5	6.5

* Variable definitions are based on the JPR study. The variables used in the NJPS study are similar, but not always identical.

Factor Analysis of Measures of Jewish Identity

The descriptions given above assume a factorial structure for Jewish identity that may not be valid. Although previous studies generated a simple, three-factor model of identity (with belief, practice, and ethnicity as the main dimensions), the present sample is certainly more heterogeneous than those obtained in previous surveys, and the data set is considerably richer. Some further analysis is therefore justified.

TABLE 14.5
Factors Underlying Jewish Identity: All JPR Variables Included

	Factor 1	Factor 2	Factor 3
Synagogue member	.89252		
Frequency of attending Seder over a number of years	.84755		
Refrains from work on Rosh Hashana	.78588		
Strictness of Synagogue movement (4–point scale)	.76251		
Frequency of lighting Shabbat candles in home (3–point scale)	.72533		
Proportion of friends who are Jewish (5–point scale)	.71528		
Fasts on Yom Kippur	.68699		
Prefers to stay home Friday nights	.67742		
Strictness of observance of Kashrut	.65994		
Number of Jewish organizations belonged to	.64817		
Frequency of Synagogue attendance (5–point scale)	.63268	-.30765	
Importance of Jewish home life to sense of Jewish identity (3–point scale)	.52326		
Supports Jewish charities	.49811		
Refrains from seasonal Christmas activities in home	.45820		
Reads Jewish publication regularly	.44501		
Judged importance of Jews marrying within the faith (5–point scale)	.43981		.35544
Extent to which Torah is seen as word of God (3–point scale)		.71019	
Level of agreement that universe created by chance (5–point scale)		-.66164	
Level of agreement that prayer helps overcome problems (5–point scale)		.62337	
Degree to which Sabbath commandment rated irrelevant (4–point scale)		-.60956	

The first analysis is based on a subset of seventeen identity variables chosen to match almost exactly the measures used by Wilder (1996) in her analysis of the 1990 National Jewish Population Survey (NJPS). Table 14.4 gives a comparison of the Miller et al. (1996) (JPR) and NJPS findings, based in each case on an unweighted, least-squares extraction with oblique rotation.

There is a remarkable similarity between these two data sets. In both cases most of the variance is explained by a single factor made up of virtually the same variables. This factor conflates two logically distinct constructs: light rituals (e.g., attending a seder, celebrating the Jewish New Year) and ethnic identity variables (e.g. organizational membership, social ties with Jews). Anticipating what is to come, this main factor might be defined as "behavioral ethnicity" where the behavioral variables comprise simple rituals or Jewish social behaviors.

The second factor, again for both the American and British samples,

TABLE 14.5 cont'd
Factors Underlying Jewish Identity: All JPR Variables Included

	Factor 1	Factor 2	Factor 3
Irrelevance of faith in God to being a good Jew (5–point scale)		-.60378	
Drives on Shabbat		-.57422	
Level of agreement that Jews have special relationship with God		.55835	
Degree to which 1st Commandment rated personally relevant (5–point scale)		.51514	
Importance of Israel to sense of Jewish identity (3–point scale)			.63212
Importance of "feeling Jewish inside" to sense of Jewish identity (3–point scale)			.61513
Importance of closeness to other Jews to sense of Jewish identity (3–point scale)			.61064
Level of agreement that an unbreakable bond unites Jews (5–point scale)			.56652
Importance of Jewish art/culture to sense of Jewish identity (3–point scale)			..51925
Rated importance of Jewish survival (5–point scale)			.51245
Salience of Jewishness vs. Britishness as component of identity (3–point scale)			.49220
Extent to which Jewish consciousness pervades everyday thoughts (4–point scale)	.36068		.48424
Preference for Jewish vs. non-Jewish social ties (3–point scale)			.42190
Level of agreement that Jews can only depend on other Jews (5–point scale)			.42170

comprises more intensive ritual and religious performance (e.g., separating milk and meat, engaging in Jewish adult education).

There is a suggestion that a few rituals which load partly or wholly on the light rituals factor in the United Kingdom (e.g. lighting candles, kosher meat) have "migrated" to the intensive factor in the United States. This presumably reflects the more advanced state of secularization of the American Jewish population. Overall however, both surveys suggest that the simple distinction between ritual practice and ethnic belonging is unrealistic. The performance of light rituals appears to be more closely allied to expressing one's ethnic identity than fulfilling a religious obligation, and only the more demanding rituals appear to be motivated by religious intentions.

Of course, the dimensional structure of Jewish identity is not an absolute; it depends on which variables are included in the factor analysis. Wilder's study does not include any measures of religious belief, and this makes it difficult to interpret the overall pattern of relationships. Fortunately the JPR survey allows a richer analysis, the results of which are summarized in table 14.5.

Here I have included all those variables that might conceivably reflect an aspect of Jewish identity. Despite this exhaustive approach to variable selection, the first factor to emerge is again a reflection of behavioral ethnicity incorporating light rituals and organizational/social Jewish behavior. The second is a more devotional or religious variable incorporating Jewish religious beliefs (like the divine origin of the Torah) and strict rituals (like not driving on the Sabbath). I have called this variable religiosity. The third factor reflects a sense of ethnic belonging which is more cognitive and devoid of ritual action, incorporating, for example, "feeling Jewish inside" and "having a bond with fellow Jews." This has been labeled mental ethnicity.

These findings take us some distance from the simple model assumed at the outset. Practice, belief, and ethnic identity do not emerge as pure dimensions, but the new structure has a compelling logic of its own, particularly in the context of the progressive secularization of the community. Here we see that simple rituals align themselves with other forms of ethnic behavior, and appear to be simple expressions of group membership, devoid of religious significance. More demanding ritual performance is aligned with belief as a combined expression of religious theory and practice. And internal thoughts and feelings about one's Jewish identity represent a kind of 'virtual' ethnic identity having neither religious significance, nor practical expression, but constituting a psychological state of belonging. This is an interesting finding, supporting Dr. Azria's suggestion (see Azria 1998, this volume) that feelings of Jewishness are relatively independent of practical action. It underlines the basic dilemma of the continuity debate, that the promotion of ethnic identity does not necessarily promote Jewish participation, and conversely that a movement towards assimilation and outmarriage does not necessarily erode mental ethnicity.

Determinants of Jewish Identity Behaviors

The progressive secularization of the British Jewish community raises the same questions about the Jewish future that have been hotly debated in the United States. I shall not consider here the competing interpretations of the American data (see, for example, Eisenstadt 1990, Cohen 1988), but it is clear that these arguments cannot be transferred wholesale to the British case. Most critically, in the United States there is a high proportion of Jews concentrated in particular geographical, social and occupational niches, and this creates a set of structural pressures that serve to reinforce and preserve a distinct ethnic community (Goldscheider and Zuckerman 1984; Wilder 1996). This happens even in the absence of any religious dimension to Jewish life, and creates the possibility—at least in principle—of a self-perpetuating secular Jewish community. In the United Kingdom, only about 20 percent of the Jewish population live in predominantly Jewish areas (containing more than 50 percent Jewish households) and the number of Jews in the population is such that even in the most "Jewish" professions such as law and medicine, Jews constitute only a small minority of the total work force. Thus, in the British sample (unlike the NJPS), higher education is negatively correlated with Jewish identity; and this means that the most talented members of the community are more prone to assimilation and outmarriage.

These issues cannot be discussed fully in the present context, but they underline the need to examine the key determinants of Jewish identity, and to consider strategies for continuity that may need to be dedicated to the British case.

On the basis of a series of multiple regression analyses, I have examined the impact of the following variables on measures of Jewish belief, practice, and ethnic identity:

- Parental religiosity
- Experience of Jewish schooling
- Involvement in Jewish youth movements
- Parental membership in a synagogue
- (Perceived) consistency of parents' Jewish outlook
- Level of secular education
- Gender

The findings essentially replicate earlier studies of British Jews (Schmool and Miller 1994; Miller and Schmool 1992) showing that parental religiosity is the most potent determinant of Jewish identity. This factor accounts for between 15 percent and 25 percent of the variation in the respondents' beliefs, practices, and ethnic involvement—and in all cases the effect is in the expected direction; that is, more religious homes generate higher levels of commitment. Even in the case of intermarriage, which is likely to be strongly influenced by chance events—and which is notoriously difficult to predict—about

10 percent of the variance can be traced to the religious character of the home.

Other factors, such as Jewish schooling and youth group involvement, account for very little variation (1 percent – 3 percent) once parental religiosity has been taken into account. As indicated above, high levels of secular education are associated with lower levels of identity, but the effects are modest except at the very highest levels of academic attainment.

The near-neutral effects of Jewish schooling are sometimes regarded as controversial, but they have been replicated now in three different British samples. Obviously the findings are historical, reflecting the impact of Jewish schooling in the 1970s and 1980s, and cannot be regarded as a commentary on contemporary educational programs. They also appear to contradict the NJPS findings (Fishman and Goldstein 1993), which showed significant positive effects of Jewish schooling, but this study confounds home background and Jewish schooling, making it impossible to assess schooling independently of other factors.

Looking specifically at intermarriage in the British sample, Jewish schooling appears to have no effect whatsoever on marriage choice, once parental religiosity is partialled out. However, although the aggregate effect is zero, it is possible to detect some positive (and negative) influences within particular subgroups. Thus, attendance at a Jewish school is associated with a reduction in intermarriage among those from Orthodox homes; a similar but much smaller reduction is found among people raised in traditional homes, and a significant *increase* among those raised in secular or Progressive homes. These differential effects are clearly of practical importance and merit more detailed investigation.

Concluding Remark

The data on Jewish schooling seem to pose a particular dilemma when taken in conjunction with the earlier findings on religious transformation. The problem is that Jewish schools are bound, almost by definition, to seek to promote distinctly religious expressions of Jewish identity. Meanwhile, among the non-Orthodox majority, it seems likely that religious constructions of Jewishness are giving way to ethnic forms of identification. Now if Jewish schools were having difficulty transmitting religious identity in the 1970s and 1980s, how can they hope to succeed in the new, more secular environment of the 1990s. But equally, if Jewish schools were to seek to transmit a purely ethnic variety of Jewishness, how can they remain Jewish schools? The answer—perhaps unattainable—is to devise a strategy that promotes religious identity alongside ethnic identity, but without internal conflict.

Note

1. Director of the Community Research Unit, Board of Deputies of British Jews.

References

Azria, Régine. 1998. "The Diaspora-Community-Tradition Paradigms of Jewish Identity: a Re-Appraisal." Paper presented at the International Workshop on Jewish Survival: The Identification Problem at the end of the 20th Century. Bar-Ilan University, 18–19 March 1997.

Cohen, Steven. 1988. *American Assimilation or Jewish Revival?* Bloomington: Indiana University Press

Eisenstadt, S. 1990. "The Jewish Experience with Pluralism." *Society* 28: 21–33.

Fishman, S. and A. Goldstein. 1993. *When They Are Grown They Will Not Depart.* Research Report No. 8, Cohen Center for Modern Jewish Studies, Brandeis University.

Goldscheider, Calvin and A. Zuckerman. 1984. *The Transformation of the Jews* Chicago: University of Chicago Press.

Levy, S., Levinsohn, H. and E. Katz. 1993. *Beliefs, Observances and Social Interaction Among Israeli Jews.* Guttman Institute Report: Jerusalem

Liebman, C. and Steven Cohen. 1990. *Two Worlds of Judaism.* New Haven, CT: Yale University Press.

Miller, Stephen and Marlena Schmool. 1992. "Survey of U.S. Synagogue Members." In *A Time for Change: The United Synagogue Review.* London: The Stanley Kalms Foundation.

Miller, Stephen, Marlena Schmool, and A. Lerman. 1996. *Social and Political Attitudes of British Jews: Some Key Findings of the JPR Survey.* JPR Report No. 1, February.

Schmool, Marlena and Stephen Miller. 1994. *Women in the Jewish Community: Survey Report.* London: Office of the Chief Rabbi.

Wilder, E. 1996. "Socioeconomic Attainment and Expressions of Jewish Identification, 1970 and 1990" *Journal for the Scientific Study of Religion* 35 (2):109–127

15

Identity Quest among Russian Jews of the 1990s: Before and After Emigration

Larissa I. Remennick

Introduction

The demise of the former Soviet Union (FSU) and the Communist Bloc in the late 1980s and early 1990s marked the onset of a mass resettlement directed from Eastern Europe to the West. The immigration of over 600,000 Jews from the FSU to Israel, and over 300,000 ex-Soviet citizens (mostly Jewish) to the United States from 1989 onwards formed the backbone of this East-West migration (Israel Ministry of Absorption 1996; Chiswick 1997). Plans and attitudes towards emigration have been shown to be one of the basic determinants of the Russian Jewish identity (Brym and Ryvkina 1996; Brym 1997). The purpose of this article is to review the main factors that shape Jewish identity among Russian-speaking[1] Jews, both those who have remained in the FSU, and those who moved to Israel or North America, and to show how the issues of identity influence the pace and character of their acculturation in the host countries.

Formal or "Imposed" Jewish Identity

Jewish identity has never been a matter of choice for Jews of the FSU. From the mid-1930s, internal passports of Soviet citizens included a "nationality" entry, meaning ethnic affiliation. At the age of sixteen everyone was ascribed the ethnicity of his or her parents; in cases of mixed marriage, either ethnic group could be chosen by an adolescent. Thus a person whose parents were both Jewish entered Soviet society officially defined as a Jew. Young people who could choose between Jewish and non-Jewish affiliation in most cases registered as Russians, Ukrainians, etc., in order to avoid a negative label which might hinder their future education and career prospects.[2] Admittedly, the Russian chauvinism of the authorities inherited from the Czarist past caused many other non-Slavic minorities (e.g., Caucasian and Asian) to experience tacit discrimination cynically pursued under the name of the "national policy." Yet, the position of Jews on the scale of ethnic intolerance has always been outstanding. Given virtual destruction of all religions by the communists, and forced secularization of the population, Judaism under Soviet power turned from religious into purely ethnic affiliation.

Thus, Jewish identity was imposed on Soviet Jews beyond or against their will, and some of them spent much effort trying to get rid of this "birthmark" that hampered their upward mobility: they Russified their family names, took literary pseudonyms, or bribed officials to change the item on their internal passport. Thus the Jewish question was reinvented and sustained by the Soviet regime, pulling Jews together due to their common problems in the anti-Semitic environment rather than through shared faith and cultural tradition. Jean-Paul Sartre's saying that Jews acquire and maintain their group identity mainly due to anti-Semitism is, therefore, fully applicable to Jews of the FSU.

Demographic and Socioeconomic Profile

Individuals who have two Jewish parents, register as Jews and call themselves Jewish in the census are called "core" Jews. The "enlarged" Jewish population includes also persons with one Jewish parent or grandparent and non-Jewish family members. According to the microcensus of 1994, the number of core Jews in Russia was 409,000 (compared with 570,000 in 1989, at the onset of the great exodus), while the enlarged Jewish population was estimated at double that size, between 700,000 and 800,000 (Tolts 1996). Due to increasing numbers of mixed marriages, consecutive birth cohorts are ever more diluted—that is, the number of core Jews is shrinking while the enlarged Jewish population is growing larger. In 1994, 63 percent of Jewish men and 44 percent of Jewish women in Russia were married to non-Jews, compared to 51 percent and 33 percent, respectively, in 1979. Reflecting this trend, the proportion of children who are partly Jewish has been growing. From 1988 to 1995, the percentage of children born to Jewish mothers and non-Jewish fathers, out of all children born to Jewish mothers, rose from 58 percent to 69 percent. According to the 1994 microcensus, only 11 percent of children under age 16 born to mixed couples, were registered by their parents as Jewish, and at the age of 16 only about 6 percent chose to be identified in their passports as Jews (Tolts 1996).

As in most other diaspora countries, Jews of the FSU are characterized by low fertility and low mortality, which combine to produce high average life expectancy and rapid aging of the Jewish population. It should be noted that, during the last decade, life expectancy of Russian Jews exhibited a much weaker downward trend than that of the country's general population (the latter plummeted to 64.6 years for both sexes while the former remained virtually unchanged at 71.5 years). Thus, the Russian Jewish population has an extremely old age composition, which drifts further upwards due to very low fertility. Between the late 1980s and the mid-1990s, the average number of children born to Jewish mothers (total fertility rate) fell by 46 percent, from 1.5 to 0.8. This was more dramatic than the decrease in fertility rates within the general population of Russia, which fell from 1.9 to 1.25 during the same period. By the mid-1990s, crude death rates among Russian Jews surpassed crude birth rates by 27 units, leading to a steady decline in the size of the Jewish population. About 40 percent of this decrease between the 1989 census and 1994 microcensus is accounted for by the negative vital balance, while 60 percent are explained by emigration. Similar processes are observed in the Jewish population of most other former Soviet republics (Tolts 1996).

Among the socioeconomic characteristics of the ex-Soviet Jews, urban lifestyle and high level of formal education stand out. Over 95 percent of Soviet Jews were urban residents, and the majority lived in the capitals (54 percent in Moscow and St. Petersburg) and other big cities. Throughout the Soviet period, Jews were the single most educated ethnic group in the country (a statistic which Soviet authorities were highly reluctant to publicize). Despite multiple invisible and intricate barriers to higher education designed by the Soviet bureaucracy for Jews, well over half of Jewish youths received academic degrees, and in certain birth cohorts the percentage of Jews with higher education exceeded 75 percent (Tolts 1997). Needless to say, the amount of effort and personal resources invested by Jewish families in their children's education and vocational advancement was immense. Higher education was traditionally regarded by Russian Jews as the highest social and personal value, and, in pragmatic terms, as a ticket into "decent society." The economic rewards of education (if any, since the Soviet *intelligentsia* was typically low-paid) were of secondary importance (Ritterband 1997; Brym 1997). Although finding suitable jobs for young professionals with a "problematic fifth paragraph" (a common Soviet euphemism for Jews) was always a tightrope, their merits gradually won them a respectable status in many professions. Jews were prominent in the ranks of Soviet scientists, engineers, physicians, journalists, musicians, artists and other liberal professions, albeit not among politicians and diplomats (for these fields have always been off limits to them). Altogether, around 80 percent of Russian Jews had white-collar occupations. Soviet Jews of Caucasian and Asian origin, who comprised about 5 percent of the Jewish population of the FSU on the eve of the last exodus (Tolts 1997),[3] were traditionally less inclined toward formal education, and tended to work as artisans and craftsmen (shoemakers, hairdressers, etc.) or engage in trade and small business.

Hence, Soviet Jewry of European descent is characterized by rapid aging, small family size and persistent investment in education and white-collar work or professional careers. Negative vital balance and emigration combine to drain the remaining blood out of what was only several decades ago the world's second largest Jewish community. The third force involved in this process is rapid assimilation.

The Issues of Perceived Jewish Identity

We have observed that a negative official label was attached to being a Jew. How did this affect the psychological dimension of Jewish experience in the FSU? As in other diaspora locations, Jews of the FSU have generally been ambivalent, and at times torn between, their self-perception as Russian-Soviet people and as Jews. The two self-concepts were contradictory, if not mutually exclusive, since the mainstream ideology and the spirit of Soviet education and culture were those of "internationalism"—the proclaimed equality of all nations, large and small, in the workers' state. All expressions of nationalism among smaller ethnic groups were suppressed as backward and politically dangerous, while at the same time the authorities turned a blind eye to Russian chauvinism, and promoted total Russification across the U.S.S.R. The hypocrisy of the "internationalist" policy found its most vivid expression in state anti-Semitism, overt in the late Stalin period and mostly covert afterwards.

Since the late 1930s, the system of Jewish schools ceased to exist, as did synagogues and rabbis[4]; Yiddish gradually vanished from the lives of educated urban Jews; the study of the Hebrew language was virtually prohibited during the time of the anti-Zionist campaign after the Six Day War in Israel. Completely detached from their religious and cultural roots, Soviet Jews became fully assimilated (but not equal) Soviet citizens. Therefore, the lines of Jewish identity formation for the young people were solely, or mostly, negative; that is, they were based on the perceived status of a discriminated minority with shared problems and ways of coping, rather than common faith, interests, and activities.

Several recent sociological surveys among Russian-speaking Jews in Russia, Ukraine, and Belarus (Brym and Ryvkina 1996; Brym 1997) have documented a very low level of positive Jewish involvement in Jewish tradition and culture. In Robert Brym's words, most ex-Soviet Jews are only "pragmatically" Jewish—they merely recognize their Jewish origin and are ready to use it in certain cases or for certain purposes (mainly related to emigration). In the survey of 1995, 95 percent of respondents thought of themselves as wholly or partly Jewish, but just over 20 percent said they plan to learn Hebrew or Yiddish, and about 12 percent said they celebrate High Holidays or are raising their children in the spirit of Jewish traditions. Only 8 percent said they participate in at least one Jewish organization, 4 percent regularly read the Jewish press and fewer than 1 percent attend synagogue regularly. Reflecting seven decades of state atheism, only 14 percent of the sample expressed any kind of religious feelings, and, among the latter, more were interested in Orthodox Christianity than in Judaism (Brym and Ryvkina 1996).

The experience of anti-Semitism is an important determinant of Jewish identity in the FSU. Those who experienced greater exposure to overt anti-Semitic policies or suffered from the general climate of anti-Semitism show stronger Jewish identity than those who did not. On one hand, growing Slavic nationalism and the revival of the Orthodox Church in the post-socialist states generally reinforced anti-Semitic feelings on a daily level. On the other hand, state, or political, anti-Semitism gradually waned and many opportunities in business, communications, foreign affairs, administration and other realms that were formerly closed to Jews now opened up. Weighing the balance of these opposing trends, and responding to the growing amount of anti-Semitic propaganda in the streets and in the nascent free press, 81 percent of respondents in Brym and Ryvkina's study felt that Russian attitudes towards Jews have worsened over the past decade (Brym and Ryvkina, 1996). It is important to remember that this portrait of post-Soviet Jewry refers to the mid 1990s, after several years of the alleged post-Communist "Jewish cultural revival" so eagerly anticipated by Israeli and American Zionists. It seems that positive sources of the Jewish identity are as weak in the 1990s as they were in the decades of state anti-Semitism.

In their analysis of variance of the strength of Jewish identity by respondents' personal and social characteristics, Brym and Ryvkina (1996) found six principal determinants: the mother is a core Jew; Jewish upbringing in childhood; higher exposure to anti-Semitism; higher level of formal education; marital partner is a core Jew; and plans to emigrate. Among these factors, marital endogamy and the intention to emigrate were the most consistent predictors of a stronger Jewish identity.

The attitude towards leaving the country of their birth, an option open to Soviet Jews in the 1970s, and then reopened for several ethnic groups—including Jews—in the late 1980s, has always formed an important axis of Jewish identity. For some Jews, the desire to emigrate was there; they were only waiting for the gates to open. For many more, though, this vital decision evolved slowly, bound up with tormenting doubts, since so much in the potential émigré's life, and his children's welfare, was at stake. Age was a crucial determinant in this decision-making process: older Jewish professionals with higher achieved status and greater material wealth (which was non-transferable abroad, like state-owned apartments and *dachas*[5]) too much to lose, while the gains were questionable. For Jewish youngsters, the uprooting was less painful since they aspired to upward social and economic mobility in the West. In between these groups, middle-aged Jews had a hard time weighing their prospects upon resettlement, and all the pros and cons of leaving or staying. The younger generation has gradually left during the great post-Soviet exodus. Among other arguments against emigration among Jewish professionals is the growing realization, based on friends' and colleagues' experiences and on "field visits" to Israel and America, that their professional skills and human capital are of limited convertibility outside Russia.

In this light, it is quite understandable that among the respondents in Brym and Ryvkina's survey of 1995, only 25 percent expressed their definite intention to emigrate, while another 17 percent said they had not yet decided. This is significantly less than the 39 percent potential émigrés in the earlier survey by Brym in Moscow, Kiev, and Minsk (Brym 1997) and likewise less than the 33.5 percent reported by Gitelman and Shapiro in their 1993 survey (cited in Brym 1997). By and large, the emigration potential of the former Soviet Jewry shrank dramatically during the last 7–8 years. Extrapolating their 1995 sample data on the general Jewish population of Russia, Brym and Ryvkina (1996) estimated the size of the emigrant pool at about 121,000 (including 50 percent of those yet undecided). Assuming the continuation of current trends, this means that the emigration flow will go on at a varying pace to the year 2008, when the remaining Jews in Russia will be either too old to move, or deceased.

Another important indicator of Jewish identity among potential emigrants is their emigration destination: Israel, North America, or Europe. In the emigration wave of the 1970s, over 75 percent of Soviet Jews who were permitted to leave settled in the United States. In the last exodus, the choice of destination was significantly limited after the United States introduced strict immigrant quotas and truncated refugee programs. As a result, the ratio was reversed and about 70 percent of the post-1989 emigrants arrived in Israel. In Brym and Ryvkina's sample of 1995, half of those wishing to emigrate chose Israel and another half other countries, mainly the United States.[6] The expressed wish to settle in Israel in a half of potential émigrés of the mid-1990s probably reflects their pragmatic estimate of low chances of entering Western countries (where immigration policy is highly selective) as well as the phenomenon of chain migration (families and friends are already in Israel and it is more reasonable to join them). This assumption is corroborated by Brym and Ryvkina's results of regression analysis of the determinants of chosen destination among those planning to emigrate (defined dichotomously as "Israel" versus "other countries"). They found four factors significantly and independently associated with the choice of Israel as a future homeland: stronger Jewish identity, older age, having close relatives in Israel, and regarding resettlement in Israel as personally advantageous (Brym and Ryvkina 1996).

The choice of destination has also been influenced by the socioeconomic characteristics of various sectors of Jewry in the FSU. The data recently published and analyzed by Mark Tolts (1997) point at significant differences in occupational structure between Moscow and non-Moscow Jewry. These differences reflect the well-known cultural and intellectual gap between the capital and the rest of the FSU, which extended itself into the post-Soviet period. Capitalizing on advantages and broad professional opportunities of the capital, Moscow Jews (who comprised 33.4 percent of the total Jewish population in 1989) were disproportionately represented among scientists, artists, and those employed in education, medicine, culture, and public administration (about 50 percent of Moscow Jews worked in these occupations). Jews living outside Moscow more often had engineering and technical occupations in industry (30 percent versus 16 percent in Moscow). Jews of St. Petersburg (20.3 percent of the total Jewish population) occupied an intermediate position between Moscow and the periphery in terms of their occupational opportunities. The recent industrial crisis was a serious push for the emigration of non-Moscow Jews during the 1990s. The Jews of Moscow and St. Petersburg had broader options for vocational change, participation in new businesses and other opportunities concomitant with economic liberalization; since these changes have been more significant in the capital and the second-largest city. The consumer market is also much weaker in the periphery than in the center. Altogether, these factors led to the ever growing proportion of provincial Jews in the post-Soviet emigration to Israel, while the proportion of Moscovites halved between 1989 and 1993 (33.8 percent versus 17.1 percent). It is also suggested that more educated and professionally successful Jews of Moscow and St. Petersburg preferred to move to the West (where more of them also had relatives and friends), while the provincial Jewry found it easier to resettle in Israel (Tolts 1997).[7]

Russian Jews as Immigrants: The Identity Quest Continues

When Russian-speaking Jews joined the ranks of their fellow Jews in North America and in Israel, both parties suddenly realized how wide is the cultural gulf separating them. As Paul Ritterband put it in *Russian Jews on Three Continents*,

> Soviet and American Jews have grown up in vastly different worlds. There is much in their life experiences which makes them incomprehensible to one another. Yet, on another level, they have grown up in worlds that are similar in their common break with pre-modern Jewish society and its larger socio-political context. The Jewish *in imperio*, the self-governing Jewish enclave within the larger society was nullified as much by John Locke as it was by Vladimir Ilyich Lenin . . .Despite their differences, the ex-Soviet and American Jews have much in common as modern Jews. They are both high achieving, have a low fertility rate and are sober. By and large, they share a gene pool and some common ancestral memories, vague as they may have become over the generations. (Ritterband 1997:338)

Despite great differences in the national, socioeconomic, and cultural contexts of the acculturation process undergone by ex-Soviet Jews in Israel and in North America, there are many similarities in immigrant Jews' destinies outside the FSU. Let me outline the main common features of this process, and show how Soviet-type Jewishness interacts with host cultures and undergoes gradual change. Among many dimensions of this process (economic, cultural, religious, etc.), I will only touch upon those related to the issue of Jewish identity.

Stemming from Brym's definition of Russian Jewish identity as a "pragmatic" one, one can observe that many Soviet immigrants were quite happy to leave this "birthmark" behind them the moment they crossed the border, and enter their new life first and foremost as professionals seeking integration, or nascent entrepreneurs seeking success. Barry Chiswick, who reviewed recent studies of social-occupational mobility of Russian immigrants in America (of whom about 80 percent are Jews), notes:

> Reflecting norms prevalent among them in the Soviet Union, Soviet Jews are reported to place great value on occupational status, for themselves and their children, because of the attendant prestige and sense of self-esteem, which they apparently respect over and above the purely monetary rewards. However, they have difficulty in adjusting to the American market-place, particularly in utilizing their high level of skills, as well as in adapting to the wide range of options in all spheres of life and the high degree of mobility. (Chiswick 1997:236)

This observation mainly refers to highly educated Jews from Moscow and other large cities, while provincial Jews are less set upon regaining and advancing their professional status, and may instead be more interested in immediate monetary rewards. Generally, Soviet Jews have demonstrated great vocational flexibility as immigrants, both in America and in Israel. Specifically, they showed interest in opening private businesses, despite the virtual absence of business experience in the FSU and the lack of initial capital. This is how a traditional Jewish entrepreneurial propensity unexpectedly came to the surface. In two largest centers of Russian Jewish settlement in the United States, New York City, and Los Angeles, 15 percent and 25 percent of the immigrants, respectively, were self-employed according to the 1990 census (Gold 1997). By the mid-1990s these figures have probably increased as more Jews with the post-Soviet business experience entered the country. In Israel, the rates of self-employment are even higher due to the lesser scope of employment opportunities in the public sector and severe competition for jobs in large private companies (Israel Ministry of Immigrant Absorption 1996).

Let us cast a brief glance at the issues of the Russian Jewish community formation in the countries of the post-Soviet Diaspora. I will mainly rely on the studies of sociologist Steven Gold and anthropologist Fran Markowitz about Russian Jews in the United States, bearing in mind that the processes of adjustment and interaction with the hosts are mainly shaped by the immigrants' Soviet cultural heritage, and hence are rather similar across national borders. Depicting the initial encounter between American and Russian Jews after the onset of mass immigration, Gold observes:

> The initial (and ongoing) hope of the American Jewish community regarding Soviet Jews was that they would be passionately interested in living a Jewish life, and, accordingly, would quickly join the American Jewish community . . . By the late 1980s, however, it was generally accepted that most Soviet Jews were interested neither in religion nor in joining American Jewish life, at least in the way that the American community had envisioned. (Gold 1997:261)

American Jewish academics and community activists further forecast that, "Because Jews are noted for their organizational proclivity, communal concern and ability to be successful in the midst of anti-Semitic circumstances, . . .Soviet Jews would form organized communities in the United States" (Gold 1997:262). In Israel, the great post-Soviet Aliyah was anticipated to be a magnified replica of the Zionist Aliyah of the 1970s. Neither of these hopes have materialized; this mass and non-selective migration wave consisted of pragmatics rather than idealists, swept out of Russia by the socio-economic and ethnic crises. The forms of social participation and ethnic networking among ex-Soviet Jews turned out to be distinctly different from those accepted in the West. Perhaps the most outstanding feature of the Russian Jewish community in both countries is the weakness or virtual absence of formal organizations. Instead, the Russian Jewish "community" is based solely on the tendency to settle in the same neighborhoods and rely on informal peer networks (Markowitz referred to this phenomenon when she called her book about Soviet Jews in New York, *A Community in Spite of Itself*). Ties with family and friends are extremely important for immigrants as a source of information and support, and form the basis of the "community." Gold, who studied Soviet Jewish enclaves on both U.S. coasts, describes them as

> ... loose networks of émigrés representing a wide variety of occupations and regional origins, various degrees of religious identification and different outlooks on adjustment to the U.S. Intense interaction among members is frequent ..., a fairly high level of institutional completeness exists. For example, in West Hollywood or Brighton Beach, a Soviet Jew can interact with neighbors, shop for food, clothes or appliances; see a doctor or a dentist, attend religious services, read a newspaper, watch cable TV, visit a local park to play dominoes ..., all without speaking a word of English. Services such as child care and auto repair are also provided by one émigré to others ... Social activities and the selection of mates and companions are often focused within this collectivity. While resettlement services are available, many émigrés supplement them with community connections so that they can reduce the cultural and linguistic problems inherent in interactions with American service providers. (Gold 1997: 263–4)

The process of sociocultural ghettoization of "Russians," also apparent in Israel and in other host countries, is probably inevitable, at least during the initial years following resettlement (Zilber 1997). On one hand, it serves as a coping and survival tool for the émigrés (especially older and less adjusted ones), but, on the other, it leads to self-isolation and hinders integration into the host society. In both the United States and Israel, the assimilative zest of the hosting Jewish community, with its emphasis on religion, community participation and traditional values, was scorned by the newcomers and caused their further estrangement from the mainstream society (Remennick 1996; Amir et al. 1997). Soviet Jews in America were additionally rejected by the Jewish community because of the ideological conflict around the "dropout" problem—American Jews' disapproval of "Russians" who failed to resettle in Israel. This stance is viewed by most Soviet immigrants as sheer hypocrisy and a double-standard. As one émigré interviewed by Gold in California put it, "Why should they sit in Beverly Hills and accuse me of not going to Israel when I left Russia with $120 and they have all the money in the world?" (Gold 1997:276). Ironically enough, similar accusations of lacking Jewish fervor are being directed at Russian immigrants in Israel. It seems that Russian Jews are destined to remain permanent outsiders: in the FSU they were Jewish outcasts, in Israel they became "Russians," and in America they were received as the local community's "stepchild" who failed to meet its best hopes. Stalin's ideologists were probably not far from the truth labeling Soviet Jews as "rootless cosmopolitans."

Based on his interviews with recent émigrés, Gold (1994, 1997) offers several explanations of the ambivalence about more formal social membership among ex-Soviet citizens. First, it reflects a strong negative reaction against the kind of forced collectivism that was a common part of life in the FSU. Membership in the organizations like Pioneers and Comsomol was mandatory from childhood, later the Party and the Profsoyuz (Workers' Union) joined the list. Paying the dues, participating in endless meetings, and coercive "volunteering" caused permanent scorn and aversion; the figure of the "social activist" is associated with officialdom, demagoguery ,and hidden self-interest. Conversely, the lack of social organization is linked to freedom in the minds of many émigrés, and this is what they sought in the West.

For the same reason, the Russian Jewish community lacks generally accepted leaders and experience in creating voluntary associations. Additionally, the need for creating self-help groups (common among new immigrants in order to counter poverty and discrimination) is reduced due to the organized provision of resettlement services by Jewish agencies in the United States and by state bodies like the Ministry of Absorption in Israel. Also, volunteering time and work for the sake of self-chosen (and not imposed from above) common cause is a novel social experience for the people from the FSU, where civil society has been dormant for decades. Financial insecurity and tight time budgets of recent immigrants also preclude them from voluntary activities. Finally, the predicament in community self-organizing stems from the great heterogeneity of regional, cultural, and occupational origins within the last wave of immigrants, making it difficult to find common denominators. Therefore, when attempts to organize for mutual benefit do take place, they usually occur within particular social-occupational or regional strata of "Russians"—among small business owners, medical professionals, or immigrants from the zone affected by the Chernobyl nuclear disaster.

Political organizations, which require a higher level of unification and ideological consensus, are usually weak and short-lived "due to the climate of individualism and competitiveness that is pervasive in the enclave" (Gold 1997:270). When Russian Jews naturalize and show interest in politics, they usually exhibit conservative and right-wing views; in America they vote for the Republicans, in Israel, for Likud and other nationalist (but nonreligious) parties. The recent success of the Israeli "Russian party" ("Israel ba-Aliyah" which is part of the nationalist governmental coalition) in the 1996 parliamentary elections reflected deep disappointment of recent immigrants with the existing absorption policies. The collective impulse to promote the "Russian cause" in Israel drew on the example of other ethnic-based parties, successful in lobbying for their communities' interests. It should be noted, though, that most of this party's leaders are Soviet immigrants of the 1970s, many of whom were active in dissident or refusenik organizations in their Soviet past (Natan Sharansky is the best-known of them). Post-1989 immigrants, who are even more atomized and self-centered, showed less enthusiasm in joining the ranks of this party, although many voted for its leaders.

Language forms the central axis of personal and ethnic identity. Russian Jews are, at the same time, one of the finest products of the Russian culture and its prominent creators (the Jewish origin of many important Russian writers, poets and journalists causes intense hatred among Slavic patriots). The link between educated Russians, of Jewish or any other origin, and the Russian language as their cherished intellectual asset is very strong and unchallenged even by years of life abroad. The first generation of immigrants in all countries of the post-Soviet Diaspora are persistent in their use of Russian at home and with their co-ethnics, which in many cases hinders their progress in learning English or Hebrew, and hence slows down the pace of social integration and widens the generation gap. In the 1990 U.S. census, former Soviet immigrants (mainly Jews) have been found to be fairly proficient in English as the language of external use, but only 3.8 percent spoke English at home (versus 30 percent among other European immigrants). Over 30 percent of Soviet immigrants spoke little English or none at all (Chiswick 1997). In Israel, where Russian newcomers form about 15 percent of the Jewish population and for every fifth Israeli Russian is a mother tongue, Russian-speakers have developed a multifaceted subculture with its own press, TV programs, a theater, etc. The Hebrew-speaking majority perceives this "linguistic separatism" as a sign of low commitment to the Jewish and Israeli national cause, lack of gratitude to the host society, or even arrogance towards it (Ben-Rafael et al. 1997; Zilber 1997). Clear signs of cultural retention and affiliation with the Russian language in the second generation of Russian Israelis have been found by Fran Markowitz in her 1993 field work among ex-Soviet adolescents who came to Israel under the Jewish Agency -sponsored program Na'ale (Markowitz 1997) and in Rita Sever's study of Russian students' integration in Israeli high schools (Sever 1997).

Both Gold (1997) and Markowitz (1993) stress that, despite low levels of Jewish education, Soviet Jewish émigrés in the US are in many ways more "ethnic" (in terms of their involvement with their co-ethnic persons, networks and views) than many American Jews. Thus, the New York Jewish Population study of 1990–91 (cited by Gold, 1997) has shown that more Soviet Jews who emigrated after 1965 than all Jews could speak Yiddish (42 percent versus 38 percent), regularly read the Jewish press (49 versus 41 percent), said that all or most of their close friends were Jewish (96 versus 66 percent), and opposed intermarriage for their children (58 percent versus 36 percent). Markowitz describes how Russian Jews in the United States have created their own version of Jewish rituals, such as bar- and bat-mitzvahs and weddings with Russian-speaking American rabbis in Russian restaurants.

> Symbolically blending and reconciling Jewish and American identities in the context of a Russian nightclub/restaurant demonstrate that the [bar-mitzvah] child, and by extension the family and all others present, are fully accepted as Jews in America, and also, that being Jewish is worthy and fun. (Markowitz 1993:161)

All this, though, applies more to the Soviet émigrés of the 1970s who settled in Russian Jewish enclaves such as Brighton Beach. Many of those who joined the Brighton Beach colony upon migration, and remained there for decades, belong to the less educated provincial Jewry (the so-called Little Odessa), which has always been more traditional than the Jews of Moscow and (then) Leningrad. The latter keep their distance from Brighton Beach (symbolizing in their eyes not only the place but the whole lifestyle), and their attachment to Judaism is often limited to sending their children to Jewish Sunday school around bar-mitzvah age (twelve or thirteen). In their cultural habits the educated immigrants of the 1990s are closer to the Russian *intelligentsia* than to U.S. Jewry (Gold 1997; Ritterband 1997; Brym 1997). Similar variance in terms of participation in Jewish life probably exists among the post-1989 immigrants in Israel, although there is less of a geographic segregation between the educated elite and the rest of Soviet Jews. They live in the same neighborhoods, their children attend the same public schools, but their social networks are distinct. Yet, many sociological studies among Russian immigrants of the most recent wave in Israel failed to account for multiple sociocultural differences among them.

Concluding Remarks

It is impossible to cover a topic as complex and multifaceted as Russian-Jewish identity in the aftermath of the great East-West migration in a short article. I have tried only to highlight the main issues and the way they are reflected in today's social research in the FSU, America, and Israel. Each of these issues merits individual study; several such studies among Russian Jews in the West are currently underway.[8] A fruitful direction which future research may take is the establishment of a multinational research network in the principal countries of Russian Jewish resettlement, in order to follow and compare their acculturation patterns in various national contexts.

Soviet Jewish identity has been shaped by several external forces: cultural alienation, secularization, Russification, and ambient anti-Semitism. These forces combined to produce the self-concept of Judaism as a mainly negative identity to be concealed and diluted by mixed marriage, name change and other means of social mimicry. Soviet Jewish identity was also a pragmatic one, in terms of readiness to capitalize on one's Jewish label when doing so would be beneficial (e.g., the chance to emigrate or to receive benefits from foreign Jewish organizations). For decades, Soviet Jews recognized each other and stuck together through common troubles, using the skills of social maneuvering and coping, rather than via shared faith or lifestyle. The recent revival of Jewish religion and tradition, mainly sponsored from abroad (by American and Israeli Jewish agencies), has been superficial and driven by fashion rather than genuine interest (see survey data on p. 8, above; Brym and Ryvkina 1996).

As a result of negative migration balance due to continuous emigration, the Jewish population of the FSU has been dramatically reduced; it is also aging. Members of the younger generation, who were more mobile and possessed convertible social and professional skills, have gradually left the country; the more Jewish Jews opted for Israel, while the more cosmopolitan ones headed to the West. The remaining Jews are either old or fully assimilated, and only about one quarter of them plan to emigrate.

Upon crossing national borders, Russian Jews are confronted with another dimension of their identity conflict: the need to fit into the Jewish society that sponsored their resettlement. Their lack of interest in Judaism and community organizations caused severe disappointment among U.S. Jews. In Israel, cultural and linguistic self-isolation is regarded as a great challenge to the dominant "melting pot" ideology. Transferring their dislike of formal organizations to their new environment, Russian Jews rely instead on informal personal networks, and cherish their individuality. The future will show what kind of transformation the Russian Jewish resettlers of the 1990s will undergo. Let me close with another quote from Steven Gold's article in *Russian Jews on Three Continents*:

> They want to be accepted [by host societies] on their own terms. They care deeply about their European way of life and, while grateful to America for the opportunities and freedom it offers, they strongly guard their independence from established Jews whom they see as overzealous in planning their acculturation. Like previous waves of immigrants, they will shape a community and identity that is uniquely their own—in their own way and in their own time. (Gold 1997:280).

Notes

1. The Russian language and cultural tradition is the principal unifying characteristic of diverse immigrant groups coming from various parts of the FSU (less so for the Jews of the Caucasus and Soviet Central Asia).
2. "Clean" documents, though, did not spare one the trouble of street anti-Semitism. As the popular Soviet saying goes, "they hit you on the face, not on the passport."
3. Among the post-1989 Soviet immigrants to Israel, the proportion of non-Ashkenazi Jews is much higher (up to 20 percent) because the regions of their settlement in the Caucasus and Uzbekistan became the arena of ethnic conflict and war, causing most Jews to flee.
4. One synagogue was usually left open in every big city, in order to demonstrate "the freedom of religion" in the Soviet Union to the outer world. The same policy

was followed towards Moslems, Buddhists, and the Russian Orthodox Church.
5. Economic liberalization during the early 1990s made it possible for those leaving the FSU to privatize and sell their property for hard currency, significantly improving their well-being after emigration.
6. In the earlier study of Jews in Moscow, Kiev and Minsk (representing over 55 percent of the FSU's Jewish population), Brym found that only 8 percent of the total sample planned to emigrate to Israel, while 21 percent wanted to move to the West (Brym 1997).
7. Moscow and St. Petersburg Jewry tended to respond more actively to any new opportunity to emigrate (due to both greater access to information and personal resources); since by late 1989 Israel had become virtually the only option, many of them embarked upon Aliyah. Later on, they were the first ones to receive discouraging information on professional employment and other problems in Israel, which made them stay or try other destination countries.
8. For instance, R. Brym teamed up with several Russian immigrant sociologists in order to study the issues of integration and identity among ex-Soviet immigrants in Toronto. This is an important enrichment of the research scene, since Canada has become one of the primary destinations for Russian Jews.

References

Amir, Delila, Larissa I. Remennick and Yuval Elmelech. 1997. "Educating Lena: Women Immigrants and 'Integration' Policies in Israel—The Politics of Reproduction and Family Planning," pp. 495–509 in N. Lewin-Epstein, Y. Roi, and P. Ritterband (eds.), *Russian Jews on Three Continents: Migration and Resettlement.* London: Frank Cass.

Ben-Rafael, Eliezer, Elite Olshtain, and Idit Geijst. 1997. "Identity and Language: The Social Insertion of Soviet Jews in Israel," pp. 364–388 in N. Lewin-Epstein, Y. Roi and P. Ritterband (eds.) *Russian Jews on Three Continents: Migration and Resettlement.* London: Frank Cass.

Brym, Robert J. and Rosalina Ryvkina. 1996. *Russian Jewry Today: A Sociological Profile.* Sociological Papers, vol. 5 (1). Ramat Gan, Israel: Sociological Institute for Community Studies, Bar-Ilan University.

Brym, Robert J. 1997. "Jewish Emigration from the Former USSR: Who? Why? How Many?" pp. 1777–193 in N. Lewin-Epstein, Y. Roi, and P. Ritterband (eds.), *Russian Jews on Three Continents: Migration and Resettlement.* London: Frank Cass.

Chiswick, Barry R. 1997. "Soviet Jews in the United States: Language and Labour Market Adjustments Revisited," pp. 233–260 in N. Lewin-Epstein, Y. Roi and P. Ritterband (eds.) *Russian Jews on Three Continents: Migration and Resettlement.* London: Frank Cass.

Gold, Steven J. 1997. "Community Formation Among Jews from the Former Soviet Union in the US," pp. 261–283 in N. Lewin-Epstein, Y. Roi and P. Ritterband (eds.) *Russian Jews on Three Continents: Migration and Resettlement.* London: Frank Cass.

———. 1994. "Soviet Jews in the United States," pp. 3–57 in *American Jewish Yearbook 1994.*

Israel Ministry of Absorption. 1996. *Immigrant Absorption: Situation, Problems, Goals.* Jerusalem: Israel Ministry of Absorption.

Markowitz, Fran. 1997. "Culture Change, Border Crossing and Identity Shopping:

Jewish Teenagers from the CIS Assess Their Future in Israel," pp. 344–363 in N. Lewin-Epstein, Y. Roi and P. Ritterband (eds.) *Russian Jews on Three Continents: Migration and Resettlement*. London: Frank Cass.

———. 1993. *A Community In Spite of Itself: Soviet Jewish Émigrés in New York*. Washington, DC: Smithsonian Institute Publications.

Ritterband, Paul. 1997. "Jewish Identity among Russian Immigrants in the United States," pp. 325–343 in N. Lewin-Epstein, Y. Roi and P. Ritterband (eds.) *Russian Jews on Three Continents: Migration and Resettlement*. London: Frank Cass.

Remennick, Larissa I. 1996. "Immigration and Gender: Russian-Speaking Women in Israel." *East European Jewish Affairs* 26(2): 41–52.

Sever, Rita. 1997. "Learning from Experience: Israeli Schools and the Task of Immigrant Absorption," pp. 510–540 in N. Lewin-Epstein, Y. Roi and P. Ritterband (eds.)*Russian Jews on Three Continents: Migration and Resettlement*. London: Frank Cass.

Tolts, Mark. 1997. "The Interrelationship Between Emigration and the Socio-Demographic Profile of Russian Jewry," pp. 147–176 in Lewin-Epstein, Y. Roi and P. Ritterband (eds.) *Russian Jews on Three Continents: Migration and Resettlement*. London: Frank Cass.

———. 1996. "The Jewish Population of Russia, 1989–1995." *Jews in Eastern Europe* (The Hebrew University of Jerusalem), no. 3 (31).

Zilber, Carmel. 1997. "Little Russia in Israel." *Yediot Aharonot*, June 1.

16

Concluding Remarks:
Patterns of Jewish Identity

Ernest Krausz and Gitta Tulea

"The story of Jewish survival is so strange, unique and vast that it strains our imagination to the limit. Even the events of a single century, our own, defy sober description." Thus Chief Rabbi Jonathan Sacks relates to the extraordinary phenomenon of Jewish survival. He calls Jews "a singular people." They are, he says, "part of a collective history and destiny, perhaps the strangest and most miraculous the world has ever know," as seen in their ability to withstand all odds during a very long history of dispersion, persecution and crises (Sacks 1994:6–10). The question is how they will overcome and survive the crises and challenges which started two centuries ago with the emancipation in Europe, followed in this century by the barbaric events of the Holocaust. Are the establishment of the State of Israel and the signs of religious and Jewish cultural renewal in the midst of strong currents of assimilation and integration into the non-Jewish world perhaps evidence of continuing Jewish resilience?

We may distinguish between two kinds of survival or extinction which merge into each other: the physical and the sociocultural. For instance, the Holocaust, which physically wiped out thriving Jewish communities, also put an end to the whole era of Jewish cultural creativity, evidenced in the heights reached in Rabbinical literature and thinking in Eastern and Central Europe, effervescent Yiddish literature, fervent Zionism, intense Jewish communal life, and so on. More recently, demographic decline in the Jewish populations of the Western world, due to the effects of modern urbanized society and the serious inroads of assimilation, has weakened and sometimes threatened the very existence of communal life. How can these threats to Jewish continuity be contained and eventually overcome?

We felt that it was important to pose such value-loaded questions about the future of Jewry. But it was not the purpose of our workshop to come up with practical answers or suggestions. Our aim was to review the current situation by focusing on one unifying theme: namely, Jewish identity. This, we thought, would sharpen the central issue, for it is a truism that Jewish survival depends primarily on the survival of Jewish identity. Of course, in some circumstances it is the lack of Jewish identity that ensures physical survival in the face of persecutions, exterminations, forced conversions, or the complete repression of Jewish religion and culture. Good examples are the Marranos of Spain or those Jews in the former Soviet Union who are no longer aware of their Jewish or partly Jewish origins. However, the bulk of world Jewry now lives in the open democratic societies of the West, where they are free to identify as Jews and organize their lives as such, and in Israel where being Jewish is consistent with the raison d'être of the Jewish state. Although constantly threatened with physical destruction by external forces, Jews in Israel are able to defend themselves. Yet in both these centers, which can be characterized as postmodern societies, the question of the survival of Jewish identity looms large, since this identity faces the challenges of assimilation in the Diaspora and secularization in Israel.

It might be argued that the challenges to Diaspora Jewish life can be met by means of adjusting Jewish identity to the conditions prevailing in the so-called advanced societies on the eve of the third millennium. In such a society, one is free to choose one's identity, including one's Jewish identity, from a variety of possible identity types, according to one's predilections. It may be an overstatement to suggest that each individual chooses and shapes his self-identity in a completely free manner, since even in the most advanced Western societies, a range of collective identities prevail and impose normative patterns. Hence Diaspora Jews can choose from a whole array of possible identities. Bernard Lazerwitz and colleagues point to such a possibility of free choice in American society where one's affiliation with a religious denomination is a matter of personal voluntary decisions (Lazerwitz et al. 1998). One can imagine a continuum which would stretch from the sharply segregated Hasidic community, which, as William Shaffir demonstrates, prevents assimilation or even minimal acculturation by insulating their members from the secular influences of the host culture (see his chapter in this volume), continuing through the various shades of Jewish denominations including the Orthodox and the Progressive, and all the way to marginally identified Jews— people who are fully integrated into non-Jewish society but still acknowledge that they are Jews, without, however, being in any way affiliated to Jewish organizations, groups or Jewish social networks, and without engaging in any social act which could be labelled as "Jewish."

Between the two extremes there is a broad middle ground, composed of traditionalists and modernists—"those who feel strongly Jewish but recognize that they need to make some accommodation with modern life"—as against those who are secular and feel fully identified with the larger society in which they live, feeling themselves to be British, French or American, but who nonetheless "are unwilling to let go of some lingering sense of their Jewishness" (Cooper and Morrison 1991: 3). If we add to this the fact that it is not just the Jewish religion but also Jewish ethnicity or minority status, and the support of Zionism and Israel, which combine in different degrees to make up Jewish types of identity in the Diaspora, we arrive at what appears to be an inordinately complex and fragmented set of Jewish identities in contemporary society. Personal identity could thus be Jewish at the core, enveloped in various ways by elements of the surrounding non-Jewish culture, or else the latter elements could form the basis of one's identity, whilst Judaism, Jewish ethnicity, Jewish historical links, and Jewish culture become minimal and peripheral. Complexity and fragmentation are found in Israel too, ranging from ultra-Orthodox anti-Zionists and religious nationalists, through the various traditionalists, to the secularists, finally reaching the extreme of an Israeli identity culturally devoid of Jewishness. It is true that using such stereotypes creates a somewhat exaggerated impression of a decentralized and disunited Jewish people, conflict-prone and lacking a clear direction in the unavoidable struggle for survival.

But do some of the more straightforward and inclusive definitions of Jewish identity provide a better description of reality? Take Isaiah

Berlin's view that a Jew is "a person whom others normally take to be a Jew" (Tamir 1996: 46), or Max Beloff's definition, which links Jewish identity to religious communal organization and the resulting ethnicity (Beloff 1994: 36). Such definitions cannot be more than starting points in an analysis of Jewish identity, which in this day and age must be examined in terms of a variegated Jewish world and whose concomitant process of Jewish identification involves most complex psychological and social dynamics. It is for this reason that we have devoted a good part of our workshop to discussing theoretical and paradigmatic frameworks within which the analysis of Jewish identity can be pursued.

One such framework is offered by S.N. Eisenstadt's analysis of Jewish history from the point of view of "Jewish civilization." This overarching concept is both ontological and inclusive, taking into account transmundane aspects as well as social reality. Eisenstadt highlights its enduring nature saying that only if one looks at Jewish historical experience in civilizational terms "may one begin to cope with the greatest riddle of that experience: namely, with its continuity despite destruction, exile, loss of political independence and loss of territorial continuity" and despite the great changes occurring in postmodern society (Eisenstadt 1992: 2). Many other writers have also stressed that Jewish identities are in constant flux, continually being defined and redefined according to different social circumstances, including the effects of other cultures, economic and technological developments and political conditions, taking into consideration both anti-Semitism and Arab-Muslim antagonism toward Israel (Tamir 1996; Schweid 1994; Putnam 1993). One could suggest here the construction of a typology of Jewish identity which would distinguish, between the various types of Jewish identity. Yet one can also point to something unifying in Jewish identity, something that transcends all the changes and persists over the generations—a specific collective Jewish identity. What we have in mind is Jonathan Webber's use of the concept of *klal yisrael*, "the belief in the ultimate unity of the Jewish people despite all its disparate manifestations in time and space. Without this overriding concept of *klal yisrael* and a long view of the spiritual requirements of Jewish survival, is there not a danger in seeing the diversity of the contemporary Jewish experience as being little more than of exotic, ethnological or antiquarian curiosity?" (Webber 1994: 26). Jonathan Webber's reflection raises the issue of what the effects of the current constructions of Jewish identity will be for Jewish identities in the future; and in particular, whether a unifying bond, in the form of an overall collective identity, will continue to hold together the Jewish people and thus enhance its ability to survive in the twenty-first century and beyond.

References

Beloff, Max. 1994. "The Jews of Europe in the Age of a New Volkerwanderung," p. 36 in Jonathon Webber (ed.) *Jewish Identities in the New Europe*. Washington, DC: Littman Library of Jewish Civilization.

Cooper, Howard and Paul Morrison. 1991. *A Sense of Belonging—Dilemmas of British Jewish Identity*. London: Weidenfeld and Nicolson (in association with Channel Four Television, Ltd.)

Eisenstadt, S. N. 1992. *Jewish Civilization—The Jewish Historical Experience in a Comparative Perspective*. Albany: State University of New York Press.

Lazerwitz, Bernard J., Alan Winter, Arnold Dashefsky and Ephraim Tabory. 1998. *Jewish Choices—American Jewish Denominationalism*. Albany: State University of New York Press.

Putnam, Hilary. 1993. "Judaism and Jewish Identity" in David Theo Goldberg and Michael Krausz (eds.) *Jewish Identity*. Philadelphia: Temple University Press.

Sacks, Jonathan. 1994. *Will We Have Jewish Grandchildren? Jewish Continuity and How to Achieve It*. Ilford, Essex: Vallentine Mitchell.

Schweid, Eliezer. 1994. "Changing Jewish Identities in the New Europe and the Consequences for Israel" in Jonathon Webber (ed.) *Jewish Identities in the New Europe*. Washington, DC. Littman Library of Jewish Civilization.

Tamir, Yael. 1996. "Some Thoughts Concerning the Phrase, 'A Quest for Identity'" in Y. Kashti et al. (eds.) *A Quest for Identity—Postwar Jewish Biographies* (Studies in Jewish Culture, Identity and Community).Tel Aviv: Tel Aviv University (School of Education).

Webber, Jonathan. 1994. "Introduction," p. 26 in Jonathan Webber (ed.) *Jewish Identities in the New Europe*. Washington, DC: Littman Library of Jewish Civilization.

Additional Reading

Birnbaum, Pierre and Ira Katznelson, eds. 1995. *Paths of Emancipation*. Princeton, NJ: Princeton University Press.

Heilman, Samuel C. 1995. *Portrait of American Jews—The Last Half of the Twentieth Century*. Seattle, WA: University of Washington Press.

Klein, Emma. 1996. *Lost Jews—The Struggle for Identity Today*. Houndmills, Basingstoke and London: Macmillan Press Ltd.

Liebman, Charles S. and Elihu Katz. 1997. *The Jewishness of Israelis*. Albany: State University of New York Press.

Wistrich, Robert S., ed. 1995. *Terms of Survival—The Jewish World since 1945*. New York: Routledge.

Contributors

Régine Azria Docteur en sociologie, chargée de recherche au C.N.R.S. (Centre National de la Recherche Scientifique) Paris, France

Benjamin Beit-Hallahmi Professor of Psychology, University of Haifa, Israel

Eliezer Ben-Rafael Professor of Sociology, The Weinberg Chair of Political Sociology, Tel-Aviv University, Israel

Leo Davids Associate Professor of Sociology, Atkinson College of York University, Toronto, Canada

Christie Davies Professor of Sociology, University of Reading, England

Eva Etzioni-Halevy Professor of Sociology, Bar-Ilan University, Ramat-Gan, Israel

Julius Gould Chairman of Trustees, Social Affairs Unit; Emeritus Professor of Sociology, University of Nottingham, England; formerly Research Adviser, Institute of Jewish Affairs, London

Samuel C. Heilman Harold Proshansky Professor of Jewish Studies and Sociology, Queens College, The City University of New York, United States

Irving Louis Horowitz Hannah Arendt Distinguished Professor of Sociology and Political Science at Rutgers—The State University of New Jersey, United States

Ernest Krausz Professor of Sociology and Director, Sociological Institute for Community Studies, Bar-Ilan University, Ramat-Gan, Israel

Stephen H. Miller Dean, School of Social and Human Sciences, City University, London, England

Solomon Poll Professor Emeritus of Sociology, University of New Hampshire, United States

Larissa I. Remennick Assistant Professor, Department of Sociology, Bar-Ilan University, Ramat-Gan, Israel

Rabbi Naftali Rothenberg Senior Fellow at the Van Leer Institute, Jerusalem, Israel

Stuart Schoenfeld Associate Professor, Department of Sociology, Glendon College, York University, Toronto, Canada

William Shaffir Professor of Sociology, McMaster University, Hamilton, Canada

Stephen Sharot Professor of Sociology, Department of Behavioural Sciences, Ben-Gurion University of the Negev, Beer-Sheva, Israel

Gitta Tulea Senior Researcher, Sociological Institute for Community Studies, Bar-Ilan University, Ramat-Gan, Israel

Index